BłT
2/31/12
26.00

W9-CBU-936

WITHDRAWN

COACHING CONFIDENTIAL

Also by Gary Myers

*The Catch: One Play, Two Dynasties, and the Game
That Changed the NFL*

COACHING CONFIDENTIAL

INSIDE
THE FRATERNITY OF
NFL COACHES

GARY MYERS

CROWN
ARCHETYPE
NEW YORK

BALDWIN PUBLIC LIBRARY

Copyright © 2012 by Gary Myers

All rights reserved.
Published in the United States by Crown Archetype, an imprint of the
Crown Publishing Group, a division of Random House, Inc., New York.
www.crownarchetype.com

CROWN Archetype and the Crown colophon are registered trademarks
of Random House, Inc.

Library of Congress Cataloging-in-Publication Data is available upon
request.

 ISBN 978-0-307-71966-9
eISBN 978-0-307-71968-3

Printed in the United States of America

Book design by Lauren Dong
Jacket design by Michael Nagin
Jacket photography © Getty Images

10 9 8 7 6 5 4 3 2 1

First Edition

To Allison, Michelle, Emily, and Andrew

CONTENTS

As soon as Tom Brady's Hail Mary pass hit the ground in the end zone on the final play of Super Bowl XLVI, it was madness in Indianapolis for Tom Coughlin.

The New York Giants' coach had just defeated Bill Belichick and the Patriots in the Super Bowl for the second time in five seasons. Now it was total chaos as confetti came flying down from the rafters and the field was flooded by media, television cameras, and whoever else managed to get onto the floor of Lucas Oil Stadium. Coughlin came off the sidelines to seek out Belichick.

He found him, and they shared a long embrace. Years earlier, under Bill Parcells with the Giants, Coughlin was the receivers coach and Belichick was the defensive coordinator and secondary coach, and they would script practices with their units going against each other, which helped them prepare for the upcoming opponent. They won the Super Bowl together in 1990.

The postgame celebration is what all coaches dream about as they are dragging their families from city to city as they go from job to job in their quest to become an NFL head coach and one day ascend to the podium at midfield after a Super Bowl and accept the Vince Lombardi Trophy. They work ridiculously long hours in a business with a high rate of divorce. Parcells, Belichick, Jimmy Johnson, Jim Fassel, Sean Payton, and Jeff Fisher are among those who had their marriages end while they were coaching. Not only has Coughlin's marriage endured, but football has brought his family closer together. His daughter became pregnant at Boston College, and the father was Chris Snee, an outstanding guard on the BC football team. The Giants drafted Snee in the second round of the 2004 draft, but it was not done as a favor to Coughlin. Giants management gave him veto power over the pick if he felt having Snee on the team would make things too uncomfortable. Coughlin gave his approval, and Snee married Coughlin's daughter before training camp his rookie year and went on to become an All Pro player and a starter on two Super Bowl teams.

Coughlin's first Super Bowl victory over the New England Patriots, who were less than a minute away from completing their undefeated 2007 season, was one of the greatest upsets in pro football history. Winning another after the 2011 season elevated Coughlin into the elite status of coaches who have won multiple Super Bowls and put him in position to be considered for the Pro Football Hall of Fame after his coaching career was over.

After the trophy ceremony, Coughlin was led to the NFL Network set near one of the end zones. As he finished the interview with Marshall Faulk and Deion Sanders, he saw a man waiting for him. It looked like he wanted to give him a hug. Coughlin was in a huggable mood.

"I'm hugging signposts at that time," he said, laughing.

He was caught up in the moment, and it was hard to blame him. He nearly had been fired after the 2006 season. He had one year left on his contract, and the Giants, who either extend their coaches or fire them with one season remaining, basically made him re-interview for his job and then tacked on just one year to his deal. That was a vote of little confidence. He responded by winning the Super Bowl. The Giants, however, were a big disappointment in 2008 and lost their only playoff game. They didn't make the playoffs in either 2009 or 2010 and then, after a 6–2 start in 2011, lost four games in a row. Once again, Coughlin's job was in jeopardy. The players knew it, too. They had Coughlin's back and won three of their last four games to win the NFC East, then beat the Falcons, Packers, and 49ers in the playoffs and the Patriots in the Super Bowl.

Coughlin came off the NFL Network set and was able to get a closer look at the man who wanted to hug him. "This guy is waiting for me with these big glasses and a clock on his chest," he said.

It wasn't a piece of jewelry. It was a clock. What the hell: Coughlin gives him a hug after the man grabs him and wraps his arms around him. "As I walk away, one of my kids says to me, 'Dad, do you know who that was?'" Coughlin said. "'No, I don't.'"

He was told it was Flava Flav, the hip-hop star. He didn't think much about it, but it was out of character for this father and grandfather who rarely ventures out of his comfort zone to be standing on the field embracing a man with a big clock around his neck. "It's pretty funny to think of Coach Coughlin and Flava Flav hugging it out," Eli Manning said later.

As Manning was getting ready to leave the stadium, he realized he had not seen Coughlin since the game was over. He walked into the coaches' dressing room and sat with the only head coach he's had in the NFL. "I talked to him for a long time," Manning said. "He definitely was very excited. He had a big old smile painted on his face."

Coughlin arrived back at the Giants' hotel at 12:30 a.m. and skipped the team party. His wife, Judy, had arranged for a private party for family and friends. By midday Monday, the Giants were on their team charter for the two-hour flight back to New Jersey.

"The next day we're on the parade, and Brandon Jacobs reaches down and grabs a man by the hand and pulls him up," Coughlin said. "He's on the float."

He was laughing hard as he finished the story. "It was Flava Flav," Coughlin said.

He had given his team a history lesson before they boarded

the buses to take them to downtown Manhattan for the ticker tape parade through the Canyon of Heroes. He told them about Dwight Eisenhower and Neil Armstrong taking the same route. He could have told them about the Giants and Yankees, too. "It's the greatest feeling in the world," he said.

Winning the Super Bowl, being the best in the business, makes all the work it takes to get there worthwhile. If the job was just Sunday afternoons, it wouldn't be so demanding. But it involves so much more. *Coaching Confidential* takes a behind-the-scenes look at the compelling and frantic world of NFL head coaches. I interviewed some of the biggest names in football in a three-year journey to find out what their lives are all about. The list starts with Tom Coughlin, Sean Payton, Bill Parcells, Jimmy Johnson, Mike Holmgren, Rex Ryan, Tony Dungy, Joe Gibbs, Mike Shanahan, and Andy Reid but certainly does not end there.

I provide details about Payton's meetings with the NFL that preceded his being suspended for the 2012 season. But just as important is a long sit-down I had with Payton two months before he won the Super Bowl as he was on the verge of becoming one of the stars of the coaching profession as an engaging, likable, and brilliant offensive strategist and risk taker. After he won it all, he got carried away with his self-importance, and his sense of entitlement and his arrogance went off the charts.

Gibbs was elected to the Pro Football Hall of Fame after he first retired from the Redskins after winning three Super Bowls with three different quarterbacks. But his best coaching job might have been in the fourth year of Gibbs 2.0 in the last month of the 2007 season, when the Redskins played with a broken heart and went on a surprising playoff run after their teammate Sean Taylor was murdered during a home invasion late in the season. Gibbs's compassion and personal frailties showed his strength as a leader.

Dungy and Reid unfortunately had one thing in common: heartache brought about by their children. Dungy's son James committed suicide. Reid's sons were jailed for incidents that involved drugs. Dungy's decision to counsel Michael Vick after he was released from prison and Reid's understanding of how inmates transitioning back into society need a helping hand were the driving forces that brought them together. I spent a lot of time with Dungy and Reid peeling back the layers of the way their experiences with their own children helped lead Vick to Philadelphia.

Tragically, Reid's oldest son, Garrett, twenty-nine, was found dead on the morning of August 5, 2012, in his dorm room at Eagles training camp at Lehigh University in Bethlehem, Pennsylvania. He had been assisting the team's strength and conditioning staff. Reid did not mention drugs three days after his son died, but he said, "It's a sad situation, and one my son has been battling for a number of years. Our family has been battling. It doesn't mean you stop loving your son, because that's not what you do. You love him and a lot of families deal with this type of thing. It's a sad situation."

Dick Vermeil doesn't run away from the label. He is the poster child for coaching burnout. But in *Coaching Confidential*, you'll find out how his inner turmoil led to his being unable to get out of his car one day when he pulled up in the parking lot at Veterans Stadium and face the pressures of his job. You'll also find out why, after fifteen years away from the NFL, he finally came back, leading to his greatest triumph and the biggest regret of his career.

Patriots owner Robert Kraft, who deserves to be in the Hall of Fame one day, has managed three of the biggest names in the coaching business: Parcells, Pete Carroll, and Belichick. At dinner one night, Kraft told me one of the first things Parcells wanted him to do when he bought the team in 1994 was sell 1 percent to his good friend and confidante Tim Mara, the former co-owner of the Giants.

Three of Parcells's guys—Lawrence Taylor, Phil Simms, and Curtis Martin—tell what it was really like playing for the Tuna. Jimmy Johnson takes you deep into his thought process in deciding to deal Herschel Walker in what turned out to be the greatest trade in NFL history. Shanahan reveals that he feared that a practical joke he pulled on Al Davis would result in Davis's death. What's it like to be fired? Brian Billick received his pink slip and an $18 million golden parachute. The NFL is all about coaches and quarterbacks, and no relationship was more volatile than that of John Elway and Dan Reeves, but no quarterback made his coach laugh the way Brett Favre did to Mike Holmgren.

In my more than thirty-five years covering the NFL, the most poignant moment was sitting with Tom Landry in his office the morning after he was fired by the Cowboys as he stuffed twenty-nine years of memories into boxes. "Amazing how much you accumulate for that many years," Landry said. "You wonder why you never cleaned out your files before."

When I called Pete Rozelle at home the night Landry was fired, he said, "This is like Lombardi's death." It was a shocking reminder to every man who has ever stood on the sideline: if it can happen to Landry, it can happen to me. There are retired coaches and fired coaches and enduring coaches and aspiring coaches. There are control freaks and delegators. There are winners and there are losers. A who's who in the coaching fraternity is opened up in *Coaching Confidential*.

The completed and often circuitous journey to the podium right after the clock at the Super Bowl says zero is a road traveled by the chosen few. Coughlin and Belichick have won five between them, but each was fired from his first NFL head coaching job. The survival rate is low, but the payoff is high.

"It's well worth it," Coughlin said. "I'll take the lumps to get what's at the end of the rainbow anytime."

FROM THE SUPER BOWL TO SUSPENDED

In mid-March 2012, Sean Payton was walking briskly through the hallway on the sixth floor of the NFL's midtown Manhattan headquarters at 345 Park Avenue. He was taking a quick break from a meeting with Commissioner Roger Goodell that was the equivalent to a student being called into the principal's office.

Payton had a card key in his left hand as he passed through a reception area on his way to a bathroom just beyond locked glass double doors. He stopped for a moment to chat with a familiar face and kept on going. The league had moved a few blocks uptown nine months earlier from its offices at 280 Park Avenue, where it did business during most of Paul Tagliabue's time as commissioner and Goodell's first five years.

The look on Payton's face didn't lie. He was worried.

"Has Roger informed you of the discipline?" he was asked.

"No," he said.

He swiped the key, went through the glass doors, and two minutes later was passing back through the reception area on his return to Goodell's office. He was meeting with his professional executioner. It was barely two years since Goodell had handed him the Vince Lombardi Trophy after the New Orleans Saints' feel-good Super Bowl victory over the favored Indianapolis Colts. Now Goodell was giving Payton one last chance to plead his case for leniency before he would hand out the first suspension of a head coach in the NFL's ninety-two-year history.

The reception area in the league's new office was state of the art. Payton glanced at the immense high-definition flat screen television with square panels. The picture covered almost an entire wall. Naturally, it was tuned to the NFL Network. If Payton had taken a seat on one of the leather couches and kept Goodell waiting just a few minutes, he could have seen himself as the lead story on the network's news updates. It was the second meeting between Payton and Goodell after an NFL investigation had uncovered one of the biggest scandals in league history. The Saints had been accused of setting bounties on opposing players in a pay-for-injury performance scheme for the previous three seasons, including their dramatic Super Bowl season of 2009. Payton hadn't been part of the bounty meetings, which the league said was run by defensive coordinator Gregg Williams and funded by Williams and the players, but he had gotten himself into deep trouble by not putting an end to it when he was told the league was investigating in 2010 and then not being forthcoming about what he knew in his initial meeting with the league investigators in New York in 2012. Goodell demands honest answers to questions, and the NFL believed Payton was not telling all that he knew to the commissioner.

Payton must have felt that the Lombardi Trophy, which he said he slept with and joked that he slobbered on the night the Saints won the championship, made him bulletproof. The Saints were aware the league was investigating them shortly after the Super Bowl, but Payton was intoxicated with success and the league felt he ignored its warnings. If Payton could not control Williams, he could have fired him. His self-importance came through in the first meeting in New York, when he spoke with league security. He was spitting smokeless tobacco into a Styrofoam cup. It's a good thing Goodell was not present for that portion of the meeting or he would have tossed him out of the office and personally escorted him onto Park Avenue.

No one person is bigger than the league. It doesn't matter if you are at the head of the class in the next generation of great coaches, already have won a Super Bowl ring, make $5 million a year, and helped in the healing process of one of the great natural disasters in the country's history. The NFL will not let its $9 billion a year business be brought down by a group of renegade coaches and players.

Payton had become one of the faces of the league after the Saints did their part in helping the city of New Orleans get over the devastation of Hurricane Katrina that ravaged the Big Easy in 2005 one year before he arrived. Until then, Payton was known for being a scab quarterback for the Chicago Bears during the twenty-four-day players strike in 1987, being close friends with Jon Gruden, and doing good work as the Giants' offensive coordinator when they went to the Super Bowl in 2000 but then being run out of New York by Jim Fassel two years later when he was demoted from his play-calling duties. If it's true that things eventually work out for the best if you keep working hard, leaving New York and going to work for Bill Parcells when he was hired as the Dallas head coach in 2003 was the best thing that ever happened to Payton. They had no connection other than that they had worked for the Giants at different times. They hit it off right away.

Having Parcells on his résumé was a good thing for Payton. Just one season with the Cowboys had put him in position to be offered the Raiders' head coaching job by Al Davis. But the Raiders had become a burial ground for coaches, and Payton turned down Davis and kept building his portfolio working for Parcells. He had been instrumental in recruiting Tony Romo to sign with the Cowboys as a free agent after he went undrafted in 2003 and then played a big role in his development that led to Parcells benching Drew Bledsoe early in the 2006 season and elevating Romo to the starting quarterback job. By then, Payton was in New Orleans and had tried and failed to acquire Romo in a trade shortly after he took the Saints job and before signing Drew Brees as a free agent.

Payton had an edge to him that Parcells loved, and they did have some things in common. Parcells lost both his parents during the 1983 season with the Giants. Payton lost his mother during the 2002 season with the Giants. Fassel had given him the play-calling duties after his own mother died in 1999. He took the play-calling responsibilities back just eleven days after Payton's mother died. Payton, who previously had lost his dad, considered Parcells a father figure. Parcells has three daughters and treated Payton like the son he never had. It was Payton's confidence that allowed him to turn down the Raiders job; he knew that if he stuck with Parcells, a better opportunity would come his way. Two years later, after the 2005 season, he interviewed in Green Bay and New Orleans. He was crushed when the Packers hired Mike McCarthy, the 49ers' offensive coordinator. That was the job Payton wanted, and he got the news from Packers general manager Ted Thompson while he was in New Orleans interviewing with the Saints. But he could have the Saints job if he wanted it. At the time, it was far from the most attractive spot in the league. The city was still trying to rebuild after Katrina, and the Saints were coming off a 3–13 season in which they spent the year based in San Antonio and played all their games on the road.

It was Payton's belief in himself and his arrogance, a trait that later would betray him, that led him to accept the ultimate coaching challenge. He packed up his young family from a beautiful suburb in Dallas where they were very happy and moved to New Orleans, where reminders of Katrina and the havoc it had caused were all around. In his first season, Payton had the Saints in the NFC championship game, where they lost to the Bears in Chicago. Considering how far the Saints had come in one year, it was a tremendous achievement. By his fourth season, he won the

Super Bowl, just as his mentor Parcells did in his fourth season with the Giants.

Payton needed his second trip to New York to be more productive than his first when the league had summoned him and Saints general manager Mickey Loomis to headquarters without telling them why. They knew the league had reopened the bounty investigation, but the invitation was not specific. They were caught off guard when they were peppered with questions from the NFL's security department when they met individually in a conference room down the hall from Goodell's office. The security staff shared some of the evidence it had gathered with Payton and Loomis. Goodell was not in the meeting, but after the security staff finished each interview, Goodell was brought in to speak with Payton and Loomis one on one. There had been talk around the NFL that after he won the Super Bowl, Payton was so full of himself it was bordering on unbearable and now he didn't appear credible when he denied knowledge of what was going on in the defensive meeting room.

Payton had his hand in everything related to his team, and the league found it hard to believe that something that was so blatantly in violation of NFL rules was going on in his building and he had no idea. Paul Hicks, the league's executive vice president of communications and public affairs, kept a copy of Payton's book *Home Team: Coaching the Saints and New Orleans Back to Life*, which Payton wrote after the Saints won the Super Bowl. Hicks and one of his staff members went through it and took notes on passages where Payton discusses his attention to detail. Hicks then reported back to Goodell, who had not read the book. The commissioner asked several sources he trusted how likely it was that Payton was in the dark while Williams and the defensive players were setting bounties on some of the biggest names in the league. The conclusion was that Payton had to have known what Williams was doing even if he was trying to distance himself from Williams, because nothing happened with his football team without his knowledge.

Payton had requested this second meeting with Goodell. They had spoken on the phone several times. Payton asked if they could get together while Goodell was in Florida attending committee meetings in advance of the league meetings later that month in Palm Beach. But Goodell was going to be tied up with the committees, so Payton arranged to come back to New York the next week. Saints owner Tom Benson was also in the league offices that day but met separately with Goodell. Payton was casually dressed for the occasion in a sport shirt and a pair of slacks. After returning from the men's room, he settled back into Goodell's office for another thirty minutes of trying to explain himself. The commissioner was beyond angry. He is a man of principle, an admirable trait passed down from his father. His mission was to make the game safer for the players, and here was Williams running a system that encouraged players to hurt other players; players accused of committing unforgivable player-on-player crimes when they were supposed to be a fraternity that played hard but clean; and the head coach, a Super Bowl winner, not stopping it. Other than players or coaches betting on games, which would destroy the integrity of the league, it doesn't get much worse than players trying to hurt one another in a game that is already ultra-violent. It was now clear to the league that the Saints' strategy was to pin the blame on Williams, who had left after the 2011 season.

Payton couldn't have felt good as he looked around Goodell's corner office, which overlooked Fifty-First Street and Park Avenue. It's a big office, just about as big as the one he had at 280 Park, and plenty large enough to have a desk on one side and a conference table all the way across the room. There is a big screen television to the right of a desk surrounded by photos and books. There's a collection of footballs. On one wall is a copy of the *Congressional Record*. Goodell's father, Charles Goodell, was a congressman from upstate New York when he was appointed by Governor Nelson

Rockefeller to fill a U.S. Senate seat after the assassination of Robert Kennedy. He took office two months after Kennedy's death. Goodell was a Republican. Kennedy was a Democrat. As Kennedy's replacement, Goodell angered President Richard Nixon and Vice President Spiro Agnew with his opposition to the Vietnam War. The *Congressional Record* means a lot to Roger Goodell. It contained the original copy of Bill S. 3000, sponsored by Charles Goodell, which proposed an end to the funding for the war.

The administration targeted him as a turncoat, a Republican turned liberal. Agnew called him the Christine Jorgensen—famous for a sex change operation from male to female—of the Republican Party. "We're five boys; we're a pretty tight-knit group," Roger Goodell said. "Somebody attacks your father, you're upset. The five of us were ready to go. My father would always laugh it off. It never got under his skin. He would understand that he was being attacked politically, but he never took it personally. The Goodell boys did."

Charles Goodell's stance on the war wound up costing him the Senate seat. He had the nomination of the Republican and Liberal parties in 1970 but split the liberal vote with Democrat Richard Ottinger, allowing the conservative James Buckley to win. "It was difficult on one level, but it was educational and important from a principle standpoint," Roger Goodell said. "He stood up for what he believed in regardless of the consequences. He knew what the consequences were going to be."

Charles Goodell died in 1987. He was just sixty years old. By then, his son was working in the NFL office after a massive job-seeking letter-writing campaign—he bombarded league executives with more than forty letters—that wound up getting him an entry-level job, stopping the letters and rewarding his perseverance. Roger Goodell had long ago told his father of his career goal. He wanted to be the commissioner of the NFL.

As Payton sat at the big conference table, he could catch a glance over his shoulder at the reason Goodell was so infuriated.

It was the reason he should not count on leniency. Mounted on the wall was a metal replica of the NFL shield. Goodell is consumed with his responsibility to protect the shield. The Saints and Payton had done huge damage to the shield. Any degree of contrition Payton would show would be measured against his motive: Was he saying things Goodell wanted to hear so that Goodell would go easier on him when he decided on the discipline?

The culture of the team had gone way off course. The Saints thought they were above NFL rules and were trying to set their own. They were sticking it in the league's face after being told in 2010 that NFL investigators were on to them. Everything that happens with a football team is the responsibility of the head coach. That goes for everything from calling for the game-changing onside kick to start the second half of the Super Bowl against the Colts that had Parcells raving about Payton's "balls" to being aware that your defensive coordinator has set up a system to reward players $1,000 for "cart-offs," when the opposing player is carried off the field, and $1,500 for "knockouts," which sidelined them for the rest of the game. The league's investigation revealed the pool might have reached $50,000 or more at its height during the 2009 playoffs and that linebacker Jonathan Vilma in 2009 offered $10,000 to anybody who knocked Cardinals quarterback Kurt Warner out of the NFC divisional round or Vikings quarterback Brett Favre out of the NFC championship game. Warner was crushed after throwing an interception as he ran to make the tackle early in the second quarter but remained in the game through three quarters, when the Cardinals trailed by 35 points. Favre took every snap but absorbed several vicious hits. The Saints won the game in overtime. Vilma denied the allegations and sued Goodell for defamation of character.

There were impressive names on the Saints' bounty list: Favre, Aaron Rodgers, Warner, and Cam Newton. In the league's initial statement, it said, "Although head coach Sean Payton was not a direct participant in the funding or administration of the program, he was aware of the allegations, did not make any detailed inquiry or otherwise seek to learn the facts, and failed to stop the bounty program. He never instructed his assistant coaches or players that a bounty program was improper and could not continue."

Just two days after Payton left Goodell's office, the commissioner handed out the penalties. It was damning. He suspended Payton for the 2012 season, but in effect it was an indefinite suspension. Payton had to apply for reinstatement after the 2012 season. If he didn't follow the guidelines during his time away from the Saints, he would be subject to further penalties. "Anything that happens in the framework of your team and your program, you're responsible for, and that's a lesson I've learned," Payton said.

Goodell did hand an indefinite suspension to Williams, who had left the Saints after the 2011 season to rejoin his friend Jeff Fisher, who had been hired to coach the St. Louis Rams. Assistant head coach Joe Vitt, who was supposed to be Payton's eyes and ears on the defensive side of the ball, was suspended for the first six games of the season. General manager Mickey Loomis was suspended for the first eight games. The Saints organization was fined $500,000 and docked two draft picks. The investigation produced fifty thousand pages of documents.

"When interviewed in 2012, Sean Payton claimed to be entirely unaware of the program, a claim contradicted by others," the NFL said after the penalties were announced. "Further, prior to the Saints' opening game in 2011, Coach Payton received an email from a close associate that stated in part, 'PS Greg [sic] Williams put me down for $500 on Rogers [sic].' When shown the email during the course of the investigation, Coach Payton stated that it referred to a 'bounty' on Green Bay quarterback Aaron Rodgers."

In the early part of 2010, the league said Loomis advised Payton that the NFL office was investigating allegations concerning a bounty program. The league said Payton met with Williams and Vitt before they were interviewed and advised them, "Let's make sure our ducks are in a row." In a tersely worded section of a press release, the NFL then said, "Remarkably, Coach Payton claimed that he never inquired of Coach Williams and Coach Vitt as to what happened in the interviews, never asked them if a 'pay-for-performance' or bounty program was in fact in place, and never gave any instructions to discontinue such a program."

Goodell had been on a two-year campaign to make the game safer. He upset players, particularly Pittsburgh linebacker James Harrison, by fining them big chunks of their salaries for hits that crossed the line. The Saints had picked the wrong time and the wrong issue and definitely the wrong commissioner to challenge. Goodell was not moved by the "Free Sean Payton" T-shirts that had surfaced in the French Quarter. Goodell was taking a strong stand even if it was unpopular in the city that was hosting the next Super Bowl.

"We have thirty-two clubs. We have rules in the league. When rules are violated for three consecutive years and they deny it, there are going to be consequences," Goodell said. "That's the way it works. We have fans in thirty-one other markets that want to make sure the game is played the right way. I know the fans in New Orleans are frustrated by what happened, and I understand that. They also want the game to be played the right way. We're going to ensure that. My job is the credibility of the NFL."

Goodell didn't back down when Payton, Vitt, and Loomis filed appeals and came to New York two weeks later after the suspensions were announced to have their cases heard individually as they pleaded for lighter sentences. Nothing changed. Williams didn't even bother filing an appeal. On the day his appeal was heard, Payton exited through a side door of 345 Park Avenue and jumped into a waiting car, avoiding the media contingent that was waiting for him.

Sean Payton's fall from grace was dramatic. He went from being the life of the party to slipping out side doors. He must have thought that the Lombardi Trophy he slept with was his kryptonite to Goodell's Superman and that it would be the shield that protected him.

Not even his plan to have Parcells pinch hit for him for the 2012 season worked. After saying he had an obligation to help out his friend, Parcells elected to stay retired. Vitt was elevated to interim head coach for the 2012 season except, of course, for the six games for which he was suspended. Offensive line coach Aaron Kromer was named to step in for Vitt. Goodell suspended Vilma for the entire 2012 season, defensive lineman Anthony Hargrove for the first eight games (he signed with the Packers after the 2011 season but was cut by Green Bay in training camp), defensive end Will Smith for the first four games, and linebacker Scott Fujita for the first three games (he signed with the Browns after the 2009 season). Two days before the start of the 2012 regular season, a three-member appeals panel lifted the players' suspensions based on jurisdictional issues, leaving open the possibility for Goodell to again impose penalties. The ruling did not impact the suspensions of Payton, Vitt, or Loomis.

"Sean does have an arrogance about him," said one coach who worked with him in the NFL. "After success, you feel like you are untouchable. He's got that in him. There is one side of me that says that isn't Sean. The other side says that is Sean. At some point, he thinks he's smarter than everybody else. He always seems to start humble and turn arrogant. He was part of a cover-up. For somebody to totally disregard what the league or his owner told him to do, that is arrogant.

"Sean is a good person. But good people can make mistakes."

Before Sean Payton's fall, there was his rise.

Payton had had his doubts about taking the Saints job and moving his wife and two young children into an area others were moving out of as fast as they could. The football part was the kind of challenge that inspires coaches looking to make a name for themselves. The Saints were not a bad team, but they were in a bad situation. The Saints left the Gulf Coast early for a preseason game in Oakland to make sure they were out of town before Katrina arrived in New Orleans on August 29, 2005. They didn't return as a team until 2006. Nearly two thousand people died from the hurricane and the flooding it caused. The damage was over $100 billion.

The Saints set up headquarters for the 2005 season in San Antonio, where owner Tom Benson has strong business ties. There was talk that Benson wanted to permanently move the Saints to San Antonio after Katrina, but that eventually died down. The NFL did not want Benson abandoning New Orleans. That would have been another nightmare for a region that needed all the support it could gather. The 2005 season was so disjointed for the Saints that they had no chance to succeed. They worked out of a hotel in San Antonio. Their home opener against the New York Giants was relocated to Giants Stadium with the Saints as the home team. Of course, they lost that game. Their other "home" games were played in Louisiana State University's Tiger Stadium in Baton Rouge and the Alamodome in San Antonio. After winning just three games and losing thirteen, they fired coach Jim Haslett. They were moving back to New Orleans shortly after the season, and they needed a bright, fresh new face of the franchise.

Payton had personally seen how a community rallied together under the most heartbreaking and gut-wrenching circumstances. He was with the Giants after 9/11. The Giants played the season-opening Monday night game in Denver on September 10, 2001. Their United team charter flight left right after the game and touched down at Newark early the next morning. After taxiing, the plane arrived at the gate at 6 a.m. United Flight 93, a scheduled 8 a.m. flight to San Francisco, was parked two gates away. Of course, the Giants' coaches, players, and staff thought nothing of it. It was a normal Tuesday morning at Newark. The

Giants had lost the game to the Broncos and after the long four-hour flight in the middle of the night the players just wanted to get home, get into their beds, and get some sleep. The preparation for Sunday's home opener against the Packers would begin Wednesday. A bus pulled up on the tarmac to transport the players back to their cars, which they parked at Giants Stadium for road trips. Many of the front office executives parked their cars at the airport and exited through the terminal. Surely, they passed some of the passengers who had arrived early for Flight 93. Forty-six minutes into that flight, the hijackers overpowered the crew. The passengers then overpowered the hijackers, and the plane, which the hijackers were trying to divert to Washington, where the target was thought to be the Capitol or the White House, crashed in a field in Shanksville, Pennsylvania. Many of the Giants coaches went to their offices straight from the airport, and soon word spread throughout the building about the planes crashing into the World Trade Center. Jim Fassel quickly went up to the roof of the stadium with a member of the team's film crew, who had a high-powered lens, and they were able to see the smoke coming from the area. It was only twelve miles away. The Giants would have a daily reminder of the hole in the New York skyline because downtown Manhattan was in clear view from their grass practice field in the stadium parking lot.

The country went into crisis management after 9/11. "For the Giants, it was so close to home," Payton said. He took mental notes on how things were being done from an organizational standpoint. "In regards to how you present it to the team, you spend the proper time with the tragedy and then shift back to 'We still have to prepare here,' " he said.

The Saints' front office remained in San Antonio immediately after the 2005 season, getting ready for the move back to their headquarters on Airline Drive down the road from Louis Armstrong New Orleans International Airport. Their two-story facility had been used as a staging area by the Federal Emergency

Management Agency. They had taken over the building. The locker room, the weight room, the training area, the coaches' offices, and the executive offices were all used by FEMA. The Superdome was a shelter for residents whose homes had been destroyed. Payton's first meeting with general manager Mickey Loomis was in San Antonio. He flew back to Dallas that evening while Texas was playing the University of Southern California in the 2005 national championship game at the Rose Bowl. It was just a quick get-to-know-you session with Loomis because Payton was flying in the morning to Green Bay to meet with Thompson. He spent the night prepping for his Green Bay interview. Payton returned to New Orleans the next week for his first visit after Katrina.

"It was tough to go home and talk about it with my wife. We were concerned how we were going to make this work. We felt confident enough that ultimately we would find a place to live," Payton said. "In fairness to Mickey and the organization, they did a good job of not trying to sugarcoat."

Loomis took him on a tour of the city. "It was awful," Payton said.

He accepted the job before his wife, Beth, even made a trip to New Orleans. "We just built a new home in Dallas, and we never moved in," he said. "We lived in Dallas for three years, and after the second year we started to build a home a couple of blocks from the home we were living in. It literally just got completed a week before I was offered this job. We ended up selling both homes. That was tough."

The Paytons found a home in a very nice area across Lake Pontchartrain. It's a long bridge across the water, and it took Payton forty-five minutes to get to work. After the 2010 season, the Paytons made the decision that Beth and the kids would live back in Dallas while Payton stayed in New Orleans. He had talked about that arrangement before accepting the job, but the Saints did not endorse it. Now that he had coached the Saints to the

Super Bowl championship, he had a little more leverage. More than a year before the family moved back, Payton said of Dallas, "It was a place that we really enjoyed, and probably at some point in our future we will end up going back there." Beth and the kids were in Dallas during the 2011 season while Sean was coaching the Saints. But the most dramatic change in Payton's life came after the season. First, Goodell suspended him for the 2012 season. Then, in June, Payton filed for divorce from Beth. She filed a counterpetition. They had been married nearly twenty years. His job and his marriage were no longer there.

But on this day Payton is sitting in the Saints cafeteria. It is December 2009. His team is 12–0 and will finish 13–3 and beat the Cardinals and the Vikings in the playoffs at the Superdome and then beat the Colts in Super Bowl XLIV in Miami. It would be years before he would be called to meet with the NFL's security team.

Payton thought it was a great idea to hire Williams after the 2008 season. Williams, the former Buffalo Bills head coach, was the first assistant hired by Joe Gibbs when he returned to the Redskins in 2004. Williams was considered the heir apparent whenever Gibbs decided to retire again. When Gibbs left after the 2007 season, Williams was interviewed four times by the Redskins. But he was not hired amid reports, which he strongly denied, that he was disrespectful to Gibbs during the interview process. Gibbs had wanted Williams so badly in 2004 that he flew to Buffalo on Redskins owner Daniel Snyder's private plane to recruit him. Snyder gave Williams a deal averaging $1.15 million per year, which was more than he was making in Buffalo. Tom Coughlin, just hired by the Giants, had also contacted Williams about joining his staff.

When Gibbs left the Redskins after four seasons, Williams had one year remaining on his contract, but once the Redskins knew they were not hiring him, they released him from any obligation and allowed him to start looking for work. It sent up an immediate red flag when Snyder elected not to hire Williams, especially when he hired the unproven Jim Zorn instead. Williams went to Jacksonville on a one-year deal and was a coaching free agent again after the 2008 season.

Payton had an opening after firing defensive coordinator Gary Gibbs, who had been with him on Parcells's staff in Dallas. Williams had a reputation of putting together excellent defenses. His players always spoke highly of him. Payton knew that with Brees at quarterback, all he needed was a defense that would not force Brees to put up video game numbers and the Saints would be Super Bowl contenders.

Payton had never met Williams before he interviewed him. "I had been on teams that played against his defenses," Payton said. "Always at Washington, regardless of personnel, they played hard and were very respected. We knew there were some other places he was going to visit. It got to where, all right, we're ready to make an offer."

The Packers, Texans, and Titans were also interested. Williams had been the defensive coordinator for the Tennessee Titans before the Bills hired him as their head coach in 2001; he got the job instead of John Fox, who had just been to the Super Bowl with the Giants. Williams lasted just three years in Buffalo and had a 17–31 record. Williams and Titans coach Jeff Fisher were best friends, and it seemed logical in 2008 that he would go back with Fisher. That was what he did right after the 2011 season when Fisher was hired in St. Louis, but the indefinite suspension he was handed by Goodell forced Fisher to make other plans.

Payton had just signed a new five-year $28 million contract that paid him $5.6 million per year. The Saints were prepared to offer Williams a three-year deal at $1.25 million per season. Payton didn't think Williams would accept, not with three other teams also interested. The going rate was $1.5 million per year for a veteran coordinator. "I wanted to make sure we weren't going to lose this guy to another team because we were light $250,000," Payton said.

He called Loomis. It was a Friday night, and he felt Williams was close to making his decision. Payton really wanted Williams, a move that might have paid off in a Super Bowl championship but eventually did major damage to Payton's career.

"Hey, let's get to a million five. I don't want to lose this guy. There's a number of coordinators making a million five. I'll throw in $250,000 of my own money," Payton said.

"Let me talk to Mr. Benson. Call me back," Loomis said.

Benson gave the okay. Payton called Williams. It was their first conversation about money. "It's going to be a million five per year for three years," Payton said.

The next morning, Payton called Loomis. He wanted to make sure his $250,000 contribution was just for one year. The Saints would be on the hook for the entire payment in the second and third years. Payton was not surprised that the Saints took him up on his offer. "It was all good," he said. "I just signed a contract for about $5.5 million a year. I wanted Mickey and Mr. Benson to feel like, 'I'm in with this hire. Let's go.' "

Payton never told Williams he was paying part of his salary. Around the Super Bowl that season, ESPN reported that the Saints had reimbursed Payton the $250,000 in week nine. Williams already was paying dividends. The Saints wound up number one in the NFL in point differential and number three in turnover differential. Tracy Porter clinched the Super Bowl when he intercepted Peyton Manning and returned it 74 yards for a touchdown with just over three minutes remaining.

At the time, it seemed like the best $250,000 Payton would ever spend. But Williams wound up costing him more than twenty times as much in salary for 2012 that will never be reimbursed. Shortly after the 2011 season, Williams was gone, out of town before the bounty scandal erupted. People close to Payton said that even before the Saints got in trouble with the league, he had no intention of asking Williams to return in 2012.

The Saints' 2011 season ended in the divisional round of the playoffs in San Francisco, a crushing 36–32 loss. New Orleans took leads with 4:02 and 2:37 remaining, but each time Williams's defense gave up a touchdown, first on a 28-yard run by Alex Smith and then on Smith's 14-yard touchdown pass to Vernon Davis with just nine seconds left in the game.

Nearly three months after that game, a damaging audiotape surfaced of Williams meeting with the defensive players at their San Francisco airport hotel the night before the loss to the 49ers. The audio became public on the same day Payton was appealing his suspension to Goodell. It was bad timing for Payton, but Goodell knew about the tape before it went viral on the Internet. The recording was made public by filmmaker Sean Pamphilon, who was working on a documentary about former Saints special teams star Steve Gleason, who had been diagnosed with Lou Gehrig's disease. The tape reveals Williams calling for his players to target Smith, running back Frank Gore, tight end Vernon Davis, and wide receivers Michael Crabtree and Kyle Williams.

"We've got to do everything in the world to make sure we kill Frank Gore's head. We want him running sideways. We want his head sideways," Williams was heard saying. He then said, "We hit fucking Smith right there," while pointing to his chin. "Remember me. I got the first one. I got the first one. Go lay the motherfucker out." When he said "I got the first one," Pamphilon said, Williams was rubbing his hands together like the sign for money. He encouraged his players to "affect the head. Continue, touch and hit the head," coming off the pile. He said they needed to hit wide receiver Kyle Williams early—he'd had a concussion problem during the season. Then, talking about Crabtree, he said, "We need to decide whether Crabtree wants to be a fake-ass prima donna or he wants to be a tough guy. We need to find that out. He becomes human when we fucking take out that outside ACL [anterior cruciate ligament]."

In the recording, Williams told the Saints, "Kill the head, the body will die." He also said, "Respect comes from fear" and "We never apologize for the way we compete."

It was the last game Williams coached for the Saints. It was too late to apologize. The damage had been done. Payton wound up in the NFL office three times. He had his team taken away from him for the 2012 season. It was his fault. The coach is responsible. The lesson learned: it was the worst $250,000 he never spent.

Payton's career derailed when the bounty scandal was revealed. It was a condemnation of him as an administrator more than of his ability to coach the game of football. At the time of his suspension, he was in the upper echelon of NFL coaches along with Bill Belichick, Tom Coughlin, Mike Tomlin, and Mike McCarthy. He inherited a program in New Orleans that was about as low as it gets in the NFL. The city was in a shambles; it was not going to be a place that would attract free agents, and players with young families would be reluctant to relocate even though their inclination is always to follow the money.

The Saints needed star power. They also needed a quarterback when Payton arrived in 2006. He immediately thought about trying to persuade Parcells to trade him Romo, who had yet to take over as the Cowboys starter. Payton was the point man when Romo signed with the Cowboys as a free agent in 2003 after he went undrafted following his career at Eastern Illinois, which is where Payton went to college. Payton was on the phone with Romo during the last two rounds and knew that if he didn't get drafted, the Cowboys would face competition to sign him. As soon as the draft was over, Payton was back on the phone with Romo.

"Hey, I know you're disappointed. Do me one favor here. You got all these teams calling you. Just look at the depth chart of every one of these teams," Payton told him.

The Cowboys' depth chart: Quincy Carter, Clint Stoerner, Chad Hutchinson. That was not an intimidating cast of characters. "If you can be smart enough here, be smart enough not to let the signing bonus get in the way, you'll pick the right spot," Payton said. "Now I know it's the Dallas Cowboys and Bill Parcells, but you need to make this decision based on where you can make a team and compete."

Free agents in 2003 would get $2,500 to $5,000 as a signing bonus. The Cowboys offered Romo a bonus of $10,000. "High for a free agent," Payton said.

There were four or five other teams offering $10,000. The Cowboys increased their offer to $15,000. Parcells got on the phone with Romo. Jerry Jones got on the phone. Payton was working hard on Romo. Then Payton heard that one team, which he believed was Arizona, had jumped its offer to $25,000.

"Tell him, shit, we'll match it," Jones said.

"Honestly, Mr. Jones, I think we're going to get him at 15. I think he wants to come. He's smart enough to know this is a good opportunity," Payton said.

Ten minutes later, Romo called back and accepted the Cowboys' offer. Payton had been in Dallas only a couple of months, but he had made a friend in Jones, who loves money. "To this day, Jerry says 'I didn't know you very well, but you saved me $10,000,' " Payton said.

It made sense that after working in practice with Romo for three seasons, Payton would be interested in bringing him to New Orleans. Aaron Brooks started thirteen games and Todd Bouman started three games for the Saints in 2005. They needed a quarterback. "Dallas wasn't going to part ways with Tony," Payton said. "We made inquiries."

Parcells liked what he saw in Romo. He had signed Drew

Bledsoe, his former Patriots quarterback, in Payton's last year in Dallas but invested enough time in Romo over three seasons and decided not to give up on him. Early in Romo's fourth season, Parcells benched Bledsoe and promoted Romo to the starting job.

Payton needed to find an alternative. The Saints had the second pick in the draft and would have their choice of quarterbacks Vince Young, Matt Leinart, and Jay Cutler. Payton could pick any of the three and try to develop him into a winning quarterback. But there was an intriguing free agent. Drew Brees had put together two consecutive fabulous seasons with the Chargers—he threw for a total of fifty-one touchdowns and just twenty-two interceptions and was selected to play in the Pro Bowl each year—but in the final game of 2005, he tore the labrum in his right shoulder and suffered a partial tear of his rotator cuff. His shoulder was dislocated. He had been hit in the end zone by Denver safety John Lynch. The ball came loose, and Brees went after it. Broncos defensive tackle Gerard Warren landed on Brees.

"Obviously, I'd like to get this thing operated on as soon as possible," Brees said after the game. "We're all very optimistic. The doctors are very optimistic, saying that this is something that they've seen before, done before. It shouldn't be a big deal."

It gave the Chargers the perfect opportunity to part with Brees. They had drafted Eli Manning first overall in 2004 and within the hour had traded him to the Giants for Philip Rivers. Manning didn't want to play in San Diego, and the Chargers were not going to risk having him sit out the season and go back in the draft the next year. They drafted Manning knowing the Giants wanted him. The Giants selected Rivers for the Chargers and then consummated the deal with the Chargers. San Diego coach Marty Schottenheimer had coached Rivers in the Senior Bowl, and the Chargers loved him.

Rivers's holdout as a rookie lasted deep into training camp, which prevented him from competing for the starting job and precluded San Diego from trading Brees. He responded by throwing twenty-seven touchdowns and only seven interceptions, and Rivers couldn't get off the bench. In his first three seasons, Brees had twenty-nine touchdowns and thirty-one interceptions, which is why San Diego wanted Rivers. Brees won eleven of his fifteen starts in 2004 and kept the starting quarterback job. San Diego used its franchise tag on Brees in 2005, and he signed a one-year $8 million contract. Rivers attempted only thirty passes in his first two seasons.

But Brees's shoulder injury changed everything. Chargers general manager A. J. Smith wasn't going to franchise Brees again, not when he had suffered a major injury and not when he wanted to get Rivers on the field anyway. San Diego wished Brees well, and he became a free agent. He went to Birmingham, Alabama, where famed orthopedist Dr. James Andrews rebuilt his damaged throwing shoulder.

Brees was the perfect quarterback for Payton—if he was healthy. If Payton had Brees's talent, it's how he would have played the game. The Saints and the Dolphins were the only teams interested. Payton flew to Birmingham in Benson's plane and picked up Brees and his wife, Brittany, and brought them to New Orleans. "We had a well-planned day," Payton said. "We wanted to make sure he saw the challenges we had."

Payton had never met Brees. "I knew of him and scouted him, and his work habits were unbelievable," he said.

Just a couple of months earlier, Payton hired Pete Carmichael Jr. off the Chargers staff to be his quarterback coach. He had been the quality control coach in San Diego. He later became the Saints' offensive coordinator. Payton was just putting together his offensive playbook and was going to be flexible with the terminology. They had a Powerpoint presentation prepared for Brees on his visit. Once Brees signed, they gave him input on how he wanted certain plays labeled. "If I called a play Sail and Drew called it Flutie, then we will change it to Flutie," Payton said. "We're all going to learn it for the first time; the protection system and the run game were set up. But where we could take plays he was familiar with in San Diego and use that same terminology, it just made sense."

Payton and Brees spent three hours on football to make sure he understood that Payton had a plan and that it could work if Brees was the quarterback. Payton helped the Giants get to a Super Bowl with Kerry Collins, and in his first year in Dallas, he squeezed a playoff year out of Carter. After working on selling himself as the right coach, Payton had to persuade Brees and his wife that New Orleans was going to be the right place to raise a family. Payton drove the Breeses to the North Shore, about forty-five minutes from the Saints' complex. They looked around some subdivisions, and then it was Payton's intention to drive them to their hotel before having dinner at 7 p.m. The problem was that Payton was not yet familiar with the area and got lost on the way back. He made it to the twenty-one-mile bridge over Lake Pontchartrain without a problem. "It's just a long, long flat bridge," Payton said. "So we came across the causeway heading to the facility, and I got off on the wrong road. I knew better. I should have had somebody with me that knew the area. So we're driving, we're driving. It wasn't twenty minutes out of the way. Now we're about fifty minutes. And I'm looking in the rearview mirror, and poor Brittany is dosing off. I'm on the cell phone with Mickey, and he's trying to get me back. So instead of being back by three, it's four thirty."

Payton couldn't help thinking that on his first big free agent recruiting venture he had lost his man. "I thought we've got no chance," he said.

Payton salvaged the night with a dinner reservation at Emeril's, one of the best restaurants in the French Quarter. The next morning, Brees was on a flight to Miami, which was considered his preferred destination. The Dolphins also were considering former Vikings quarterback Daunte Culpepper, whose season ended in 2005 when he tore three knee ligaments. Even so, the Dolphins doctors considered Culpepper less of a medical risk than Brees, and Miami never offered Brees a contract. It was a decision that sent the franchise reeling. Instead of signing Brees, whose shoulder was fully healed in time for him to participate in training camp, they sent a second-round draft choice to the Vikings for Culpepper, who started and played in only four games in his single season with the Dolphins, which was cut short by shoulder and knee problems.

One week after Payton got lost driving him around New Orleans, Brees called back to say he was accepting the Saints' offer.

"I just felt that energy in New Orleans," Brees said. "From the very beginning there was a genuine feeling that they wanted me there. They believe I can come back from this shoulder injury and lead them to a championship. They were as confident as I am, and that meant a lot."

Brees signed a six-year $60 million contract. The only risk was the $8 million signing bonus. Once Brees showed he was healthy, and that didn't take very long, he was a bargain.

He led the Saints to the NFC championship game in his first season in New Orleans and was the Super Bowl MVP in his fourth season. He was devastated when Payton was suspended in 2012 and has come to his defense. Payton reached out to Bill Belichick to consult with him on how to handle the public side of the fallout from the scandal. Belichick once was fined $500,000 by Goodell after the Patriots were caught videotaping opponents' defensive signals, a violation of NFL rules. Goodell did not suspend Belichick, although the punishment would have fit the crime.

"Once you get to the top of the mountain, you've got to begin the journey to go back up," Payton said.

He was talking about his team. He could have been talking about himself.

THE PHONE CALL

Joe Gibbs caught the football world looking the other way in 2004 when he finally relented to the full-court press put on by Redskins owner Daniel Snyder and jumped out of the NASCAR pits to come out of retirement and coach the Redskins once again. Snyder idolized Gibbs as a kid growing up in Silver Spring, Maryland, and purchased the team in 1999, seven years after Gibbs left. It had been more than ten dreary years for the 'Skins without Joe.

The Redskins were in serious need of instant credibility by 2004. Snyder was only thirty-three years old when he became the owner. With his tender age, lack of experience in the football business, and abrasive personality, he quickly developed a reputation as an impetuous and impossible person to work for and a man no coach would want in control of his football future.

Gibbs was an icon. He had won three Super Bowls with the Redskins and had done it with three different quarterbacks: Joe Theismann, Doug Williams, and Mark Rypien. His third Super Bowl followed the 1991 season. In 1992, Gibbs formed the Joe Gibbs Racing Team, and after spending one more year with the Redskins, he decided to devote all his attention to NASCAR. The Redskins promoted defensive coordinator Richie Petitbon to replace Gibbs, but he was gone after one season when Washington went a dismal 4–12. Next, Jack Kent Cooke went outside the organization for Norv Turner, who had just helped the rival Cowboys win Super Bowls two years in a row. His work in developing Troy Aikman was instrumental in returning Dallas to prominence.

By the time Snyder became Turner's boss, he was entering his sixth year as the Redskins' coach and had not made the playoffs. It's inevitable in the NFL that coaches will be fired, especially when a new owner puts down a good chunk of his life savings and expects instant gratification. The clock was ticking on Turner the moment Snyder signed the last piece of paper on his purchase. He received a stay of execution when the Redskins made the playoffs in Snyder's first season and then won a playoff game, but he was gone with three games to go in 2000. Snyder had been looking for the right time to fire Turner, and that came after a loss to the Giants that made the team's record 7–6. Terry Robiskie finished out the 8–8 season as the interim coach.

Snyder went for a big name when he hired Marty Schottenheimer, but when a power struggle ensued after another 8–8 season, Schottenheimer was fired. Snyder thought he won the lottery when he hired Steve Spurrier, who just ten days earlier had surprisingly resigned after twelve years coaching at the University of Florida, his alma mater. Spurrier built a powerhouse in Gainesville and had been highly sought after in the NFL, but he repeatedly refused to leave the comfort zone he established in Florida. Besides, coaching in the NFL would drastically reduce the number of tee times Spurrier could fit into his schedule during the season and in the off-season. Spurrier lasted only two years in Washington—7–9 and 5–11—and left when it was clear that NFL coaching life was not for him: training camp, the regular season, the NFL Combine, free agency, the draft, minicamps, organized team activities (OTAs)—that didn't leave a big window for setting up tee times. He made $10 million for his twelve victories and soon was back in college coaching at South Carolina.

Now Snyder was in a jam, and his idol bailed him out. He found

Gibbs at a time in his life when he was willing to get back into the grind. Not surprisingly, Gibbs was successful in the racing business. His team won the Sprint Cup Series in 2000 and 2002, and by 2004 Gibbs felt comfortable relocating back to Virginia from Charlotte. Could his Redskins enjoy the same success again?

Snyder made him the highest paid coach in the NFL with a five-year $28.5 million deal. For that price, he also bought himself a lot of goodwill with Redskins fans. Gibbs was beloved in Washington. Snyder was not, but he hit a home run. It was an excellent public relations move even if there were doubts about Gibbs's ability to recapture his old magic after being gone so long. It wasn't the first time Snyder had tried to persuade Gibbs to come home and save the Redskins. Now he was going to get his chance, and even after being out of football for the last eleven seasons, he was a better choice than Jim Fassel, Dennis Green, and Ray Rhodes, the other candidates interviewed. Gibbs brought instant credibility.

The money was great, and Gibbs hired his son Coy to be on his staff. Coy wanted to get into coaching, and this gave Gibbs a chance to ease his son into the business and keep his family close to him. But he also was putting his reputation on the line by giving this another shot. He was already in the Pro Football Hall of Fame. Anything short of a fourth Super Bowl title to go with the three Vince Lombardi Trophies that were sitting in the lobby at Redskins Park would be a disappointment.

"There is no net," Gibbs said. "I am hanging. There is nothing down there to catch us. That may be the biggest thrill. Knowing how hard it is and to get the chance to do something super-hard. It's probably going to be one of the toughest deals you can imagine."

At his introductory news conference on January 8, 2004, many of Gibbs's former players came by to lend their support, including Darrell Green, Art Monk, and Gary Clark. Gibbs spoke for forty-five minutes without naming one current Redskins player. He had a lot of catching up to do. But he didn't become one of the all-time best coaches in NFL history by cutting corners. He would put in the hours, Snyder would spend the money, and pretty soon the fans would be singing "Hail to the Redskins" and really mean it.

Gibbs had a formidable challenge. He had been gone from the league since 1992, and a lot had changed in the way the NFL conducted business. It was a different game. There was free agency and the salary cap. It was the new world of NFL finances and player movement. The Redskins were a dominant team in the twelve seasons Gibbs coached them in Act 1—they made the Super Bowl four times and won three of those games. But now he was inheriting a team that had made the playoffs just once in the little more than a decade during which he was gone.

The good news was that the Redskins were bad enough in 2003 that Gibbs inherited the fifth pick in a draft loaded with talented players. Mississippi quarterback Eli Manning went first to the Chargers, Iowa offensive tackle Robert Gallery second to the Raiders, Pittsburgh wide receiver Larry Fitzgerald third to the Cardinals, and North Carolina State quarterback Philip Rivers fourth to the Giants. The Giants immediately traded Rivers to the Chargers along with picks in the first, third, and fifth rounds for Manning, a daring move that paid off with two Super Bowl titles in Manning's first eight seasons.

The three best players left on the draft board when it came time for Paul Tagliabue to announce the Redskins' pick were quarterback Ben Roethlisberger from Miami of Ohio and safety Sean Taylor and tight end Kellen Winslow from the University of Miami. The Redskins had selected quarterback Patrick Ramsey with their first-round choice in 2002. He was a developing player. That ruled out Roethlisberger, which became a mistake when Ramsey turned out to be a dud and Big Ben won two Super Bowls in his first five seasons. The Redskins gave strong consideration to Taylor and Winslow. They selected Taylor, a phenomenal athlete, perhaps the next Ronnie Lott. Safeties are a low-priority position and usually do not get taken very high in the draft. Lott was the overall eighth pick by the 49ers in 1981, and he began his career at cornerback, a more valued position. But he made the Hall of Fame because he was one of the greatest safeties to ever play the game.

The Redskins spent a lot of time in Miami with Taylor before the draft and felt confident that he was going to be a big-time player for them. They decided he was their guy. But once they selected him, he was difficult for Gibbs to read. "He was kind of standoffish. It was hard for me to get in contact with him," Gibbs said. "He wouldn't return phone calls. Now once you got him on the field, he was great. As a matter of fact, this guy loved football. He felt like he was made to play football. He probably could have been a running back; he could have been a heckuva receiver. We played him some at receiver. He was obviously a great safety. But he also could have been a corner. Real competitive."

Taylor's personality didn't change much in his rookie year: great player, tough to get to know. But he was the foundation that Gibbs knew he could build his defense around even though Taylor was running into problems off the field. Gibbs suspended him one game his rookie year after Taylor was arrested for driving under the influence, charges that later were dropped. Taylor's father, Pedro, was the chief of police in Florida City, and so he should have known right from wrong, but he was a young man with a lot of money in his pocket and was still trying to figure things out. The NFL fined him $71,764 for violating the personal conduct policy when he was charged with a felony count of aggravated assault with a firearm for brandishing a gun in 2005. Taylor took a plea agreement of two misdemeanors and received eighteen months probation. He had been fined seven times by the NFL for late hits. He spit on Tampa Bay Buccaneers running back Michael Pittman in a playoff game after the 2005 season. Like a lot of players, Taylor needed to grow up. He came out of Miami after his junior season and was just twenty-one years old when he entered the NFL. The football is always the easy part.

It's being out on their own, the new and vastly improved financial situation, the after-hours temptations—those are the things that often provide the biggest impediment to success.

Gibbs was not only a great coach but very spiritual. He had a way of reaching his players, even those who seemed lost. Taylor was putting his people skills to the test. "The way you react to him is you're trying to win him over," Gibbs said.

If Taylor felt people around him were trying to take advantage of him and in return he was not trusting, Gibbs at least wanted Taylor to trust him. So Gibbs made a special effort with him. "You get a player like that, and all of a sudden he's got a lot of money in his deal, so you are trying to work through that," Gibbs said. "This guy could be a very, very valuable part of what we're doing here in the future. When you got him on the field, he really was a leader right off the bat. You're wanting to develop a relationship with him as a coach. Every player is not going to love his coach, but you want his respect and to have a chance. You are kind of wanting all of them to love the Redskins and have a great relationship with you. That's not going to happen, but you would like to win most of them over."

The Redskins were just 6–10 in Gibbs's first season. Not to worry. He had been only 8–8 in his first season with the Redskins in 1981 after losing the first five games. He won the Super Bowl in his second season. That season was reduced to just nine games as a result of the fifty-seven-day strike, turning the year from the usual marathon into a sprint. Redskins fans knew Gibbs was the real deal when he beat Tom Landry in the NFC championship game and then one week later beat Don Shula in the Super Bowl.

Once again, in his second act, the Redskins improved in Gibbs's second season. In 2005, the Redskins were 10–6 and made the playoffs as a wild card. They beat the Bucs in the first round before losing to the Seahawks. Back on the NASCAR circuit, Gibbs's team won its third Sprint Cup Series championship. It was a good year.

Gibbs started to notice a change in Taylor before his third season. Taylor had met Jackie Garcia while they were at Gulliver Prep high school in Miami. Taylor was infatuated. She was the niece of the actor Andy Garcia. He came home and told his grandmother about Jackie and said that he had to learn how to speak Spanish. They had a daughter, also named Jackie, in May 2006 after Taylor's second year with the Redskins. He embraced fatherhood. That changed his demeanor. He also was letting Gibbs into his life.

"He had his first child, and you'd see him walk around with that little girl," Gibbs said. "He started coming to our chapel services, and I felt there was real change in his life. The next thing, he walked down the hall and said, 'Hey coach, how you doing?' It was just a real change at how he looked at things."

Taylor was having his best season in 2007. The Redskins were 5–3 at the halfway point after an overtime victory against the Jets. But late in the third quarter the next week against the Eagles, Taylor sustained a sprained knee. Without him, the Redskins gave up 20 points in the fourth quarter and lost. Taylor told defensive coordinator Gregg Williams that he didn't expect to be out very long.

"Hopefully, Sean will be fine," cornerback Shawn Springs said. "He looked like he'll be fine. I wouldn't doubt that he'll be right back out there."

Taylor did not play the next week against the Cowboys in a tough 28–23 loss in Dallas. Terrell Owens caught four touchdown passes from Tony Romo as the 'Boys took advantage of the Redskins being without their best defensive player. Washington had now lost two games in a row and desperately needed Taylor to return to the field. They were in Tampa the next week, and once again Taylor was not healthy enough to play. When the Redskins were losing to the Bucs, Taylor was back home in Miami with Jackie, his fiancée, and their eighteen-month-old daughter, taking care of some personal business with his house, which had been broken into the previous week. It was Thanksgiving weekend. He had arrived in Miami on that Saturday. After watching the Redskins lose their third straight game the next day, he went on a thirty-mile bicycle ride. Maybe that workout would accelerate his return to the field. His team desperately needed him. But he would never play again.

The knee injury that kept him away from his team would cost him his life.

The phone call.

It comes after midnight, and it's the call every mother and father fear when their children are out of the house. It's the call every coach fears when his players are not under their control. You can't watch them 24/7. Nothing much good ever happens after midnight, especially when you are dealing with young men in their twenties, many of whom are millionaires, already with more money than they dreamed they would make in a lifetime.

Giants coach Tom Coughlin got the phone call in 2008 that Plaxico Burress, who had been a close friend of Sean Taylor, accidentally shot himself in the leg on the night after Thanksgiving at a midtown Manhattan nightclub. He never played for the Giants again, and his absence cost them a chance to repeat as Super Bowl champions. The phone rang in the home of Baltimore Ravens coach Brian Billick after midnight, a few hours after the St. Louis Rams defeated the Tennessee Titans in Super Bowl XXXIV in Atlanta in 2000. Billick's best player, Ray Lewis, was in trouble in Atlanta after a street fight outside a nightclub in upscale Buckhead at 4 a.m. left two men stabbed to death. Lewis and two friends were charged with murder, felony murder, and aggravated assault. Lewis was jailed for nearly three weeks before he was released on $1 million bond. He posted $200,000 in cash. His mother had been waiting for him in Honolulu for Pro Bowl week at the time he was arrested. He never made it. The phone rang so late in the Billick house that he knew there was a problem.

"Both my daughters, who were living at home at the time, were home," he said. "I knew this was about my team. You don't get a call that late when it's not about one or the other. You knew it wasn't going to be good."

Billick didn't have a lot of information initially, but the Ravens organization placed its faith in Lewis. "The hard thing is there was no one to call for reference to say, 'Okay, what happens when your best player is indicted on two counts of murder? How did you handle this?' What was the case study? It had never happened before."

Four months later, Lewis reached an agreement to plead guilty to misdemeanor obstruction of justice and avoided jail time. The murder charges were dropped.

There is nothing in the playbook, nothing one coach can learn from another, that Gibbs could reference to help him deal with the phone call he was about to receive. The Redskins returned from Tampa on the night of November 25, 2007, after losing to the Bucs. They were reeling at 5–6, the last two losses without their brilliant young safety Sean Taylor, who had become a team leader.

Gibbs's phone rang at six o'clock on the morning of November 26. It was Dan Snyder. It could not be good.

"Sean has been shot," Snyder said.

"How bad is it? Where is he shot?" Gibbs said.

"He's shot in the leg," Snyder said.

Gibbs's first thought was, okay, it's only the leg; Sean is going to be fine. This was a strong twenty-four-year old athlete. He might need time to recover, but at least he hadn't been shot in the head or the chest. Gibbs didn't have enough information. "Not realizing exactly where he got shot and the fact that he bled so much," Gibbs said.

Taylor was in bed with his two Jackies in his house in the upscale area of Palmetto Bay when he heard intruders. He reached for a machete that he kept by the bed for emergency situations. This was an emergency. The house had been burglarized on November 17, but no one had been home. A kitchen knife had been left on the bed. The intruders clearly didn't expect anybody to be home this time, either. Taylor played for the Redskins, and he was not supposed to be in Miami.

Taylor tried to block the bedroom door. Two shots were fired. One hit the wall. The other hit Taylor in the leg in the upper thigh area near the femoral artery. Jackie called 911 on her cell phone at 1:40 a.m. Taylor was airlifted to the trauma unit of Jackson Memorial Hospital.

He underwent seven hours of surgery beginning at 5:30 a.m. He lost a massive amount of blood and required seven transfusions. His heart stopped beating twice during surgery. He was unresponsive and unconscious when he came out of surgery. Back at Redskins Park, Gibbs and team chaplain Brett Fuller addressed the players at noon and told them Taylor was in critical condition. Snyder flew to Miami in his private plane and took running back Clinton Portis and others with him. Portis and Taylor were tight from their days together at the University of Miami. Portis played the first two years of his career with the Denver Broncos but was traded to the Redskins for cornerback Champ Bailey two months before the Redskins selected Taylor in the first round.

Portis had seen the change in his friend. "It's hard to expect a man to grow up overnight," he was quoted in the *Washington Post*. "But ever since he had this child, it was like a new Sean. And everybody around here knew it. He was always smiling, always happy, always talking about his child."

There was a shred of optimism when it was reported the night of the surgery that Taylor squeezed the doctor's hand and made facial expressions. It was false hope. He was dead at 3:30 the next morning.

The coaches' manual does not provide instructions for how to handle a locker room in mourning when a teammate is shot to death in the middle of the season. There was no crisis management team to call in. Football teams are like families. At least the good ones are.

"We wind up losing Sean. You never plan for that," Gibbs said. "Coaches go through a lot of things, but you don't go through that. We certainly didn't have a plan. You just kind of embark on something like that, and you just try to do the best you can to handle it from day to day."

Gibbs's strength held the Redskins together during the week. He was the leader, the foundation of the organization. The players and staff looked to him for guidance.

Gibbs didn't second-guess the organization's decision to allow Taylor to return to his Miami home instead of forcing him to remain in Virginia to keep rehabilitating his knee. "I never really did think a lot about that," Gibbs said. "It was a decision where we felt it was best for him personally. He wanted to get the situation squared away with his house so he could come back and be more focused on football."

Gibbs knew his players and knew this was going to be the toughest challenge he ever faced as a head coach. "Our players were distraught," he said. "Looking them in the eye, you see it had a huge impact on them."

If the season had not slipped away already, it was surely hanging by its fingertips on the edge of a cliff with a three-hundred-foot drop. Gibbs was always adept at finding ways to motivate his team. He was such a good coach that he often could impose his will on the other team by the sheer brilliance of his game plans. Defenses knew that Gibbs loved the counter trey, a misdirection running play, and that he loved it even more when he had John Riggins. Nobody could stop it.

This was different. It had nothing to do with X's and O's. This took Gibbs out of his comfort zone. Less than a week after Taylor died, the Redskins were playing a home game against the Buffalo Bills. If they had any desire to remain in the race for a wild-card spot, it was imperative that they beat the Bills. But they had to play with broken hearts, the most debilitating injury of all. Gibbs says Taylor is one of the top five athletes he's ever coached, but it was more than that now. There was a death in the family. A young lady lost her fiancé. A little girl lost her father. Parents lost their son. And Redskins Nation lost one of its best players. How could the Redskins summon the strength to play a football game? During the week, Gibbs had Portis and Santana Moss, another player from Miami, speak to the team about Taylor. Gibbs was dealing with fifty-two personalities who would all attempt to process the loss in their own way.

The Redskins distributed white towels with Taylor's number 21 to the fans at FedEx Field. Taylor's locker was encased in Plexiglas. There was a four-minute video tribute to Taylor prior to the game and the Redskins' marching band wore black hats. Defensive coordinator Gregg Williams elected to open the game with only ten defensive players for the first play. The eleventh spot belonged to Taylor; his replacement, Reed Doughty, stood on the sidelines. Williams made the decision without first consulting with Gibbs. He had described Taylor as being like a son to him, and this was his way of honoring him. "He was going to ride with us one more time," Williams said.

Buffalo's Fred Jackson ran for 22 yards against the ten-man defense.

It was a strange game. There were ten scores: eight field goals, a safety, and a touchdown. The only touchdown, a 3-yard run by Portis, had given the Redskins a 16–5 lead with 5:42 left in the third quarter. Buffalo moved to within 16–14 on three field goals by Rian Lindell. But now the Bills were on the Redskins' 33 with eight seconds to go after Buffalo quarterback Trent Edwards spiked the ball to stop the clock.

As Lindell was about to attempt a 51-yard field goal, Gibbs called time-out. Freezing the kicker at the last possible moment had become the trendy thing to do in the NFL. There was a new rule in the NFL allowing coaches to call time-outs from the sidelines. Denver's Mike Shanahan began the freezing the kicker movement earlier in the season. Lindell went through with the kick anyway, and it was good. Good move by Gibbs. The points came off the board. There is also a rule in the NFL that you are prohibited from calling consecutive time-outs. Gibbs didn't know the rule and called time-out again to ice Lindell just before Lindell would have attempted the kick a second time. Gibbs thought the official on the sideline had given him the okay. The flag went up, and Gibbs's heart sunk. He had blown it. The unsportsmanlike conduct penalty cost 15 crucial yards, moving the ball to the 18-yard line. Lindell then drilled a 36-yard field goal to win the game.

"I will never forget it," Gibbs said.

He was sixty-seven years old. His age had nothing to do with him blanking out on the rule. Less than one week earlier, one of his best players had been murdered. He won't use that as the reason. He says he wasn't distracted. "I just think it was a terrible mistake," he said. "There was no excuse for it. I did it. I don't think you make an excuse for something like that."

It had been the worst week in Redskins history. It wasn't supposed to end with the iconic coach, the glue of the Redskins, losing the game. "When I first saw the commotion, I was hoping it had been a procedural penalty on Buffalo," left guard Pete Kendall said after the game. "After that, after it was explained, my first thought was I felt for whoever called that. To find out that it was Coach Gibbs, after the week that he's been through, my heart just breaks for him."

In the end, it did come down to Gibbs making a mistake. But it would have been tough for the Redskins to beat any team that day, even a team as poor as the Bills, who finished 7–9 that season. The Redskins were still in pain. Gibbs knew by looking at his players before the game that "they were wanting to, but just couldn't. It just wound up being a huge disappointment for all of us."

And the players knew by looking at his face that he was tired and worn out. Gibbs had been through a lot in the last week. The team had been through a lot. Now there were whispers that his blunder against the Bills was proof that he never should have returned to the sidelines. Had the game passed him by? It was the same criticism Tom Landry faced at the end of his twenty-nine-year run as the Cowboys' coach. This is a results-oriented business, and when the team is not having success, it's the coach who gets the blame. This was new for Gibbs. In his first life with the Redskins, he was considered an innovative coach. When he walked away two months after the 1992 season, he left at the top of his game. He wanted more time with his family—that's what they all say—and had driven himself so hard that leaving when he did was the right thing to do. He had taken the Redskins to the playoffs eight times and won three Super Bowls in twelve years. He said his decision had nothing to do with his health, his racing team, or the Redskins. It was simply family-related. His son Coy was playing at Stanford, and Gibbs had seen him play only twice. He felt guilty.

Gibbs did reveal that late in the 1992 season he had been unable to sleep and had developed a nervous twitch, which ultimately was blamed on exhaustion. His decision to leave shocked the Redskins simply because so much time had passed since the end of the season. But after a family vacation in Vail, Colorado, his mind was made up. It was time to go.

"Every year, we get away and talk about it," Gibbs said at the farewell news conference in 1993. "We always reach the same conclusion. This year, it was different. The boys didn't encourage me one way or another, but they understood when I told them what I was thinking. I think Pat's happier than anyone. This isn't an easy lifestyle for a coach's wife. The coach is the guy who stands up and hears everyone tell him how great he is. The wife is the one waiting at home alone while the coach is spending every night at the office."

When he returned to the Redskins, Gibbs promised his wife

he would stop sleeping in the office. It was a promise he could not keep. Gibbs knew only one way to do it and was not making any concessions to his age. Besides, Pat was spending a lot of her time surrounded by family back home in Charlotte, so Gibbs knew he wasn't leaving her alone in Virginia.

After the loss to the Bills, the record was 5–7 and the Redskins players had every reason to pack their bags and wait for the end of the season. And now they were facing another challenging week—emotionally and physically. The day after the loss, Snyder flew the entire team and members of the organization on a 747 to Miami for Taylor's funeral. "I wanted everybody to pay respect to a fallen hero of the Redskins," Snyder said. "We hopefully did a respectable job of paying respect to Sean's family. I think I was very responsible for making sure we did everything first class with dignity and pride."

He is sitting in his large office at Redskins Park talking about Taylor and how he still thinks about him all the time. He points to his desk. "It's a picture of me and Sean Taylor," he says.

In addition to the Redskins family, more than twenty players from around the NFL attended the three-hour service. And on Thursday that week, the Redskins were playing at home against the Bears. Two games in five days with a funeral in between for a fallen teammate. How much can be asked of one team, of one group of young men dealing with the death of a friend?

"It was a big challenge for the whole coaching staff and the players," Gibbs said. "By that Thursday night, they really wanted to honor Sean. It drove them. I can remember the guys were jacked."

Just as Gibbs knew by looking in the eyes of his players before the Buffalo game that they were not ready to play, he knew before the Chicago game that they were ready to do everything they could to win one for Taylor and end the four-game losing streak. If the season seemed lost at the time, it didn't mean they had to lose this game.

"It was probably one of the greatest games I've ever had a team play for me," Gibbs said.

The Redskins refused to lose. Gibbs remembers cornerback Fred Smoot coming off the field but refusing to stay in the locker room. "He's throwing up blood on the sideline," he said. Smoot had a severe stomach illness, but he returned to the game. Quarterback Jason Campbell went out with a dislocated kneecap late in the second quarter that cost him the rest of the season. But journeyman Todd Collins came into the game against the Bears "and plays one of the best games I've ever seen somebody play coming off the bench," Gibbs said.

Collins was fifteen of twenty for 224 yards and two touchdowns in the 24–16 victory. Even with the win, the Redskins were only 6–7 with no indication they were ready to go on a winning streak that could qualify them for the playoffs.

That changed the next week when they went up to the Meadowlands to play the New York Giants, who also were fighting to make the playoffs. The Giants' coach, Tom Coughlin, had barely escaped being fired after the 2006 season. New York was 9–4 after victories over the Bears and the Eagles the previous two weeks. This was not going to be an easy game for the Redskins. The best thing about playing Thursday games, as the Redskins had against the Bears, is that if you win, you have ten days to catch your breath and get reenergized coming off a victory. It's a very long ten days if you lose.

The Sunday night game against the Giants was when the Redskins started to believe again. They beat New York 22–10 on one of those nights when Giants Stadium was a wind tunnel. Eli Manning was able to complete just eighteen of fifty-three passes. Collins managed to complete only eight of twenty-five. It was an ugly game, but it enabled the Redskins to get back to .500. They no longer were an emotionally beaten-down team. Instead, they were inspired by the memory of Sean Taylor.

"The whole organization handled it exactly the right way,"

said Kendall, who was in his first year with the Redskins. "Guys were really torn up on a personal level with what happened to Sean. I remember Joe and Dan had their finger on the pulse of the team. There was a time to work and a time to do the right thing in terms of honoring Sean's memory and family. The team was able to respond right after the Buffalo game."

The Redskins then beat the Vikings, a contender for one of the two wild-card spots. That put the Skins at 8–7. The final game of the year was at home against the hated Cowboys. One of the most popular items for sale outside old RFK Stadium for those intense Dallas-Washington games was a button that simply stated: "Fuck Dallas." The same sentiment, in a more civilized tone, was printed on T-shirts: "I Root for Two Teams: The Redskins and Anybody Playing Dallas."

Nothing else really needed to be said about how the Redskins and their fans felt about America's Team. Before this crucial game against the Cowboys that would determine whether the Redskins made the playoffs, former Washington defensive end Dexter Manley, who had knocked Cowboys quarterback Danny White out of the 1982 NFC championship game, which led to the Redskins' first Super Bowl victory, took the microphone at midfield at FedEx Field and led the fans in a chant of "We Want Dallas." The Redskins were fired up and outgained the Cowboys 105–14 in the first quarter.

The Redskins caught a break because Dallas already had clinched the NFC's number one seed. That allowed Wade Phillips to rest four banged-up starters, including wide receiver Terrell Owens, who had an ankle injury. T.O. had caught the four touchdown passes against the Redskins earlier in the season. Phillips played quarterback Tony Romo through the first series of the third quarter. He left with Dallas trailing 13–3. The Redskins scored on their next possession to make it 20–3. Former Redskins quarterback Brad Johnson relieved Romo, and Washington went on to win 27–6. Dallas was held to 1 yard rushing. Collins played well again, and since taking over for Campbell, he had completed 67 of 105 passes for 888 yards with five touchdowns and no interceptions. If you take away that windy night at Giants Stadium, he was fifty-nine for eighty, an impressive 74 percent.

In the four games since Taylor's funeral, the Redskins were 4–0, and they went into the playoffs as the hottest team in the NFC. "To come back and win four games; if Joe and Dan hadn't handled that situation the way they did, it was unlikely we would have been able to do that," Kendall said. "You can't pretend it didn't happen and keep a stiff upper lip. They were able to get the team to strike the right balance between mourning Sean's loss and honoring Sean's memory."

The Redskins were in the process of writing an incredible story in the wild-card game in Seattle. They trailed 13–0 before Collins threw a 7-yard touchdown pass to Antwaan Randle El on the first play of the fourth quarter. The Redskins intercepted Matt Hasselbeck on the next possession, setting up Collins's 30-yard touchdown pass to Moss to give Washington a 14–13 lead less than three minutes into the fourth quarter.

But then things fell apart. It was as if the anguish of the events since that Sunday night after Thanksgiving in Miami had finally become too much to bear. Hasselbeck put the Seahawks on top 19–14 on a 20-yard pass to Dino Hackett with 6:06 left in the game. Seattle was successful on the two-point conversion to put the lead at 21–14. The Redskins showed they still might have a little gas left in the tank when Rock Cartwright returned the kickoff to the Seattle 44. But on first down, Collins went deep down the right sideline for Moss and was intercepted by Marcus Trufant, who returned the interception 78 yards for a touchdown to give Seattle a 28–14 lead. Collins would throw another interception for a touchdown with twenty-seven seconds remaining. The final score was 35–14. That was deceptive. The Redskins had a fourth-quarter lead, but part of the problem in the four years since Gibbs returned was the inability of Williams's defense to protect fourth quarter leads.

It was the last game of Gibbs's career. He had one year left on his contract but decided the time was right to retire again. Two days after the loss to the Seahawks, Gibbs resigned. Snyder had stayed up with him until 2:30 a.m. the night before he made his decision public trying to persuade him to return for the 2008 season.

"You can never replace Joe Gibbs," Snyder said.

It was the one-year anniversary of his grandson Taylor, then just two years old, being diagnosed with acute lymphoblastic leukemia. He was being treated back home in North Carolina with spinal taps, pills, and shots, according to the *Charlotte Observer*, which reported that Taylor was in remission by the fifteenth day of the treatments, but to prevent a relapse, the treatments continued until Taylor, the son of J. D. Gibbs and his wife, Melissa, was five years old. Gibbs called his seven grandchildren his "grandbabies" and didn't want them growing up without him. He felt guilty that he wasn't around enough for his boys. Coy already had decided coaching was not for him and returned to the NASCAR team before the 2007 season. Pat was back in North Carolina. After the loss in Seattle, Gibbs returned home to talk to his family in Charlotte to help make his decision.

"I felt like they needed me," he said.

The final month of the season allowed Gibbs to leave with his legacy intact. "I hate to leave something unfinished. I made an original commitment of five years. I felt bad about that," he said. "Pro sports has been my life."

He is a good man but left the game with a heavy heart.

"You kind of live in a little bit of fear of late night phone calls," he said.

TUNA SUBS

Bill Parcells. Pete Carroll. Bill Belichick.

Bill, Pete, and Bill were hardly Moe, Larry, and Curly. They are three heavyweight coaches. If they weren't Ruth, Gehrig, and DiMaggio, either, at least Parcells and Belichick are Pro Football Hall of Fame–caliber coaches, and though Carroll has had only moderate success in the NFL, he dominated in college football. The one thing the three had in common: they worked for Patriots owner Robert Kraft. There isn't an NFL owner who has had a more fascinating and dizzying ride with his coaches than Kraft.

"When I go into any situation, I look for stability," Kraft said. "In the NFL, more than any other business, you need stability, people who can trust one another. This is an up and down business."

Parcells had one of the biggest egos and biggest résumés. Carroll became an elite college coach, winning two national championships at Southern Cal after he left the Patriots, where he was way over his head in replacing Parcells. It was much harder following a legend in New England than creating a legacy at USC. Belichick, the sourpuss genius, guided Kraft's Patriots to five Super Bowls, winning three, in his first twelve years with the team, but his accomplishments have been tarnished by the Spygate scandal.

Kraft was in awe of Parcells, but they had an unmanageable working relationship. He thought Carroll was a prince but just didn't win enough. Belichick took his passion for winning too far and embarrassed the organization by spying on opponents, but he won for Kraft and Kraft had his back. Ultimately, the owner has to be comfortable with the coach and the coach has to respect the owner to create a winning environment.

Kraft purchased the Patriots in 1994, saving them from being moved by owner James Orthwein to his native St. Louis. Kraft owned Foxboro Stadium and refused Orthwein's offer to buy his way out of the lease. Orthwein sold the team to Kraft instead. What Kraft got was a moribund franchise with an inadequate stadium and a lackluster record. "All you did was put your heart and soul into it, turned down $75 million, paid the highest price, a quarter of a billion dollars, your wife thinks you are absolutely nuts, the team has the worst record in the last five years, hadn't sold out a season in thirty-four years, and played in an old dinky stadium," he said.

In this case, one man's garbage was another man's treasure. Kraft, from Brookline, Massachusetts, had been a Patriots season ticket holder since 1971, the year of the grand opening of not-so-grand Foxboro Stadium, the eyesore with the aluminum benches and lousy access roads in the middle of Nowhere, New England. The Patriots finally had their own home. The Boston Patriots were an American Football League original but were neglected orphans in a city infatuated with the Red Sox, Celtics, and Bruins. They bounced from Nickerson Field, to Fenway Park, to Alumni Stadium, to Harvard Stadium.

Kraft was a visionary when he purchased a ten-year option on the 300 acres of land next to Foxboro Stadium in 1985. In 1988, he paid $25 million to buy the stadium out of bankruptcy court from Billy Sullivan, the original Patriots owner. The Sullivan family took a financial beating promoting Michael Jackson's Victory Tour in 1984. The Patriots' lease on the stadium ran through 2001. That was a smart acquisition and eventually put Kraft in a position of power because he owned the stadium while Sullivan and then Victor Kiam and then Orthwein owned the team.

By 1994, New England was in danger of losing the Patriots. Did anybody really care? Kraft might have been the only one who got misty-eyed about the prospect of the bunch of misfits playing halfway between Beantown and Providence heading to St. Louis. Boston was the only city in America where the professional football team was fourth in popularity. Even when the Pats somehow became the first team to win three road playoff games to advance to the Super Bowl, they were humiliated by the Bears 46–10 in Super Bowl XX, and then were immediately embroiled in a drug controversy.

Sullivan, along with nine partners, paid the $250,000 entry fee to the AFL in 1960 for the Patriots. He sold the team to Kiam in 1988 for $83 million. Kiam then sold it to Orthwein in 1992 for $110 million. Two years later, Orthwein offered Kraft $75 million to buy out the final seven years of the Patriots' lease at Foxboro Stadium so that he could pack up the team and move it to St. Louis, which had lost the Cardinals to Phoenix in 1988. It would have been a nice return on Kraft's $25 million investment, but he said no thanks. Orthwein was the great-grandson of Anheuser-Busch founder Adolphus Busch and at one time owned 1.6 million shares in the company. Considering that Kraft subsequently transformed the Patriots into a model franchise with three Super Bowl championships and the first 16–0 regular season in NFL history, it's easy to forget how close they came to becoming the St. Louis Stallions.

Kraft refused Orthwein's offer on the stadium lease and then offered him $172 million to buy the Patriots, which at the time was the most money ever spent on a sports franchise. Orthwein accepted, and Kraft had himself a bad football team to go along with a run-down stadium right off Route 1 in Foxborough.

"I had to move fast, and I took on a lot of debt," Kraft said. "I had a chance in the '80s to buy it for a lot less money—half of what I paid for it. Then I took out the option on the land and controlled all the parking. I bought the stadium out of bankruptcy. I was working hard to get an edge to buy the team. Kiam had problems, and he brought in Orthwein. He was part of the Orthwein family, the Budweiser family, so he was moving it. Except he had to buy out my lease, and I wouldn't let him do it. I decided to step up and pay a very high price."

It was hardly the deal of the century—just five years earlier, Jerry Jones had spent only $140 million to buy the Cowboys and the lease to Texas Stadium. That was America's Team. The Patriots were Foxborough's team. In the four years before Kraft bought the Patriots, they were a pitiful 14–50. Even so, the Patriots fans were excited to have local ownership. The day after the NFL approved Kraft's purchase in January 1994, New England had one of those fabled winter nor'easters. It was a day when sitting in front of the fireplace is a more attractive option than driving out to the local ballpark to buy tickets to see a bad team. Even so, it was quite busy at the ticket office at Foxboro Stadium. An astounding 5,958 season ticket orders were processed, more than six times the Patriots' one-day record. The previous record was the 979 tickets sold when Parcells was hired in 1993.

Kraft began his business career working for the Rand-Whitney Group of Worcester, Massachusetts, a company that converted paper into packaging. It was owned by Jacob Hiatt, the father of Kraft's wife, Myra. Kraft later bought the company. They had met in 1962 at a deli in Boston. She was a student at Brandeis, and he was at Columbia and in town for the Ivy League basketball game against Harvard. They made eye contact, and Kraft later showed up at the Brandeis campus to find her. They went out on a date, and Kraft is fond of saying she proposed that night. She was nineteen years old. They had a true love affair.

I met with Robert and Myra in the summer of 2010, and we had dinner at a restaurant a few minutes from their home in Chestnut Hill, Massachusetts. Myra looked healthy and energetic. Her ovarian cancer had gone into remission, and she remained active in her philanthropic ventures. Even after finding out the next spring that the insidious cancer had returned, she insisted on keeping a commitment to travel to Israel. But Myra, who adored Robert, wasn't supportive when her husband informed her that he was buying his favorite football team. "This young lady thought I was a little cuckoo," Kraft said. "It was the first time in our marriage she questioned my business sense."

He tended to her every need at the restaurant. He ordered for her and made sure the food was cooked to her liking, not letting on how concerned he was about her health. They were married in June 1963, had four sons, and never tired of each other. They finished each other's sentences. She was a wonderful lady and the love of his life. He always called her his sweetheart. She died on July 20, 2011, about one year after our dinner.

In 2012, *Forbes* ranked the Patriots as the third most valuable franchise in the NFL and the sixth most valuable sports franchise in the world at $1.4 billion, so it turned out to be a pretty wise investment. The Patriots' biggest asset when Kraft became the owner was the Jersey guy who owned two Super Bowl rings from his eight years as head coach of the New York Giants. "You need to get people to trust in your brand, and you look at having someone like Bill Parcells as being a plus and an asset," Kraft said. "But you need a bond."

Parcells quit the Giants on May 15, 1991, leaving them in an awful bind with training camp just ten weeks away. When coaches leave, they usually make the decision within a week or two of the end of the season. But there were many factors at work with the complicated Parcells. His ally with the Giants was co-owner Tim Mara, the nephew of co-owner Wellington Mara. The Maras had an awful relationship, but Parcells managed to get along with both of them, though he was particularly close to Tim. Less than one month after the Giants beat the Bills in Super Bowl XXV, Tim Mara sold his 50 percent interest to New York businessman Robert Tisch, who had long wanted to own an NFL team. The price was $75 million, now one of the great bargains in sports. The Giants were valued at $1.3 billion in 2012 by *Forbes*, making them the fourth most valuable NFL franchise.

Wellington Mara had right of first refusal on his nephew's share but didn't have the money to finance the purchase. For the first time since they were founded in 1925, the Giants were not 100 percent owned by the Mara family. Tim's departure combined with Parcells's health issues—he soon would have several heart procedures—led to Parcells stepping down in May.

It didn't take long for Parcells to regain the desire to coach. He turned down the Bucs after the 1991 season when a deal seemed imminent. Tampa called a news conference to announce Parcells's hiring, but he changed his mind at the last minute. He then flirted with the Packers, who hired Mike Holmgren, and approached the Vikings, who hired Dennis Green, but ended up sitting out the 1992 season. The next year Orthwein offered him the chance to coach the Patriots and run the football operation. Parcells, his health under control and his competitive fire burning once again, found that very attractive. He had been the linebacker coach in New England in 1980 and enjoyed the area. He left New England after only one season when Ray Perkins hired him as the Giants' defensive coordinator, but when he was ready to coach again in 1993, the Patriots were the best fit. He inherited a 1–15 team that would have been dropped down to the second division if the NFL operated like European soccer leagues. Parcells selected quarterback Drew Bledsoe with the first pick in his first draft and was in the playoffs in his second season, which was

Kraft's first season. Everything seemed great. Yet when a rookie owner who has just bought his hometown team inherits an iconic coach used to having his own way, it's only a matter of time before the honeymoon period ends and the divorce proceedings begin. For Kraft and Parcells that took four years and one Super Bowl appearance.

Even though he had long since made his peace with Parcells, some of the stories Kraft told during dinner gave him indigestion. Almost immediately after he purchased the team, Parcells all but flattened him trying to run a power sweep. Kraft said Parcells wanted to create a layer between the two that was completely unacceptable. He remembers the conversation vividly. It took place in the first week after the sale became official. Kraft said Parcells told him, "I think it would be good if you sold 1 percent of the team to Tim Mara."

What? Are you kidding me? "Why would I do that?" Kraft said. "He said he will be between us. He wanted someone in between us. So all of a sudden, my bubble and my dream started to get shattered. I said, 'I don't want anyone between us.'"

Tim Mara was Parcells's confidant. It wouldn't have made any sense for Kraft to make him his only partner. The 1 percent share would have been worth less than $2 million and not even make a dent in Kraft's financial obligations. There was no upside to adding Mara to the family business, especially since he had a contentious relationship with his uncle Wellington, a man Kraft deeply respected. Kraft didn't need to be best friends with Parcells, but they needed to communicate. He didn't need a liaison. He's very approachable; he's not a meddler but likes to be kept informed. Parcells already was running the football side of the business, and so there was no reason to make Mara a partner and insulate Parcells from him. He didn't want Mara, just as he turned down other investors who wanted to buy into the team.

Parcells denies that he wanted Kraft to make Mara a partner and claims he doesn't recall that ever coming up. "That's bullshit.

Why would Tim Mara want to own a part of another team? His family owned the Giants," Parcells said. A high-ranking league insider corroborated Kraft's version and believes part of the motive for Tim Mara was to irritate his uncle Wellington.

"I got to give Bob Tisch the credit," Kraft said. "He said to me at the finance meeting when I was coming in for the interview, 'Look, if you don't need to have partners, don't take partners.' So I said, you know what, I'll wait. I didn't take in partners. It would be like hiring someone in between Bill and I to manage this relationship. I come in, I'm owning the team, I'm a hero in the town, I save it. I turned down the money [from Orthwein], I got a great coach. Then reality started to set in. I got a rude awakening right away."

Kraft delegates authority to the people who manage his businesses around the world. That was what he did with Parcells at first. It made sense. Rookie owner defers to Hall of Fame–caliber coach.

"I loved it that Parcells was the head coach," Kraft said. "They had a great quarterback they had drafted first overall, and they won their last four games of the year. I remember being in the elevator with my son Jonathan after that last game and saying, 'We can't let that team move.' So it was pretty exciting. And having Parcells as the coach—we were lucky to have him. He brought instant credibility to the Patriots. My experience with him, inheriting him as a coach, was probably the best thing that could have happened to me. It taught me about the NFL and how things worked."

Kraft knew he was a lucky man even if Parcells was giving him a hard time. "The odds of being in your hometown, owning your hometown team; you got a greater chance of being a starting quarterback in the NFL than owning a team," he said.

Parcells was set in his ways and not interested in changing for an owner who until now was just a fan, who could have been "Robert from Brookline, long-time listener, first-time caller."

Parcells bailed on the Giants in part because half the team was sold. He later would leave the Jets after the death of owner Leon Hess, whom Parcells greatly admired, and his estate sold the team to Johnson & Johnson heir Woody Johnson. Ownership was always an issue with Parcells. As Kraft became more comfortable, Parcells became more uncomfortable.

"I was really excited about Parcells. I got a Super Bowl coach. I got one of the best in the business," Kraft said. "But, of course, my image of him and what was reality, that was a lot different."

Kraft was eager to soak up all the knowledge that Parcells would impart. And the Tuna, a longtime nickname for Parcells, surely taught him a lesson. Kraft had his eyes opened wide. Quickly. Parcells irritated Kraft after the Patriots lost to Belichick and the Browns in the wild-card game after the 1994 season by proclaiming that he needed time to think over whether he would be back the next year. It was Parcells's second year with the Patriots, his first with Kraft. "At the end of the first year, he says, 'I don't know if I'm going to coach anymore,' " Kraft said. "Every year we went through this."

Kraft couldn't run his business that way. He needed a commitment. It's hard to plan for the future when the coach insists he's year to year. How could he let Parcells influence him to sign players to multiyear contracts when Parcells was not ready to say he would stick around long enough to coach them? Kraft couldn't afford to be caught in the trap that Parcells set for the Giants. He didn't leave until nearly four months after the Super Bowl following the 1990 season, and general manager George Young had few options and was forced to promote little-known running back coach Ray Handley, who turned out to be a disaster and was fired after two seasons.

The relationship between Kraft and Parcells began to disintegrate even before Kraft gave the final say in the draft to personnel director Bobby Grier in 1996. That led to Kraft granting Parcells's wish before the '96 season that the fifth and final year of his contract for the 1997 season, a deal he signed when Orthwein owned the team, be eliminated. The $1.2 million penalty clause for leaving early was also taken out. If Parcells didn't want to be in New England, Kraft didn't want him there. Kraft agreed to cut off the final year, but as Parcells found out after the season, that didn't mean he could just get in his car, head south on I-95, and take a job with the rival New York Jets without the Patriots being compensated. The revised contract prohibited Parcells from coaching any team other than the Patriots in 1997 unless, of course, Kraft gave his blessing.

It was clear that Parcells lost his power when the personnel department overruled him and selected Ohio State wide receiver Terry Glenn with New England's first-round pick in 1996, seventh overall. Parcells wanted to trade down and select Texas defensive end Tony Brackens, who went in the second round to Jacksonville. Parcells didn't even attend the scouting combine that year, a sure sign he was on his way out of New England.

But the problems with Kraft really started much earlier. Parcells had his run of the place the year before Kraft bought the team. Kraft had just invested a fortune and incurred a tremendous amount of debt, and he wasn't going to be an absentee owner. He wasn't looking for Parcells to kiss up to him because he was some rich guy who was now his boss, but he expected to be treated with respect.

"Look, he did great things for the franchise. He brought us instant credibility. He's an engaging personality, and he is fun to be around when he wants to turn on the charm," Kraft said. "I'm not sure he was always respectful to me."

Then, looking over at Myra, he said, "He never would talk to her, not even be polite. That's my wife. I get on the team plane with my banker, the guy that loaned me $172 million on short notice. He looked me in the eye and said, 'I'm never going to get hurt?' And I said, 'No, you won't.' The guy takes a big risk as a banker, so he comes to an away game, and Parcells wouldn't talk to him or say hello to him. It was not pleasant. He wouldn't shake hands or say hello to the CEO of one of the major banks in America. The Bank of Boston. He gets on the plane and looks the other way and won't talk to him. And we're in first class."

Then the Christian Peter fiasco created a firestorm in New England. The Pats selected Peter, a talented defensive tackle from Nebraska, in the fifth round of the '96 draft. Parcells called to welcome him to the team. Peter had a history of violence against women, and the details were chronicled in the days after the draft, causing a tremendous backlash. Myra Kraft was outraged. Within one week, the Patriots relinquished their draft rights to Peter, making him a free agent. The story goes that Myra Kraft demanded that the Patriots disassociate themselves from Peter, but that was not completely true. She did question whether her husband was aware of Peter's background. He was not. He told his coaches that if he needed "thugs or hoodlums" to win, he would get out of the business. It was the first time a drafted player was released before training camp.

Days before the draft, Kraft said the Patriots would never select troubled running back Lawrence Phillips, who was Peter's teammate at Nebraska, because he couldn't explain it to his wife. Phillips had assaulted his girlfriend.

The Patriots had a first-round grade on Peter, and when he started to slip, Kraft was told that the Patriots were going to take him in the fourth or fifth round. "What's the deal?" Kraft asked a member of the Patriots' college scouting department.

"Well, he was a frat boy," he was told. "And he grabbed some girl's tush or crotch."

When Kraft conducted his own investigation of Peter's past after the draft, he discovered that the rap sheet was much more involved. "So I went down to Bill," he said. "I said, 'Look, we are cutting this guy.' I had to show him we couldn't do things with a wink and a nod."

Kraft believes every player on his team "has my family name attached to it," he said. "I don't want thugs and hoodlums here."

Peter was gone. Former Nebraska coach Tom Osborne, a congressman, called Kraft the day Peter was cut. "He begged me and told me how great he was," Kraft said. "I said no. I got about two hundred letters from high school coaches saying thank you. That really helped us."

Parcells's reaction to losing a valuable fifth-round pick? "He was not pleased," Kraft said.

"I can't tell you anything," Parcells said by phone days after Peter was released. "Talk to someone else about it."

In training camp that summer, Parcells rode Glenn hard. When Parcells was asked when the rookie would be returning from a hamstring injury, he said, "She isn't ready yet." Nobody ever said Parcells was politically correct. "That's not the standard we want to set," Kraft said at the time. "That's not the way we do things."

Myra Kraft called Parcells's comment "disgraceful . . . I hope he's chastised for that. It was the wrong thing for anyone to say."

Despite the turmoil, the Patriots finished 11–5 and won the AFC East. By late in the season, rumors were circulating that Parcells was being romanced by the Jets and their owner, Leon Hess. The Jets had been 3–13 in Rich Kotite's first season in 1995 and were on their way to a 1–15 year in 1996. Two days before the final game of the season, Kotite announced that he was stepping down. Hess allowed him to go out with a little dignity by not saying he fired him and letting him coach the final game, which the Jets lost.

Hess knew he needed to restore credibility to the franchise. He knew Parcells was not happy in New England. He knew Parcells was a Jersey guy.

Parcells's final regular season game coaching the Patriots was also the first time he coached against the Giants at Giants Stadium. New England, which already had clinched the AFC East, fell behind 22–0 at the half but came back and won the game 23–22 with Drew Bledsoe throwing a 13-yard touchdown pass to tight end Ben Coates with 1:23 remaining. That clinched the number two seed for the Patriots and gave them a first-round bye going into the playoffs. After the game, in the visitors' locker room, Parcells sat on a bench with Kraft and explained to him the routine he would follow to get the Patriots ready for their first playoff game. They clenched hands. Parcells was glowing, and Kraft had the great Parcells taking the time to educate him. Parcells was no longer complaining about Glenn. Nobody was talking about Peter anymore. The Pats were in the playoffs, and at the time, that was all that mattered.

New England beat Pittsburgh in the divisional round and earned home field advantage for the AFC championship game when the Broncos, the number one seed, lost to the Jaguars and Tom Coughlin, a former Parcells assistant. The Patriots beat Jacksonville 20–6 and had outscored the Steelers and Jaguars 48–9 in the playoffs. They were rolling. In the fourth year owning his hometown team, Kraft was going to the Super Bowl and the Patriots were going to play Brett Favre and the Packers.

As soon as the Patriots arrived in New Orleans, the future of Parcells overshadowed the game. It was virtually a foregone conclusion by now that he was going to the Jets. Kraft and Parcells did a silly press conference together that failed to lighten the mood. "His heart was somewhere else," Kraft said. "I'm trying to protect our team. To be honest, the NFL didn't rush to our support."

There were rumors that Parcells was on the phone negotiating with the Jets while he was in New Orleans preparing the Patriots to play in the Super Bowl. "That's bullshit," Parcells said. "All that stuff about people saying I was making phone calls. That's all bullshit. That's all fucking bullshit. If they checked the fucking phone records, they know there was nothing. Not one thing on there. Nothing. Zero."

The Patriots lost to the Packers in the Super Bowl. In the locker room after the game, Parcells hugged Belichick, who had been added to his staff in 1996 after he was fired by the Browns. He didn't say anything to his players about the future. "I told them I appreciated what they had done for me this year and the effort they have given," Parcells said.

The next morning, Parcells skipped the flight home and took a private plane. Other than players headed to the Pro Bowl, everybody rides the team charter home from the Super Bowl. Outside the Fairmont Hotel in New Orleans the morning after the game, as he was getting into a sedan with his family, Kraft was asked about Parcells. "He's going to the Jets," he said with a combination of humor and disgust. Parcells met with Kraft in the days after the Super Bowl, and the divorce was official.

"Here's what I was told," Kraft said. "He took the job with the Jets in that December after Rich Kotite got fired. He didn't think we were going to the Super Bowl. What I was told is he wouldn't take the job with the Jets while there was another coach there. So they fired Kotite. That was mid-December. To be honest, that is when I learned a lot about the NFL. I figured they would enforce a contract. I think the league office wanted him in New York. I was a naive kid. The whole Parcells experience was horrible in many ways. He didn't fly back with us from the Super Bowl. He tortured me. So it got me ready for the business. His record with us was 32–32. He was a .500 coach in his years with the Patriots."

On his way out of New England, Parcells said, "It's just like a friend of mine told me: 'If they want you to cook the dinner, at least they ought to let you shop for some of the groceries.' "

If Kraft wanted him to coach, he needed to let him pick the players. "I knew I had to leave," Parcells said.

Parcells was soon in his car driving back to New Jersey but was prohibited from coaching or being the general manager of any team in 1997 without Kraft's permission. The translation: he couldn't do it without the Patriots being compensated.

Although twenty-four coaches applied for the Jets' head coaching job after Kotite made his announcement on December 20, the Jets didn't interview any of them. They had a plan devised by the team president, Steve Gutman: they would hire Belichick as their head coach and Parcells as a consultant for 1997, and then Parcells would be the coach in 1998. That would pressure Kraft into making a deal to free up Parcells immediately, the Jets hoped. "A transparent farce," Kraft said.

When they put that plan in place one week after the Super Bowl, all hell broke loose. Jets fans didn't want Belichick, who had been just 37–45 in five years as the Browns coach before joining Parcells in New England. They wanted Parcells. Kraft wanted to be made whole. He wasn't about to let Parcells pull off this charade without a fight.

The Jets offered two second-round picks and $1 million. The Patriots wanted the Jets' first-round pick, which was number one overall in the 1997 draft. Kraft mentioned that he would take Keyshawn Johnson, Aaron Glenn, or Hugh Douglas as part of the package. The Jets considered that tampering. Eventually, it was for Commissioner Paul Tagliabue to decide.

Kraft, still relatively new to the NFL's political games, felt he was at a disadvantage. "Leon Hess was one of the fair-haired boys at the league office," he said.

Tagliabue brought the parties together in a conference room at the New York law firm Skadden, Arps—they represented the league on major issues, including the United States Football League antitrust lawsuit—then sent the sides off to resolve the matter on their own. Four hours later, unable to agree to compensation, Kraft and Hess shook hands on a deal to make Tagliabue the binding arbitrator. Tagliabue knew it might come to this and was prepared to make a ruling. He awarded the Patriots a nice package: the Jets' third- and fourth-round picks in 1997, their second-round pick in 1998, and their first-round pick in 1999. The more valuable picks were saved for the later years when Parcells presumably would have made the Jets a better team. Tagliabue didn't want to strip the Jets of high first- or second-round picks that would help Parcells rebuild in his first two years. The alternative for the Jets was waiting one year and getting Parcells for free. They had promised Parcells to their fans and had to deliver. The alternative for Kraft was making Parcells sit one year and then getting nothing for him. "If we simplify it, Bill Parcells would not have coached for one year and we got four draft choices for allowing him to coach one year," Kraft said.

Not only was Parcells leaving the Patriots, he was going to a division rival. That made it much worse for Patriots fans. The way New York football fans looked at it, New England had just borrowed Parcells for the four years, and now he was coming home. The way New England fans looked at it, it was the coaching equivalent of the Red Sox selling Babe Ruth to the Yankees. Hess signed Parcells to a six-year $14.4 million contract as coach and general manager.

Hess was a hero to the long-suffering Jets fans. He was going to let Parcells do the shopping and cook the groceries and hopefully pick the menu for the Super Bowl party. "I just want to be the little boy that goes along with him and pushes the cart in the supermarket and let him fill it up," Hess said. "He's going to run the show, and it's not going to be two or three cooks in the kitchen. It will be just him."

Kraft, who was looking to protect the Patriots' interests during every step of the Parcells process, felt bloodied at the end. "I got roughed up pretty bad, and all I was doing was looking out for my team," he said. "I got the crap beat out of me because I wasn't just doing whatever Bill wanted."

Kraft eventually established a cordial relationship with Parcells in the years after he left the team. "All that being said and done, we were lucky to have him," Kraft said. "The only objection I had to him is that he was not always respectful to me or my family or people close to me."

If they had to do it over again, Kraft and Parcells admit they would have been a dynamic team. Kraft gave his coach what he needed to be successful. Parcells knew he had built a potential powerhouse in New England, and he bailed out.

"That was one of my greatest regrets," Parcells said. "I had young players, a good team. I had Ty Law, Lawyer Milloy, Shawn Jefferson, Ben Coates, Curtis Martin, Bledsoe was young. Willie McGinest. Chris Slade. Sam Gash. That was hard to give up."

When he was a candidate for the Patriots' Hall of Fame in 2011, Parcells conceded that he really didn't want to leave New England. He was insulted by having his power diminished and had not realized Kraft was going to be one of the best owners in the NFL. In the first eighteen seasons Kraft owned the Patriots, his accomplishments were outstanding: New England went to six Super Bowls, winning three, and the Patriots led the league in victories. Kraft was instrumental in ending the 136-day lockout in 2011 during a time when his wife was dying. He was also influential in the blockbuster network television contract signed after the lockout that guarantees the NFL immense profitability and popularity for years to come.

If Parcells remained in New England, it could have been he, not Belichick, winning all those Super Bowls. Who knows if he would have had the same conviction about Tom Brady to take him in the sixth round in 2000, but Parcells had put so many pieces in place to ensure success. He felt Kraft, because he was new, was letting himself be influenced by other people.

"Let's say we had a couple of domestic misunderstandings with the ownership," Parcells said. "I do regret that. Those things have since been resolved. I think retrospectively, I would have handled things substantially differently than I did. And I was always saddened by the fact that I had to leave there, and in all honesty didn't really want to. And I'm sure Bob would say something along those lines himself because we have talked about that."

Bill Walsh always regretted leaving the 49ers after they won the Super Bowl in 1988. He handed George Seifert a championship team that went on to win two more titles. Dick Vermeil never has forgiven himself for leaving the Rams two days after they won the Super Bowl following the 1999 season. Walsh and Vermeil were best friends, and they made the same mistake. Parcells was always fond of Walsh and was close to Vermeil. Coaches make emotional decisions, often involving their egos, and when they realize they should have been more flexible or given it more thought, it's too late.

"I thought I left a pretty good team there," Parcells said. "We had just been to the Super Bowl, and it was a very young team. Now we needed some more help. It wasn't a finished product by any stretch of the imagination, but we were on the way up. I don't think there was any question about that. And we needed a little help defensively and maybe another offensive lineman or two. But we had the skill people and some of the defensive pressure players in place. So I did regret that."

Parcells was never fired in the NFL. He left the Giants, Patriots, Jets, Cowboys, and Dolphins, where he ran the front office but didn't coach. All but the Dolphins were in significantly better shape when he left than when he arrived. New England is the only place he's admitted that he should have stayed.

"Hey, that's life, and you learn from things as you go on," he said. "I probably retrospectively would have approached it a little differently than what I did."

There is still a bit of sadness and regret in Kraft that it didn't work out with Parcells. "I think it would have been a great partnership," he said. "I forgot to tell you, today I love Parcells. I really believe that he knows he had something good. He was his own demon."

Stepping in and replacing a legendary coach can be a nightmare. Before the Parcells dispute with the Jets was resolved by Tagliabue, Kraft hired Pete Carroll as his new coach. Carroll had limited head coaching experience. He joined the Jets' staff as defensive coordinator when Bruce Coslet was hired in 1990. Coslet was fired after four seasons, and Carroll was promoted by Hess and general manager Dick Steinberg to replace him. Carroll was a fun guy. He had a basketball court constructed in the parking lot of the team's facility and created a diversion during training camp with bowling night, but these were still the Jets, a team with only Super Bowl III on its résumé.

The results on the field for Carroll weren't so good. The Jets were 6–5 when they played the Miami Dolphins in a crucial game late in the 1994 season. They held a 24–6 lead deep in the third quarter but lost on Dan Marino's famous fake spike play, in which he motioned as if he was about to stop the clock by slamming the ball into the ground but instead fired a touchdown pass to Mark Ingram. The Jets didn't win another game the rest of the season, finishing with a five-game losing streak, and ended 6–10. Carroll, who had three years remaining on his contract, was shocked when Hess fired him after just one season.

"I really feel no bitterness," Carroll said a few days after he was let go. "I hate talking about this. It's not worth it."

Carroll went to San Francisco to resurrect his career. The 49ers were coming off their fifth Super Bowl championship and were the model franchise in the NFL. He was hired by George Seifert as the defensive coordinator to replace Ray Rhodes, who had been hired by the Eagles to replace Rich Kotite, who had been hired by the Jets to replace Carroll. Kraft admired the 49ers, and Carroll was the anti-Parcells. He would not make the owner feel like an outsider.

But Carroll was not Kraft's first choice. He had grown close to

Belichick in his year with the Patriots after Art Modell fired him as the Browns were moving from Cleveland to Baltimore. Belichick had alienated Browns fans with his secretive ways, lack of personality, painful-to-watch news conferences, and his controversial decision to cut popular quarterback Bernie Kosar, who grew up in nearby Boardman, Ohio. Modell knew that to get started on an upbeat note in Baltimore he could not take the morose Belichick with him. Parcells threw Belichick a career-saving lifeline and brought him to New England to help with the defense for what turned out to be a Super Bowl year. Kraft and Belichick became buddies.

"We had our budget full when Belichick got fired," Kraft said. "Parcells said, 'Look, this is a guy I think we should have in the system. You talk to him and you see if you agree.' I liked him from the minute I met him. That's when I realized I would eventually hire him as a coach."

Kraft and Myra and Belichick and his wife, Debby, went to dinner after Parcells left, and Kraft explained why he had to make a clean break from the Parcells era. "I probably should have hired him," Kraft said. "But in the important decisions in life, I go with my instinct. I don't think Belichick would have been right in '96. I told him when I didn't hire him that I thought he had to work on how he handled the media, how he handled things. But the real problem I had with him was he was so tight with Parcells. I thought Parcells had stuck it to us. Belichick wanted to stay with us. He didn't want to go."

It shows the depth of Kraft's enmity for Parcells at that point that he dismissed Belichick, whom he considered a friend, "because I didn't want anything to do with Parcells," he said. "Anyone who could live with Parcells for so many years and be under his thumb, I needed someone as a head coach I could trust, and I hired a guy who is the antithesis. As soon as I met Pete, I knew I wanted to hire him."

Kraft needed to heal, and Carroll was exactly the right medicine to help Kraft get over Parcells. Carroll has an infectious personality, and players liked playing for him.

Parcells was the tough Jersey guy. He had friends in the Boston media. Carroll was California cool, and that didn't play well in one of the toughest sports towns in America. He used to wear sandals to work, not that there is anything wrong with that; it just didn't play well in Beantown. "Can you see Bill Parcells coming to a meeting in sandals?" Kraft said. "Pete is one of the truly great guys in the coaching fraternity, and I didn't give him all the support he needed. Pete was inclusive. Look, in the end, I needed someone to make me feel good. It was good for me to have a guy like Pete Carroll because he's my kind of guy. I mean, we loved Pete. You want Pete to marry into your family. I love the guy to this day. He's an awesome guy."

Kraft just didn't want him as his head coach anymore. Three years was enough. The team was going backward. Carroll won the AFC East with a 10–6 record in his first year in New England and lost 7–6 to the Steelers in Pittsburgh in the second round of the playoffs after beating Miami in the wild-card game. He made the playoffs his second year but lost in the wild-card game to the Jaguars. The Patriots won just nine games that year, and making things worse, Parcells and the Jets finished 12–4 and won the AFC East for the first time since the division was formed in 1970. New England avoided further embarrassment when the Jets blew a 10–0 second half lead in Denver in the AFC championship game and failed to make the Super Bowl. In 1999, the Patriots started 6–2 and looked like one of the better teams in the NFL, but they went just 2–6 in the second half of the season and missed the playoffs at 8–8. They had gone from eleven victories in Parcells's final season down to ten, then nine, then eight with Carroll. Kraft fired him.

"Pete was very good, but I probably went overboard in cutting down his influence over personnel to the point where I didn't give him a fair chance," Kraft said.

The scars had healed from Parcells, and Kraft felt the time was right to bring Belichick back to New England. Even though Belichick came off looking like a stooge when he ran interference for Parcells in the 1997 scam by taking the head coaching job as a way to get Parcells to New York, it wasn't something Kraft held against him. He remembered how as Belichick was leaving the Patriots, he not only spoke to him about the personnel on the team but how thorough he was in his presentation. That was his guy, and it was the right time.

It was also the start of another chapter in what had become known in the New York tabloids as the Border War between the Patriots and Jets. Parcells's move to the Jets got it started. Then in 1998, Parcells had his salary cap specialist Mike Tannenbaum construct a six-year $36 million offer sheet filled with poison pills to Patriots restricted free agent running back Curtis Martin, who Parcells drafted in the third round in 1995. Kraft didn't match the offer and received first- and third-round draft picks as compensation. Advantage: Parcells. Martin played eight years for the Jets and was elected to the Pro Football Hall of Fame in 2012.

The Jets went to the AFC championship game in 1998, and Parcells was loading up for a Super Bowl run in 1999 amid speculation that his third year back in New York would be his final year coaching the Jets. In the second quarter of the season opener against the Patriots, the Jets' season ended when quarterback Vinny Testaverde tore his Achilles chasing after a fumble by Martin and was lost for the year. Parcells lost interest for weeks, and the Jets stumbled. Not until he switched at quarterback from Rick Mirer, the player he passed over in 1993 to select Bledsoe, to Ray Lucas halfway through the season, did Parcells seem to have the old fire. Lucas went 6–3 and helped the Jets rally to finish 8–8. But it didn't prevent Parcells from quitting as the Jets coach within minutes of their season-ending victory over Seattle.

There was a reason he acted so quickly: there was a clause in

Belichick's contract that automatically elevated him to Jets head coach the moment Parcells stepped down. Hess had even given him a $1 million bonus the previous year to entice him to remain and turn down opportunities to interview for head coaching jobs. Belichick had met with Al Davis for the Raiders job that went to Jon Gruden in 1998. The bonus was intended to make it attractive for him to wait out Parcells.

The Jets knew Kraft wanted Belichick, and as soon as the season was over, Kraft faxed in the request to interview him. By that time, the Jets had activated the clause in Belichick's contract, and he was their head coach with three years remaining on his contract. The Jets denied Kraft permission. "We put in a request to talk to him, and I think as soon as we put in the request, Parcells resigned," Kraft said. "He didn't preempt me. We had it in. Parcells didn't want to coach without Belichick. I'm not looking to beat up Bill, but he didn't want to lose him."

What the Jets didn't know right away was that Belichick desperately wanted the Patriots job. On the day after the season ended, Belichick, now the Jets head coach, turned down media requests after Parcells's official announcement. The Jets said it was because Belichick wanted it to be Parcells's day. Parcells promised he would never coach again and encouraged reporters to write it on their chalkboard. Of course, with Parcells, it was always wise to keep an eraser handy. The next day, the Jets called a press conference to introduce Belichick as their new head coach.

The auditorium where the Jets held their team meetings on the second floor of Weeb Ewbank Hall was filled. This was to be Belichick's coronation. Despite his failures in Cleveland, in New York he was known for constructing the defenses that helped the Giants win two Super Bowls and for helping Parcells clean up the mess Kotite had left behind. Nobody in New York cared what happened with the Browns.

Belichick walked to the podium and began to read from a

handwritten note. He was resigning as the "HC of the NYJ." He had held the job for twenty-four hours.

Belichick stunned Gutman with his decision shortly before addressing the media in a rambling twenty-five–minute address on January 4, 2000. Hess had passed away on May 7, 1999, and the sale of the team to Woody Johnson for $635 million would be official one week after Parcells and Belichick quit. Belichick was concerned about working for a new owner. He was concerned about Parcells remaining as the general manager and being in his shadow. Parcells in essence had quit because of the uncertain ownership situation. Now Belichick was doing the same thing with a couple of other issues: He wanted to work for Kraft. He was tired of Parcells having a career crisis after every season.

"We all know how Bill is," Belichick said. "Sometimes he reacts emotionally to a loss or a bad season or a series of bad performances. Every time Bill says that, I take it with a grain of salt. It's been like that for the last twelve, thirteen years."

After Belichick made his decision public, he exited the auditorium at the Jets facility. Gutman then took the stage and unloaded on Belichick. "We should have some feelings of sorrow and regret for him and his family," Gutman said. "He obviously has some inner turmoil."

Two hundred miles away in Boston, Kraft was keeping a close eye on this latest Jets drama. "Steve Gutman thought Belichick was having a mental breakdown," he said.

He was not. He just wanted out. He made an unsuccessful bid to get the final three years of his contract with the Jets overturned by the NFL—Parcells was called as a hostile witness—after Commissioner Paul Tagliabue ruled that he could not coach another team without the Jets' consent.

Kraft was in his office in downtown Boston. It was January 25, and the season had been over for nearly a month. Former Jaguars coach Dom Capers was the fallback candidate for the Patriots.

Kraft didn't think he was going to get Belichick. In addition to Tagliabue ruling against Belichick, a judge had refused to issue a temporary restraining order that would have allowed Belichick to take another job after Belichick's attorney, Jeffrey Kessler, filed an antitrust lawsuit against the Jets and the NFL. Kessler was well known as an attorney for the NFL Players Association who was adept at giving the league a hard time. After losing his bid for the restraining order, Belichick dropped the lawsuit. His immediate coaching future was now in Parcells's hands. Could Parcells strike a deal with Kraft to set Belichick free? If not, he could make him sit. It was ironic that Parcells still controlled Belichick's fate because that was one of the reasons Belichick left the Jets.

"I'm in my office, and they said someone is calling, and they say it's Darth Vader," Kraft said. "So I knew exactly who it was."

It was Parcells, of course, and it was the first time he and Kraft had spoken in three years. The Jets had named long-time Parcells assistant Al Groh as their new head coach one day earlier after Johnson was unable to talk Parcells into rescinding his retirement to return to the sidelines. Now with all the leverage after the ruling by Tagliabue and the courts, Parcells was ready to deal. He and Kraft negotiated Belichick's release. The Jets received the Patriots' first-round draft pick, and the teams exchanged lower-round picks. "The Border War is over between the Jets and Patriots," Parcells declared.

Belichick got into his car and drove to Foxborough to close the deal. Kraft was already being second-guessed. "When I was waiting to hire Belichick, I was getting calls from the league office and my own internal organization saying you are seeing things here that no one else sees," Kraft said. "But it was my instinct."

There is little debate that "Little Bill" is an acquired taste. He is not for everybody, just as Kraft painfully found out that "Big Bill" is not for everybody, either. One of Belichick's first hires was Scott Pioli to run the Patriots' personnel department. Pioli worked for Belichick in Cleveland, and accompanied the team to

Baltimore in 1996. Belichick brought him to the Jets during that interim period in 1997 when he was the head coach and Parcells was the supposed consultant. One day at the Jets complex, Pioli started chatting up a woman named Dallas, who said she was there on business for an electronics company.

As they were talking, Parcells came out of the head coach's office.

"Oh, I see you met my daughter," Parcells said.

Pioli was floored. Dallas's last name was Parcells.

They started dating during the 1997 season, but Parcells didn't find out until after the season. Friends in the Jets' front office warned him about dating the boss's daughter, but Pioli was smitten. Scott and Dallas were married on June 11, 1999. Kraft naturally was not initially thrilled when Belichick told him he wanted to bring along the man who married the enemy's daughter.

"It shows you how I trusted Belichick when he wanted to bring in Parcells's son-in-law," Kraft said. "I trusted him to do it, although at the time, it was not something I was in support of."

Pioli was the most important part of Belichick's infrastructure. Belichick had the final say, but Pioli was not afraid to present the counterargument. The Kraft-Belichick marriage turned out to be one of the best owner-coach relationships in football history. Belichick turned out to be a combination of Parcells and Carroll. He's tough like Parcells and a control freak like Parcells. Publicly, he's cranky, but with Kraft, he's open and honest. He doesn't have Carroll's outgoing personality, but he respects his boss the way Carroll did.

"Whatever I want to know, I know," Kraft said. "Is he forthcoming? He knows what I want to know, and he tells me. He's smart because he knows it's in his interests, especially if something doesn't go right. Bill will leave me voice mails at eleven, eleven thirty at night, on his way home. Then I'm speaking to him at six in the morning. That's six days a week. That's just what it is."

Belichick had Kraft's complete backing, and Kraft gave him

the power he had taken away from Parcells and never gave to Carroll. But Patriots fans felt they had the wrong Bill when Belichick went 5–11 in his first season in 2000. He had drafted Michigan quarterback Tom Brady that year in the sixth round, the 199th player taken overall. Kraft had signed Drew Bledsoe to a ten-year $103 million contract in March 2001. Brady was an afterthought. Why not take a chance on a kid who had started some games at Michigan and showed at times he might have the "it" factor? The investment was minuscule. The first time he met Kraft, the rookie told him, "I'm the best decision this organization has ever made."

Brady had a terrific training camp in his second year in 2001. There was speculation that Belichick wanted to start him over Bledsoe in the season opener against the Bengals but backed off. The Patriots lost in Cincinnati. The second week of the season was postponed because of the 9/11 terrorist attacks. The Patriots' next game was against the Jets. Late in the fourth quarter, Jets linebacker Mo Lewis crushed Bledsoe near the sidelines. Bledsoe was sent to the hospital with severe internal bleeding in his chest. Brady was impressive in taking over for Bledsoe on the Patriots' final possession in that game, but New England still lost. At 0–2 following his 5–11 first season, there were rumors that Kraft was going to fire Belichick.

But Brady saved Belichick and turned Bledsoe into the NFL's Wally Pipp. Brady got red hot and had the Patriots rolling by the time Bledsoe was ready to return. Belichick stuck with Brady, the Patriots won the Super Bowl over the heavily favored Rams, and Bledsoe was traded to Buffalo the next spring for a number one draft pick.

Those were great times for the Patriots. Kraft had set the standard for how to run a franchise. He opened a new $325 million privately financed state-of-the-art stadium on the land he owned next to Foxboro Stadium after nearly moving the team to Hartford when he had been unable to get a deal done in the Boston area. There were even backs on the seats at the new place. The Patriots won the Super Bowl again after the 2003 and 2004 seasons, giving them three in a four-year period. Belichick was a genius. Brady was the new Joe Montana. Belichick might be uncomfortable socially, but his relationship with Kraft worked.

"Basically, similar philosophy relative to team building, organizational structure, things like that," Belichick said.

The Patriots lost in the divisional round in Denver and in the AFC championship game in Indianapolis the next two years. Disappointing? For sure. Embarrassing? Not really. The embarrassment would come during the season-opening loss to the Jets in 2007. Eric Mangini was a coach Belichick handpicked in Cleveland when he was working in the public relations department and then hired with the Jets. When Belichick returned to New England in 2000, he brought Mangini along with him from New York, and Mangini worked his way up from secondary coach to defensive coordinator.

Belichick was Mangini's role model and mentor. They had gone to Wesleyan University in Middletown, Connecticut, a generation apart. After the Patriots' loss to the Broncos in the 2005 playoffs, the Jets hired Mangini as their head coach. He was just thirty-five years old. Belichick was furious. He hated the Jets and felt that taking the job was not the proper way for Mangini to show his gratitude. They stopped talking, and their postgame handshakes—Belichick had perfected the no-look dead fish— were more anticipated than the Jets-Patriots games.

Belichick had developed the rules-breaking program of having one of his video guys tape the opponent's defensive coaches hand signals sending in the alignment. It was for future reference when the teams would meet again. Belichick would decode the signals and use the tape to his advantage, for whatever it was worth. Two problems: it was against NFL rules, and Mangini knew about it. He knew where all the camcorders and tapes were stored. Now that he was with the Jets, it didn't work to his advantage to allow Belichick to tape his defensive signals. The Jets blew the whistle on Belichick during the first game of the 2007 season. NFL security confiscated the video camera of New England video assistant Matt Estrella while the game was going on.

It was dubbed Spygate, and the scandal had such a long shelf life that you can't tell the story of Belichick's career without bringing it up. Commissioner Roger Goodell fined Belichick the maximum $500,000, the most a coach had ever been fined. He fined the Patriots $250,000 and took away a first-round pick from New England in 2008. Belichick was fortunate Goodell did not suspend him.

"Everybody has their idiosyncrasies, but if there is trust, that's the key in business, in marriages," Kraft said. "You build a sense of trust so you go through rough times. Look what happened with this bogus thing with the Jets. I stood by him pretty darn good. That was rough."

Why was it bogus? Kraft hesitates.

The restaurant is buzzing with activity. It is noisy. It was the most humiliating time in his Patriots ownership. He pauses before answering.

"How much do you think that helped us?" he said. "How much of a surprise was it to Mangini and [Jets GM Mike] Tannenbaum?"

It was against the rules. "You know how many teams steal signals? That's bupkis," Kraft said. The Patriots claim they caught the Jets illegally videotaping them in 2006 at Gillette Stadium. "We kicked them off our roof," Kraft said. The Jets insist the Patriots had given them permission to tape from that location.

The Jets had been on to Belichick's taping years earlier. Head coach Herm Edwards saw the Patriots' camera fixed on him and defensive coordinator Donnie Henderson during a game in 2004 at Giants Stadium, and they started waving to it. Clearly, Edwards wasn't concerned about any information Belichick might

be pilfering. Edwards and Belichick were friends. He never talked to him about it. He laughed it off.

Kraft questioned Belichick about his use of the videotape.

"How much did this help us on a scale of 1 to 100?" Kraft said.

"One," Belichick replied.

"Then you're a real schmuck," Kraft said.

Mangini was fired by the Jets after the 2008 season and immediately was hired by the Browns to be their head coach. After two seasons he was fired by Cleveland and went to work for ESPN. Nearly five years after turning in his former boss, Mangini had deep regrets. Belichick had given him his break in coaching, he won three Super Bowl rings as an assistant in New England, and Spygate not only destroyed his relationship with Belichick but created discussion whether the championships were tainted.

"If there is a decision I could take back, it's easily that decision," Mangini said on ESPN. He knew too much and didn't want Belichick cheating against him. That's as far as he wanted it to go. It went much further. "Never in a million years did I expect it to play out like this," Mangini said. "This is one of those situations where I didn't want them to do the things they were doing. I didn't think it was any kind of significant advantage, but I wasn't going to give them the convenience of doing it in our stadium, and I wanted to shut it down. But there was no intent to get the league involved. There was no intent to create the landslide that it has become." It also put any coach who might consider hiring Mangini on his staff in a difficult position. Could he trust Mangini not to turn on him the way he turned on Belichick? Mangini did the right thing shutting down Belichick's taping operation, but as coaches like to say, the execution was poor. Coaches are a tight-knit fraternity and Mangini turned in one of his brothers.

Maybe Kraft had blind loyalty to Belichick because he delivered three Super Bowl rings, but he never thought about firing him after Spygate. He believes Belichick wouldn't do anything "deliberately" wrong. "He would take every edge he could get, but he would never knowingly break the rules or cross the line," he said. "I know him. I'm not saying he was a choirboy."

There was never a doubt in Kraft's mind that he would support Belichick. He didn't condone what he did, but he wasn't going to end their relationship because he made a mistake. "Your wife gets very sick. You dump her? Or your kid makes a bad mistake. It's your kid," he said. "It's your family. How can you get people to dig deep and go through the wall for you if they know you're not going to be there for them when they need you? You make your decisions, you think it out, you get good people, and then you stay the course. And then the wind comes and the lightning comes and you stay the course."

Kraft one day should be in the Hall of Fame as an owner. Belichick's three Super Bowl championships as a head coach and two as an assistant will get him to Canton, too. That won't stop critics from saying that what the Patriots accomplished before the videotaping was stopped is tainted.

But as Kraft says: "That's their problem."

MIND GAMES

Lawrence Taylor, the greatest defensive player in NFL history, walked into the locker room a few days before the Giants were going to play the Los Angeles Rams in the 1989 playoffs. His locker was just a few feet from the entrance, so it was just a matter of seconds before he was able to see something he didn't recognize sitting on his stool. He picked it up. It was an airline ticket to New Orleans.

LT usually didn't need much motivation to play in a game, especially a playoff game, but Bill Parcells knew that all he had to do "was show him where the competition was" and he would respond to it. Parcells's greatest gift in his nineteen years as an NFL head coach was being able to push the right buttons with his players. Every player had a different button. He knew Taylor and Phil Simms responded to tough love mixed in with a lot of cursing, and he didn't mind when they gave it right back to him.

Parcells figured the best way to create a path to the quarterback for Taylor was to appeal to his enormous pride. LT had an overdose of athletic arrogance, and Parcells always picked the right time to tap in to it. Taylor had put Parcells through a lot with his drug problems—he was suspended the first four games of the 1988 season—but they were as close as a coach and a player could be. "I think about it all the time: if I had gone to another team, if I had gone with another coach, what type of player would I have been?" Taylor said. "I was very fortunate to have Parcells. He allowed me to do my thing. I've never been a guy who works well in structure."

When Taylor came into the league in 1981, he was immediately unblockable. He was 240 pounds of lightning-fast fury rushing the passer from his right outside linebacker spot in the Giants 3–4 defense. It took about two snaps in training camp before the Giants ended the charade that there was a competition with the veteran John Skorupan. Taylor was put right into the starting lineup. Teams tried to block him with running backs, which was a terrible mismatch. Finally, in a playoff game against the 49ers his rookie year, San Francisco's innovative coach Bill Walsh came up with an alternative plan. He would swing 258-pound left guard John Ayers into the backfield to meet Taylor head on. Soon teams would use their left tackle, always the best pass protector, as the first line of defense in trying to neutralize him. They might get backup help from a tight end or running back, but at least Taylor wasn't allowed to run over 185-pound running backs. One left tackle who had his way with LT was his nemesis, Irv Pankey of the Los Angeles Rams. Earlier in the 1989 season, Pankey had held Taylor without a sack when LT was playing with a sprained ankle. Pankey had shut out Taylor when they met in 1985. Meanwhile, Parcells was well aware of the success that New Orleans linebacker Pat Swilling, a third-round pick in 1986, had when he faced Pankey in the two Saints-Rams games in 1989. Swilling had three sacks in the first game and one sack in the other playing the same position as Taylor in New Orleans's defense. Swilling was a fierce pass rusher but was not in Taylor's league.

Pankey was an excellent player, but Taylor was having a Hall of Fame career. He just had trouble with Pankey, who at six-four and 277 pounds had one inch and nearly 40 pounds on him. Pankey was as much of a barrier as those blocking sleds they use in practice. Before Taylor arrived in the locker room the week of the playoff showdown with Pankey, Parcells put the airline ticket on the stool in front of his locker. Once he knew that Taylor had seen it, Parcells walked over to needle him.

"You get the ticket?" Parcells said.

"Yeah, what's up with that?" LT said.

As much as Taylor loved to party, he knew Parcells was not sending him to the French Quarter to get ready for the game by staying up all night on Bourbon Street.

"I want you to go down to New Orleans. Now you don't have to change jerseys, because he also wears number 56. Just give Swilling your helmet and send him up here. And you go ahead and stay down there and play for the Saints this week because I need somebody that could whip Pankey," Parcells said.

"If you wanted Pat Swilling, why didn't you draft the son of a bitch?" Taylor fired back.

Taylor was incensed. He was also fired up to face Pankey. Mission accomplished. Parcells had hit LT's sweet spot. Of course, the Saints didn't make the playoffs, so they were not even playing that week. Taylor had two sacks against Pankey even though the Giants lost the game on Flipper Anderson's touchdown in overtime.

"He was always playing head games," Taylor said. "There's a lot of guys who didn't care for Bill. I really find that amazing. Are you kidding me? For me, I couldn't imagine having any other coach. He let his players play. What else do you want?"

Parcells was not for everyone. He alienated players with his mind games. As decisive as he was managing games on Sunday, he was just as indecisive when it came to managing his career. He had four head coaching jobs and quit all four. He ruled by intimidation and had a sarcastic sense of humor that could humble his players. He had no patience for celebrity quarterbacks. He's one of the great motivators in NFL coaching history. As Parcells likes to say about players who have accomplished a lot in their careers, he has the pelts on the wall to prove it.

Taylor was part of an exclusive club. He was a Parcells guy. It's not a club to which you apply for membership, and it's harder to get into than Augusta National. The coach decides you are in, and once you are accepted, it's a lifetime membership. Taylor, Simms, Harry Carson, and George Martin were executive directors with the Giants. Curtis Martin became a charter member in New England when Parcells drafted him in the third round in 1995. Sam Gash and Troy Brown were part of the club with the Patriots. Curtis Martin later followed Parcells to the Jets, where the group expanded to include Vinny Testaverde and Keyshawn Johnson. Then it was on to Dallas for Parcells's final four years as an NFL head coach, and he initiated Demarcus Ware, Jason Witten, and Tony Romo. If there was a problem in the locker room, if a player needed peer pressure instead of Parcells pressure to get with the program, he went to the Parcells guys and said, "Fix it."

Parcells had won two Super Bowls with the Giants, got to another with the Patriots in his fourth season after inheriting a 1–15 team, and in his second season after taking over a 1–15 team with the Jets had them in the AFC championship game. Dallas was his only stop where he failed to win a playoff game, although he would have if Romo had held on to the snap for a chip shot field goal in a wild-card playoff loss to the Seahawks in what turned out to be the final game of Parcells's career in 2006. Parcells always felt that if the Cowboys had won that game, they could have made it to the Super Bowl.

What is a Parcells guy?

"Just likes football and wants to win," he said. "You got to like it. I like it."

Curtis Martin scored the winning touchdown in the first game of his rookie year. He was surrounded by reporters at his locker after the game. He had lasted until the third round because of injury concerns, but Patriots running back coach Maurice Carthon, another Parcells guy from their time together with the Giants, gave Martin high grades. He told Parcells he was going to be suspicious of Martin because "he's too good to be true." Now with Martin's locker surrounded by reporters after his impressive debut, Parcells walked by, barking as usual.

"Get away from him," Parcells declared. "He's a one-game wonder."

Martin had run for 30 yards on his first carry and 102 yards for the game. Nice way to break into the NFL, but as Parcells was fond of saying of young players who did well, "Let's not put him in Canton just yet, fellas." Martin was much more than a one-game wonder. He rushed for 1,487 yards and won the rookie of the year award. "One-Game Wonder morphed into Boy Wonder," Martin said. "He still calls me that."

Martin finished his career as the NFL's fourth leading rusher all-time with 14,101 yards, was elected to the Pro Football Hall of Fame in 2012, and picked Parcells to present him in Canton. He is a high-ranking officer in the Parcells Guy club. "It's an exclusive club in Parcells's mind," Martin said. "A lot of times, you don't come to understand until the end of your career that you are a Parcells guy. Or he even tells you that you are a Parcells guy. At these little moments, he would stop by and say a few words with a little nugget of wisdom. I use so many of Parcells's principles in my business affairs. One time he came up to me and said, 'You know, Boy Wonder, I think you got it. A lot of guys don't get it. I find it a problematical situation when I want someone to succeed more than they want to succeed.' That is what separated Parcells. He had that insight."

He knew Martin was a different kind of guy from Simms and Taylor and that penetrating his ears with four-letter words was not going to get the best out of him. "That just wasn't effective with me," Martin said.

Martin survived growing up in one of the toughest neighborhoods in Pittsburgh. Tough talk from Parcells was not going to intimidate him even though Martin had tremendous respect for him. When Martin was just nine years old, he was devastated when his grandmother was found in her apartment by his mother stabbed to death by an intruder. She was lying on her back with a knife in her chest that went clear through and was stuck in the bed. Martin had to identify the killer from mug shots. Friends of his were killed. "Growing up in a really bad neighborhood, you begin to decipher the difference between people who are book smart and street smart," he said. "You look at some coaches; they are more book smart. Parcells is more of a street smart coach. He understands all the different moving parts. I've never seen a man who has the wisdom and insight the man has about people."

When Parcells jumped from the Patriots to the Jets in 1997, he left Martin behind. But one year later, Martin was a restricted free agent and the Jets constructed a poison-pill six-year $36 million offer sheet that New England decided not to match. The Patriots took the Jets' first- and third-round picks as compensation instead, and Martin played two more years for Parcells before the coach "retired" for three seasons and then ended his coaching career in Dallas.

If Parcells had remained in New England, so too would have Martin. He was not unhappy with the Patriots. Unlike Parcells, he was very fond of owner Robert Kraft. But the Jets' money was right. And Parcells was there. "I left because of Parcells," Martin said.

If LT was the problem child son, Martin was the son who always did the right thing. Parcells had great admiration for him. "I can only tell you, he's one of those players who inspire you as a coach. He really does," he said. "From the first day I ever met him, he wanted everything I ever had. I knew he was going to put it to use. He wanted to know what to do to be successful. 'Give me what you got, coach, I'm taking it,' " he said. "He's a great kid. He's a wonderful person. I can't tell you enough about him."

Before Parcells's final season with the Cowboys, owner Jerry Jones signed wide receiver Terrell Owens, who had been a locker room problem in San Francisco and Philadelphia. He was never going to be a Parcells guy, and Jones signed him over Parcells's objections. Parcells knew Jones was consumed with bringing in T.O. and knew it was a lost cause trying to stop him. "I talked him into about seven other things," Parcells said. "He's got three or four of his really best players that I fought my ass off for. He knows that."

Witten was one of them. In the one season he coached Owens, Parcells almost never referred to him by name. It was always "the player." Parcells lasted four years working for Jones in Dallas, about three years longer than many predicted for this pairing of volatile personalities and big egos. "I really liked Jerry," Parcells said. "You know why? Jerry just wants to win. He will put his money where his mouth is."

Part of the Parcells legacy as a head coach was his job hopping. That turned off a lot of people. "Hey, that doesn't bother me at all," he said. "Our society is transient."

The Giants were angered when they found out Parcells might be trying to get out of his contract days after they won their first Super Bowl so that he could take a job as coach and general manager of the Atlanta Falcons in 1987. Commissioner Pete Rozelle had to step in and prevent Parcells from breaking his contract. Parcells tormented himself and tormented his employers with his indecision by claiming he was coaching year to year, which is not what owners wanted to hear, and by following a career path that made him and Marty Schottenheimer the only coaches in the modern era to be the head coach for four different teams. The difference was that Parcells was never asked to leave. He was never fired. He did it to himself.

On the day after the 1999 season, he stood in front of a huge media contingent in the team meeting room at the Jets' head-quarters at Weeb Ewbank Hall on the campus of Hofstra University to announce his retirement. "This is definitely the end of my football career," he said. "Bill's not coming back. You can write that on your chalkboard."

He probably meant it at the time, but he still had a lot left to give. "I never thought after I left the Jets that I would coach again," he said. "Things happen; things change."

One thing that changed: Jerry Jones offered him a four-year contract worth $17 million to coach America's Team.

Parcells is the self-proclaimed Jersey guy. He attended Colgate University, then transferred to what is now called Wichita State, where he played linebacker. He was drafted by the Detroit Lions but was cut before he had a chance to play in a game. He began his coaching career in 1964 at Hastings College in Nebraska, where he worked with linebackers. It was the first stop on a college tour that took him to seven schools. At Army, he became lifelong friends with the legendary basketball coach Bob Knight.

He was the head coach at the Air Force when Ray Perkins, the Giants' new head coach, offered him a job in 1979 as the linebacker coach. Parcells initially accepted but wound up changing his mind for personal reasons. He stayed in Colorado for one year working in real estate, which didn't provide the same adrenaline rush as coaching football. The next year, he was coaching linebackers for the New England Patriots. When Perkins had an opening for a defensive coordinator in 1981, he reached out to Parcells, who this time took the job. There was a huge carrot: the Giants were going to take Taylor, the linebacker from North Carolina, with the second overall pick in the '81 draft.

After Perkins left to succeed Bear Bryant at Alabama, his alma mater, after the 1982 season, Giants general manager George Young elevated Parcells to head coach. It was a gut-wrenching year for Parcells. It started off when he made the biggest mistake of his coaching career, picking Scott Brunner to start over Simms at quarterback. Simms had been injured for much of Parcells's first two years with the Giants. It had been Brunner who led the Giants to the playoffs in 1981 when Simms was hurt. He knew more about Brunner than about Simms and despite the huge talent edge that favored Simms, he began the season with Brunner as his starter. When Parcells realized Simms was the right quarterback for the Giants, he put him in during the third quarter of the sixth game of the season right after Brunner threw an interception. Simms completed his first four passes but had a season-ending injury when he sustained a compound fracture and dislocation of his right thumb on his fifth pass, an incompletion, when he hit the face mask of Eagles defensive end Dennis Harrison. His hand was a bloody mess from the bone that had penetrated the skin.

Before the injury, Simms had spoken about being so frustrated that he wanted to be traded. Then Parcells gave him his old job back two days before the trading deadline, and he couldn't make it through the game without getting hurt again. Even without the injury, it was unlikely that the Giants would have dealt Simms. The injury made it a moot point. The Giants lost the game to drop to 2–4 and won only one more game the rest of the season to finish 3–12–1. During the season, both of Parcells's parents passed away. When the season mercifully came to an end, Young nearly fired Parcells and hired University of Miami coach Howard Schnellenberger, who had been on the Colts' staff when Young worked in Baltimore's front office. Young thought the trauma of the 1983 season was going to be too difficult for Parcells to overcome.

"It had to be unbelievable, between his parents and the season," Simms said.

Not long after the season was over, Simms sat down with his coach. "He said one day in the weight room, 'If I survive this, I swear we are going to do it my way,' " Simms said.

Young brought Parcells back, and he did change. Parcells was close to many of the defensive players from his two years as an assistant coach. He needed to make a break and be the head coach. He did that. His relationship with Young was never the same. It was hard to overlook the fact that his boss came close to firing him during the toughest year of his life. Young picked the players, and Parcells coached them. That was about all they had in common.

"There were a lot of things that went on that year. I don't want to say it served me well, but really it probably did," Parcells said of his football troubles. "You develop an attitude that you eventually know that nobody cares and that it's a results business. Nobody is ever going to understand why things are the way they are. So you just have to try and go forward the best you can."

Simms was his quarterback despite a brief off-season flirtation that Young had with Warren Moon, who'd had a successful career in the Canadian Football League and was sought after by many NFL teams. Moon signed with the Houston Oilers. The Giants traded Brunner to the Broncos in the off-season, leaving Simms as the starter and journeyman Jeff Rutledge as his backup.

As Parcells developed as a head coach, he came to understand that creative tension produced better results. He preyed upon the insecurity of players. If his team was cruising along winning week after week, he manufactured a crisis to keep the players on edge. If they were losing, he had plenty of material at his disposal. Parcells knew Simms could take it, so he often used him for target practice. By picking on Simms, one of the faces of the franchise, the other players knew they would be held accountable.

"Every day there were two things you knew you were going to get: mental pressure and physical pressure," Simms said. "The man just didn't let up. You would see him first thing in the morning, and he would be Mr. Grumpy."

Simms would ask, "What is the crisis today?" Then Parcells would say, "The stupid offensive line stinks. My defensive backs can't tackle." Simms realized, "There is always a crisis, and whose turn was it going to be today? I hated it when it was me. It was really a tension-filled day. I would come home exhausted from the tension. Practice was real. I got nervous before the seven on sevens. I got nervous before the team drills. I knew the performance had to be good. No exaggeration, just a fact. That was his MO. He loved friction. If it wasn't there, he created it. A lot of times, I was the perfect foil."

Parcells would never let Simms relax. He was the Giants' first-round draft pick in 1979 from tiny Morehead State in Kentucky. The 49ers didn't have a first-round pick—it had been traded years earlier to the Bills in the O.J. Simpson trade—and Walsh was hoping to take Simms at the top of the second round. But the Giants took Simms seventh overall, and Walsh had to settle for Joe Montana with the last pick in the third round. The draft was being held at the Roosevelt Hotel in midtown Manhattan. That was long before the days of the Internet and an endless number of draft publications that allowed fans to familiarize themselves with all the players from big schools and small in the months before the draft. Few Giants fans knew of the existence of Morehead State and as a result had absolutely no idea who Phil Simms was. The draftniks in New York started booing when Rozelle made the announcement: "With the seventh pick in the 1979 NFL draft, the New York Giants select Phil Simms, quarterback, Morehead State."

What? Phil Simms? Maybe the Giants meant Oklahoma running back Billy Sims, who wasn't eligible to be in the draft until 1980. NFL Films was caught off guard by the Simms pick and also by the reaction of the fans in the Roosevelt's ballroom. They asked Rozelle to make the announcement again so that the fans could boo again, allowing NFL Films to capture the moment. Rozelle obliged with a big grin on his face. When Simms found out about the reenactment, he was not happy.

He became entrenched as the starter in 1984, his sixth year in the league. "We were walking out of the locker room before the opening game of the season," Simms said. "When I tell this story now to head coaches in the NFL, they laugh. But Bill says to me, 'Simms, if you don't throw at least two interceptions today, you're not taking enough chances. Take some chances now.' Wow, what head coaches say that to a quarterback?"

Simms didn't listen to Parcells. He didn't throw an interception against the Eagles. But he did throw four touchdown passes and completed twenty-three of thirty passes for 409 yards in New York's 28–27 victory. The Giants made the playoffs but lost in the second round to the 49ers. They made the playoffs again in 1985 but were shut out in the second round by that great Bears defense. The next year, the Giants were clearly the best team in football. They finished 14–2, mauled the 49ers and Redskins by a combined 66–3 in the first two rounds of the playoffs, and then beat the Broncos 39–20 in the Super Bowl.

Simms was twenty-two for twenty-five in that game—the 88 percent completion percentage is a Super Bowl record—and really could have pitched a perfect game. A case could be made that all three incomplete passes should have been caught. Was Parcells happy with Simms? When he threw a 6-yard touchdown pass on third down to wide receiver Phil McConkey that first bounced off the hands of tight end Mark Bavaro with 10:56 left to give the Giants a comfortable 33–10 lead, Simms came to the sidelines feeling pretty good about himself. He had quickly forgotten taking a 5-yard sack on a play action pass on the play right before the touchdown, which pushed the Giants from the Denver 1 to the Denver 6. It was to be the only time he was sacked during the game. Parcells, of course, didn't forget and didn't forgive.

Simms came to the sidelines and was summoned for a conference by Parcells.

"Hey, hey, come here. You can't take a sack there," Parcells said.

"Shut up. Don't be coaching me now. We just won the Super Bowl. You are going to coach me up about taking a sack? You're unbelievable," Simms said.

By then, Simms had learned to deal with Parcells picking on him. "There were probably ten guys on the team he could say anything to, brutally honest mean things, and it wouldn't be taken that way," Simms said. "Everybody understood why he said it. If he was yelling at me in front of the team, all the other players were allowed to laugh at me. He didn't care."

Did Simms ever want to tell Parcells to stick it or something worse? "I probably mumbled that under my breath every day for eight years," he said. "I once threw an awful interception, even bad for me, and oh, my God, I didn't even want to walk by him. He walks over to me and says, 'Come here a second. [Offensive coordinator] Ron [Erhardt] and I just want to know if you're watching the same game we're watching.' "

Their most public fight came in a Monday night game in Indianapolis in 1990. Simms came to the sidelines, and he and Parcells started screaming at each other. The national television cameras caught every last f-bomb. It became big news. "He knew he fucked up, and he was mad at himself," Parcells said. "He was trying to make it look like it was something else. I said, 'Go sit the fuck down.' "

Simms put the skirmish in context. "On a scale of one to ten, it wouldn't have even been point one," Simms said. "Unfortunately, it was on television. I'm definitely not proud of it. That was Bill. He egged us on. There was just a group of guys on the team he said things to that he wouldn't say to other guys. That relationship allowed us to bark back a little bit. What coach can do that in the NFL now? There might be a couple of players around the league that have a relationship with a coach where they might yell at each other for half a second."

Parcells would get on Taylor, too, even though it was hard to come down on the best player on the team, the best player in the league. On plays in which Taylor was out of position, he made up for it because he was so much better than anybody else. "Bill always got something to say. You think you are doing good and you are playing like shit, he will let you know," Taylor said. "My rookie year, he told me, 'You look like a deer in the headlights. You just look fucking lost.' We would cuss each other out all the time. At one point, we wouldn't even talk during practice, I wouldn't stand beside him. At the end of practice, all the players would pick up on it and were egging us on. They would say, 'Okay, you two, come up here and make up, get up there and kiss and make up.' It was a father and son argument."

When the Giants lined up on the sideline for the national anthem, Taylor was always by Parcells's side. "That was his way of saying, 'I'm with you.' That was kind of an unspoken thing that I liked very much and that I think he felt," Parcells said.

Before a huge December game in the 1986 season at RFK Stadium against the Redskins that would decide the NFC East champion, Parcells and Simms were in the baseball dugout, getting ready to walk onto the field. Parcells, Simms, and Taylor loved those games at old RFK, where the lower deck of the stands would bounce when the fans really got into it, which was all the time for Giants-Redskins games.

"You ready?" Parcells said.

"I'm ready," Simms said.

"You know, boy, these fans hate us so much that they like us," Parcells said.

"I think you're right," Simms said.

They walked out of the dugout together. "They started shouting, 'You motherfuckers,' " Simms said. "It made me smile. Those little things Bill would say could really disarm you and put you in a different state of mind." As soon as the words "and the home of the brave" were sung before that Redskins game, Parcells turned to Taylor. "Are you going to fucking play or not?" Parcells said. Meaning, are you going to play great? Taylor responded, "You just worry about those other sons of bitches you are coaching. Don't worry about me." Parcells smiled at LT. He showed him the competition and knew Taylor was all in. LT had three sacks and the Giants won 24–14 and then shut out the Redskins at Giants Stadium weeks later in the NFC championship game putting them in their first Super Bowl.

Parcells had a special relationship with Taylor even though he caused plenty of aggravation for the coach and the organization. LT had a drug problem, and Parcells did his best to try to get Taylor straightened out. But there were always questions whether he was enabling him by also doing everything he could to keep him on the field.

"I worried about him a lot. Of course I did. He knows that," Parcells said. "What really stings my ass is when people say Parcells looked the other way because that is so much bullshit. There's not a fragment of truth to that. Not a shred. I didn't look the other way."

What was Parcells trying to do for him? "Help," he said. "Just help. I'm not going to go on about what I did. I did a lot and tried a lot."

Taylor knew that he was protected by his production on the field. "That's a different atmosphere back in the '80s than it is now," he said. "It is not as public as it is now. You got to understand back in those days, even though you have a problem, it's all about what you are going to do on Sunday. So the people will tend to turn a blind eye to that a little bit as long as the law don't get involved. I know Bill was concerned, but hey, he had a job; he was trying to protect his job, too. He couldn't say to me, 'Are you doing drugs?' You can't say that to me. On Sunday I was making twelve tackles and two or three sacks; what are you going to say?

During that time, I'm not listening to nobody anyway. As long as I can do what I do on Sunday, what is the problem? Luckily, it didn't get really bad until after my career was over."

The mold was broken with Parcells. He was the Giants head coach for eight years. That's now a lifetime in the NFL. It allowed him to build lifelong relationships with many of his players. Even though he left the Giants after they won their second Super Bowl in 1990 and despite the Giants going into a down period with Ray Handley for two years, there was never any talk of resentment or abandonment from the Giants players. Parcells helped them turn into winners. "I love Simms. I love a lot of those guys," Parcells said. "I got the nicest letter from Simms [around 2005]. Just wonderful. It's why you coach."

Simms told Parcells in the letter how much he appreciated him. "I had a lot of those. They must think I'm going to die," Parcells said.

The Giants held a twenty-fifth anniversary reunion of their 1986 Super Bowl championship team in New Jersey in 2011. Simms said that when Parcells walked into the room, things got quiet. "Bill is here," they all whispered.

"They did it out of tremendous respect," Simms said. "They couldn't wait to see him. Listen, they all thanked him."

When the Giants lined up for a team picture at the reunion, they sat in the same spot as they had for the picture in 1986. "If they filmed it, it would have been the funniest hour on NFL Network," Simms said. "Guys were telling stories. Bill was talking about the whole team. It was pretty cool."

Hall of Fame linebacker Harry Carson was perhaps the wisest of all those Giants. "The thing we can all say about Bill is he put us in a position to win," he said.

The Parcells coaching tree has produced eight Super Bowl appearances and six Super Bowl championships, and the two losses came when one of the branches defeated the other. Combine that with Parcells's three appearances and two championships, and that's a total of 11 Super Bowls and eight championships in the first 46 Super Bowls. That means there's been a Parcells connection to nearly 25 percent of all the Super Bowls.

Bill Parcells and Bill Belichick may have been the two best coaches on any NFL staff since Vince Lombardi was running the offense and Tom Landry was running the defense as assistants for the New York Giants in the late 1950s. Parcells and Belichick first worked together as assistants for Ray Perkins with the Giants in 1981–1982 before Parcells was named head coach in 1983. He elevated Belichick from linebacker coach to defensive coordinator in 1985.

They won two Super Bowls together with the Giants and then made it to one Super Bowl with the Patriots and one AFC championship game with the Jets before their bitter parting in 2000. When they were apart, Belichick did much better. Parcells never made the Super Bowl in any of the seven seasons he coached without Belichick on his staff. Belichick made it to five Super Bowls without Parcells in his first twelve seasons in New England.

Simms says he's looked at the team picture from the 1986 championship team and wondered, "Were we that good or were we just coached that well?"

Parcells let his coaches coach, especially Belichick. In the 1990 playoffs, the Giants played a four-man front against the Bears, a three-man front against the 49ers, and then a two-man front against the Bills in the Super Bowl. Belichick devised the schemes. They all worked.

"I had a lot of faith in him, but never to the point where I didn't know or have a pulse on it," Parcells said. "The conversations were much shorter because we had been together so long. I could say, 'Bill, remember when we did this against Roy Green?' He always knew. Of course, he had ideas, too. It worked well."

The cold war between Parcells and Belichick finally ended at a

Hall of Fame luncheon for Carson in summer 2006 at Gallagher's Steak House in Midtown Manhattan. There were speeches by Parcells, Belichick, and Schottenheimer, who was Carson's first position coach after he was drafted in 1976 and helped him in the transition from defensive end at South Carolina State to linebacker with the Giants. It was a very nice affair. As it was winding down, Parcells and Belichick sat at a table with Schottenheimer and finally broke the ice. It had been six years since they had worked together or really communicated. They repaired their relationship that day.

They will always have one thing in common: they loved their time with the Giants. It was unfortunate that business got in the way of their friendship. "Hey, that's life," Parcells said. "Things go forward, and everybody has to make their own decision. So he made some of his and I made some of mine. Time goes on. It's not in anybody's best interests to have things the way they temporarily were. We were back on pretty good terms pretty quickly."

Ten former assistants of Parcells went on to become NFL head coaches: Belichick (Browns, Patriots), Tom Coughlin (Jaguars, Giants), Sean Payton (Saints), Romeo Crennel (Browns, Chiefs), Al Groh (Jets), Chris Palmer (Browns), Eric Mangini (Jets, Browns), Tony Sparano (Dolphins), Todd Haley (Chiefs), and Ray Handley (Giants). Charlie Weis, another Parcells assistant, has been the head coach at Notre Dame and Kansas, and Mike MacIntyre was hired as the San Jose State head coach in 2010. He worked for Parcells in Dallas.

There were four general managers in the NFL in 2012 who also worked in the front office for Parcells: Mike Tannenbaum (Jets), Scott Pioli (Chiefs), Jeff Ireland (Dolphins), and Trent Baalke (49ers).

Belichick has won three Super Bowls with New England. Coughlin, who joined the Giants in 1988 and was the receivers coach for their second title, won two Super Bowls with New York in his first eight years as the head coach. Payton, who worked three years for Parcells in Dallas, won the Super Bowl for the Saints.

"Obviously, Bill made some pretty good choices along the way of the people that would work for him," Coughlin said. "So you have to add that ability to his long list of things that he has done extremely well in his career."

Coughlin learned Giants football from Parcells, which means being a physical team that plays great defense and doesn't turn the ball over. "That was driven home very easily for me," Coughlin said. "We played a certain way, we practiced a certain way. We had an element of toughness about our teams. Our guys were very proud of that."

Payton was a coaching star after the Saints won the Super Bowl in 2009—and before Bountygate brought him down in 2012—and he counted on Parcells for direction as the game against Peyton Manning and the Colts approached. By then, Parcells was running the Dolphins and the Super Bowl was being played in Miami. Over a four-day stretch between the Saturday eight days before the game and the Tuesday leading up to the game, Parcells's phone kept ringing and Payton kept calling for advice. He also saw him once when the Saints worked out at the Dolphins' facility that Monday.

"I bet you the son of a bitch called me ten times. Ten. Not one. Ten. Saturday he's still in New Orleans. How about Monday? What do you think about Monday? What do you think about Friday at the end of the week? What happens if one of my guys gets in trouble? How would you handle that? Every fucking question," Parcells said. "I said I told my team that if any of you get drunk, any of you get arrested, you're going home. You're not playing in the game. You're going fucking home. So I said write it down, right now, look them all in the face, I don't care who you are. Just do it and you are going home."

Parcells also let him in on a big-game secret that obviously stuck.

"I told him you got to have balls to win this game," Parcells said. "He was asking me about all these things. You ran these fakes in these biggest games. Why did you do it? You got to have balls. But I said you got to calculate this shit. You can't just indiscriminately decide to run it. I'm sure that was in his head with the onside kick."

Payton called for Ambush, an onside kick to start the second half. The Saints recovered, and it gave them an extra possession, which they converted into a key touchdown in their victory over the Colts. Parcells pulled off a fake punt—Arapahoe in the Giants' playbook—on fourth and one from his own 46 on the Giants' first possession of the second half of his first Super Bowl against Denver. They trailed 10–9, picked up the first down and scored a touchdown, and never trailed again. It was a risky call. If the Giants had failed, they would have given John Elway a short field.

Payton never tipped Parcells off to the onside kick, but Parcells was proud of him. "I don't want any credit for any of this," he said. "This kid is his own guy. He really is. You can influence people because you do have to have balls. And your team has got to know you have them."

Parcells was not happy when Payton called a reverse in the second quarter to wide receiver Devery Henderson that lost 7 yards. He told him the day after the game, "Sean, what the fuck are you doing? You bringing out the jugglers and the clowns? Why fucking do that?"

He had warned Payton not to "start bringing extra furniture into your house now because it's not going to look good once you get it in there," meaning don't clutter up the playbook this late in the season. "You better give them a song they know by heart, but if they don't know it, the pressure of the game is going to get them," he said.

Payton said that working for Parcells "for three years, it was like law school."

Haley was hired in Kansas City by Pioli, Parcells' son-in-law, but he was fired with three games remaining in his third season, in 2011. He was then hired by the Steelers, the team his father Dick helped stock with wise personnel decisions during Pittsburgh's tremendous Super Bowl runs in the '70s, as the offensive coordinator. Parcells had given Todd Haley his first coaching job with the Jets in 1997 and later hired him in Dallas. Dick Haley worked for Parcells with the Jets as well.

"In my mind, Bill is the best there is at what he does," Todd Haley said. "I know any business he was in he would have been at the top also. He just knows how to handle people and how to push the right button, on top of knowing football as well as anyone. There isn't a day that goes by that something doesn't come up that I don't think, 'What would Bill do in this situation?' "

Parcells was just passing down wisdom he picked up along the way from Al Davis and Tom Landry, Chuck Knox, Mike Holovak, and Bucko Kilroy. He never forgot how they helped him out when he was a young head coach, and he's been committed to helping the next generation of coaches. He was touched when Payton called him the morning after the game and starting crying, telling Parcells he was a father figure to him. "I told him I was honored," Parcells said.

Parcells doesn't want to take any credit for the success of his assistants. "We all work from our experiences. Organizationally and how to approach things, they all took a lot," he said. "But they are their own guys. They have their own identity."

In the end, they are all Parcells guys.

SECOND CHANCES

The rain was slamming down on Tony Dungy as NFL officials hurried to assemble the podium for the Super Bowl XLI trophy presentation. The Indianapolis Colts had just defeated the Chicago Bears in a driving rainstorm in Miami. It was the tenth Super Bowl in southern Florida and the forty-first overall and the first played when the NFL would have been better off indoors.

There were a lot of thoughts spinning around in Dungy's mind. He and Bears coach Lovie Smith, one of his former assistants with the Bucs, were the first African-American head coaches to take their teams to the Super Bowl. That made the game historic even before it was played. Dungy then carved a deeper and unforgettable place in history as the first African-American coach to win the Super Bowl. It could have happened earlier for Dungy, but he could never get the Bucs to the next level in the six years he coached in Tampa. He turned around a moribund and ridiculed program and even brought the Bucs all the way to the NFC championship game in just his fourth year after the 1999 season, where they lost to the Rams.

The Bucs held the explosive Rams to just 11 points, but Tampa managed only two field goals. It typified Dungy's Tampa years: great defense, no offense. His offense lacked firepower and played not to lose. In the next two playoff seasons, Tampa's offense produced a total of four field goals, and the Bucs were outscored in back-to-back wild-card games in Philadelphia by a combined 52–12. There were rumors after that first loss to the Eagles that the Bucs were on the verge of being sold and the new owners wanted to replace Dungy with Bill Parcells. The team remained with the Glazer family, and Dungy remained the coach. But he was on the hot seat going into the 2001 season. Unfortunately, his team didn't play as if it were motivated to save the coach. Dungy heard the Parcells rumors again and was angered by them. This was supposed to be a fraternity, and it was bad form to covet a job that wasn't open. The Bucs went into the playoffs knowing Dungy's job was at stake, but they lost again to the Eagles, and this time Dungy was indeed fired. Parcells was the first choice of the Glazer family. Tampa thought it had a deal with Parcells—he had stood up former Bucs owner Hugh Culverhouse at the last minute in 1992—but he backed out again. Parcells was so close to taking the job that he had Mike Tannenbaum, the Jets' assistant general manager who had been Parcells's right-hand man when he was with the Jets, fly to Tampa to meet with Bucs executive Rich McKay. If Parcells had closed the deal, Tannenbaum was his choice to be Tampa's general manager. A long and winding search led the Glazers to Jon Gruden of the Raiders. He was under contract but at odds with Oakland owner Al Davis. When the Glazers offered the exorbitant price of two first-round picks and $8 million, Davis was happy to send Gruden to Florida.

It paid off immediately for the Bucs. Gruden won the Super Bowl in his first year in Tampa with the core of the team constructed by Dungy. It was made even sweeter for Gruden by the fact that the Super Bowl victory came against Davis and the Raiders. Gruden's knowledge of the Raiders' offense and quarterback Rich Gannon was instrumental in forcing the usually precise Oakland quarterback into a Super Bowl record five interceptions.

It had not taken Dungy long to find a job after the Bucs fired him. He had his choice of Carolina or Indianapolis, and who wouldn't want to coach Peyton Manning? It was an easy decision. His first season with the Colts, however, ended miserably when they lost to the Jets 41–0. The Jets were coached by Herm Edwards, a former assistant to Dungy with the Bucs and one of his best friends. A few weeks later, it got even worse. Dungy was back home in Tampa on the night the Bucs were winning the Super Bowl in San Diego. As he drove back to his house after watching the game on television with friends, it was an emotional thirty minutes in the car. Fans were celebrating in the streets of Tampa as Dungy sat in traffic. None of the fans recognized him. Gruden won with Dungy's players, but the former coach was yesterday's news. The Glazers had taken his team away from him, and now they had won it all without him.

He had put his heart into building the Bucs, made the community proud of the team, insisted that his players give back, but then missed out on the grand prize. "It was really bittersweet," Dungy said. "Not to be there to see it to fruition; it was hard. It was disappointing for me, but I was happy for the city. I was happy for the guys because you remember the orange uniforms and 22,000 people in the stands, people saying you stink. There was a little bit of a hollow feeling; as proud as I was of those guys and what they had done, it was difficult not being there with them."

Four years and nine days later, it was Dungy who was about to lift the Vince Lombardi Trophy proudly over his head with Manning, one of the greatest quarterbacks of all time, by his side. Dungy was thinking about his junior high school coaches, his high school coaches, the different teachers he'd had. He thought about Grambling's Eddie Robinson and Florida A&M's Jake Gaither and others who had coached in the historically black colleges and never were given the opportunity to coach in the NFL. "Lovie and I have been able to take advantage of the opportunity," Dungy said after the game. "But we're certainly not the best, certainly not the most qualified, and I know there's some other guys who could have done it, given the chance. So I just feel good I was the first one to be able to do it and represent those guys that paved the way for me."

He thought about the route he had taken to be a head coach in the NFL after fifteen years as an assistant with the Steelers, Chiefs, and Vikings. And he thought about failing to get a head coaching job after interviewing with the Eagles twice, the Packers, and the Jaguars and getting fired by Tampa.

Most of all, he was thinking about his father, Wilbur Dungy, who died in the summer of 2005. Wilbur was devoted to physical fitness and enjoyed bicycle riding and swimming but had been diagnosed with leukemia. He died at the age of seventy-eight. He missed by less than two years seeing his son reach the pinnacle of his profession. As he was standing on the podium with the massive amounts of confetti coming down along with all that rain, it turned out Wilbur Dungy was right after all.

"Don't worry about what's wrong; look at what's right and make it better," Wilbur had always told his son.

That was what Dungy thought to himself on the car ride home in Tampa the night the Bucs won the Super Bowl. It was how he kept calm after getting passed over for all those head coaching jobs. It was easy to doubt during those years that he would ever get his chance as a head coach or if that special moment hugging the trophy would ever come. But he didn't let it consume him. He had his faith. He had his family. Everything else would fall into place. He had an inner peace and calmness that made the many teams that interviewed him wonder if his personality was strong enough to deal with so many diverse and powerful personalities in the locker room. He wasn't a yeller or screamer. He didn't curse. Like father, like son. "My dad was really just a quiet, quiet guy," he said.

Tony Dungy was just a really nice guy, maybe too nice to handle the knuckleheads in the locker room. One time, Dungy was complaining to his father about the lack of playing time his high school football coach was giving him, and his father told him about his days as a teacher in Arlington, Virginia. It was a lesson in the inequities in life. It was 1951, Wilbur Dungy's first teaching job. This was four years before Tony was born, and Wilbur was at an all-black school because the schools were segregated and he wasn't allowed to teach in the all-white school. Every day, Dungy and his students would walk past the all-white school on their way to class. "All I could do was make sure my kids knew as much as the students in the all-white school," he told Tony. "Then, it was, what was I going to do to make the situation better?"

Make it better, he told him, and don't complain. His father told him that when he graduated from high school, he wanted to go into the service. "They wouldn't let us fly the planes, didn't want us to fly the planes, so we taught ourselves," Wilbur Dungy said.

He didn't say it was because he was African American, but it was implied. "I knew the point he was making, but I never knew it until his funeral," Dungy said. "One of his friends talked about my father being in the Tuskegee Airmen. It was an all-black kind of air force regiment. It was segregated. It was a very decorated group, but it was still segregated at the time. But I had no idea he was even involved in it. I just kind of got the message: Don't complain. Make the situation better."

Dungy always tried to make the situation better for his own children as he worked to survive in a competitive business. He never slept in his office. He drove his kids to school in the morning. He never bought into the idea that extra hours bring better results even though he was aware that his peers were picking up frequent-stay awards for sleeping in their offices. Beds pulled out from the wall. Air mattresses. Sleeper sofas. Dungy slept in his own bed every night. He encouraged his assistants to spend quality time with their families. He learned how to do it the right way playing and coaching for Pittsburgh's Chuck Noll, the only coach to win four Super Bowls. Gruden was well known for showing up at his desk hours before the sun came up.

"I felt that we could start work at 8:15 or 8:30 and get done what we needed to do," Dungy said. "I was very fortunate I was ten years with Coach Noll: two as a player and eight working for him. I saw you can win and be very successful and still have outside interests. He was a tremendous family person. He had his nephew and son working in training camp, and that made a big impression on me. Then I worked the last four before I got a head coaching job working for Denny Green, and he was the same way."

During the season, Tuesday was game plan night, and Dungy worked until 10 p.m. In other teams' offices around the NFL, that was about when coaches were ordering in late-night dinners. He stayed until 9 p.m. on Wednesday and until dinnertime on Thursday, and then on Friday the head coach's office was empty by 2 p.m. Compared with other head coaches, Dungy was working banker's hours—and winning. Nobody questioned his work ethic or his priorities. He made the playoffs in four of his six seasons in Tampa and in each of his seven seasons in Indianapolis. He was a man of faith and strong devotion to his family. Wilbur never missed any of Tony's games and attended many of his practices and still taught school, and Tony still doesn't know how he did it. "It made a big impact on me, and I always knew that's how I wanted to be," he said. "If I had slept in the office, would we have won two Super Bowls or three instead of one? I don't think so. I don't think the trade-off would have been worth it for me."

He won father-of-the-year awards. He was always there for his children. He and his wife, Lauren, had three of their own children and adopted four, the youngest in 2010. "It keeps you young," Dungy said. "At least that's what she tells me."

James was the second oldest. When he was thirteen years old, he helped his father present a Bucs T-shirt to President Bill Clinton at Tampa's training camp. James had moved with the family to Indianapolis when Dungy was hired by the Colts, but now, three years later, he was back in Tampa and enrolled at Hillsborough Community College, interested in pursuing a degree in criminal justice technology. He was planning his nineteenth birthday party for January 6, 2006. There already were signs of trouble. A few months earlier, on October 21, he told a 911 dispatcher he had taken several pills, including four hydrocodones, an addictive narcotic painkiller, and possibly naproxen, which is used for mild to moderate pain and inflammation. He told the 911 operator he was being stupid and had taken about fifteen pills and that he had called his mother back in Indianapolis, who instructed him to call 911 and said to tell 911 he needed to have his stomach pumped. He told the operator his stomach and throat were burning and he felt like he was going to pass out. He was taken by ambulance to an area hospital. He reportedly told authorities he was depressed. He recovered from the episode with the pills.

James Dungy was six foot seven, much taller than his father. He was outgoing and courteous, just like his father. There is still no explanation why he took a twenty-eight-inch leather belt and secured it around his neck and hanged himself from a ceiling fan on December 22 in his apartment at the Campus Lodge in Lutz, Florida, a Tampa suburb. It was two months after the incident with the pills. His girlfriend had gone out for a ten-minute walk and came back to find him hanging at 1:30 a.m. She used a knife to cut him down. "I think my boyfriend's dead," Antoinette Anderson cried to an emergency dispatcher. "I think he tried to hang himself or something."

The 911 operator talked her through administering cardiopulmonary resuscitation. A medical worker arrived and did CPR until a fire rescue crew pulled up and brought James Dungy to University Community Hospital, where he was pronounced dead. There was no trace of alcohol or drugs in his body. The only substances found were nicotine and caffeine. Emergency workers had injected him with medication in a failed attempt to revive him. It was an unimaginable horror. James Dungy was now a statistic. Suicide is the third-leading cause of death for fifteen- to twenty-four-year-olds, after accidents and homicide, according to the Centers for Disease Control and Prevention. There are about 4,400 suicides every year in that age group.

It was now nearly five years after James's death, and Tony Dungy was in New York City for an NBC sales meeting. He had left the Colts after the 2008 season, two years after he won the Super Bowl. He started a successful second career as an analyst on NBC's *Football Night in America* studio show. He was sitting in the lobby of a fashionable hotel next to Central Park talking about his life in football and how the fraternity of coaches was an invaluable support system after James's death, especially at the funeral in Florida.

"Like Herm Edwards," Dungy said. "The Jets played on Monday night and the funeral was on Tuesday, and I knew he was going to be there. I still don't know how he got there. Their game wasn't over until one o'clock in the morning.

"It's a neat fraternity, and you realize some of the things you go through no one else understands other than the thirty-one other guys. They know how hard you work, and they know what you put into things. When you get fired or you lose a playoff game or you had a great year and it doesn't end up the way you wanted, there are guys that have been there; they know what it's like, and they reach out to you."

Dungy and Edwards are like brothers. They first worked together on Marty Schottenheimer's staff in Kansas City in the early '90s. James Dungy used to sit on Edwards's lap when he was a little boy. When Dungy was hired by the Bucs, the first thing he did was bring Edwards with him as his assistant head coach. "Kind of puts everything in perspective when something like that happens," Edwards said after getting the news that Dungy's son had died. "You get all hung up in football, winning and losing. When you lose a child, that's tough. Pretty tough on everybody."

A few days before James's death, the Colts had suffered their first loss of the season after starting 13–0, ending their bid to be the first team to get through a regular season with a perfect 16–0 record. Dungy missed the next game in Seattle and then returned less than one week after the funeral for the final game of the regular season and then a crushing playoff loss to the Steelers.

All these years later, Dungy is reluctant to say much about the agony he and Lauren went through after their son's suicide. He had spoken quite eloquently for twenty minutes during a gutwrenching two-hour funeral service less than one week after James died. There were two thousand mourners at the Idlewild Baptist Church in Lutz. The entire Colts team attended. Commissioner Paul Tagliabue and four past and present NFL head coaches were there: Edwards, Lovie Smith, Jack Del Rio, and Dennis Green.

"Parents, hug your kids every chance you get," Dungy told the congregation. "Tell them you love them every chance you get because you don't know when it's going to be the last time."

The last time he saw James was when he dropped him off at the airport in Indianapolis around Thanksgiving. He didn't have a chance to give him a hug, and that always bothered him. He figured there would be a next time. In one of their last phone conversations, James asked his father if he would get to be on the field in Detroit if the Colts made it to the Super Bowl. Tony assured him he would but cautioned that the Colts had to get there first.

"We loved our son very much, he loved us, and we miss him terribly. James was a good young man with a compassionate heart, and we were glad to have him for eighteen years," Dungy said at the funeral. "God has him now for the rest of eternity."

His faith and his family helped him get through it. His football team, too. During the service, he specifically addressed his players.

"I want to urge you to continue being who you are because

our young boys in this country, they need to hear from you," he said. "If anything, be bolder in who you are. Because our boys are getting a lot of the wrong messages about what it means to be a man in this world. About how you should act, and how you should dress, and how you should talk, and how you should treat people. They don't always get the right message, but you guys have the right messages."

During training camp the next summer, Dungy explained to *USA Today* how he was coping with his son's death. "It's human nature to grieve, and you're going to have some pain," he said. "But then the choice is how you handle the pain. You can choose to go on and fight through it, or you can choose to succumb to it. You can't make the feeling go away. There's no Novocain or anything that can just take it away. You begin to realize that you can still function, you can still move forward."

Dungy mourned the loss of James but did not make himself feel guilty. He didn't second-guess selecting the demanding occupation of being an NFL head coach. It didn't change the way he approached his job after taking some time off. He was still an available father. His hours remained the same. Dungy always felt there was more he could do with his life than coach football, but he enjoyed the game, enjoyed influencing young lives. A few weeks after James's death, the Colts' dream of winning the Super Bowl ended in a surprising loss to the Steelers. "A couple of big disappointments," Dungy said after the game. "Obviously, this one doesn't rank anywhere close to the last one."

Just one year later, Dungy was standing in the rain in Miami. "I just have to say how sweet this is," he said. "It's tough to win. It's tough to win the Super Bowl."

The coaching fraternity is small. The jobs are coveted. They are hard to get and harder to keep. Each year at the NFL owners meetings, a group picture is taken of the thirty-two head coaches. There are significant changes to the picture every year. Some years, there is a massive overhaul with ten new faces. In a year when the owners are not in the frame of mind to pay off existing contracts, maybe there are five new faces. That's still a lot. At the league meeting in the spring of 2012 in Palm Beach, Florida, the only coach in the picture representing the same team he did in the 1999 photo was Philadelphia's Andy Reid. That was Reid's first year with the Eagles. He was a surprising hire from the talent-rich staff that Mike Holmgren put together in Green Bay. Reid worked for Holmgren for seven years, the entire time Holmgren stayed in Titletown, USA, until he left to become coach and general manager of the Seattle Seahawks.

Reid was an unknown to Eagles fans. He had served Holmgren well as his quarterback coach and then assistant head coach, but while he worked closely with Brett Favre, he was never the offensive coordinator and Holmgren called the plays. Eagles owner Jeffrey Lurie was taking a leap of faith that Holmgren had prepared Reid to be the head coach in one of the toughest sports towns in America.

Reid got off to a bad start with the cynical and demanding Eagles fans by selecting Syracuse quarterback Donovan McNabb over Texas running back Ricky Williams with the second overall pick in the 1999 draft. A Philadelphia radio station rented a bus to transport fans to the draft in New York City to boo McNabb when he came onto the stage to accept congratulations and an Eagles cap from the commissioner, Paul Tagliabue. It wasn't fair to McNabb, but he handled it well. It was just a preview of the inordinate amount of criticism he would encounter during his career with the Eagles.

Reid, of course, made the right decision. McNabb and Reid were a team until McNabb was traded in the spring of 2010 to the Washington Redskins. In McNabb's eleven years with the Eagles, they went to five NFC championship games but only one Super

Bowl, and they lost that game to the Patriots. McNabb was never fully appreciated in Philadelphia. He never played his best in the biggest games.

In the days before the Colts played the Bears in the Super Bowl, the lives of Dungy and Reid drew closer together. The unfortunate common denominator was heartache brought about by their children. Reid's sons Garrett, twenty-three, and Britt, twenty-one, got themselves into big trouble in separate incidents on the same day in suburban Philadelphia while Reid and his wife, Tammy, were vacationing in California. The Reid boys were living at home at the time of their arrests.

According to the authorities, Britt pointed a handgun at another motorist during a traffic altercation. He later was arraigned on nine counts, including making terroristic threats, possession of a controlled substance, and a felony charge of carrying a firearm without a license. Garrett was involved in a traffic accident, and police found a shotgun and ammunition in the vehicle. He told the police he had used heroin before the crash, and a blood test confirmed that he was under the influence of the drug. Garrett was arraigned on misdemeanor drug and traffic charges.

Garrett Reid said he didn't begin using drugs until he graduated from high school, but according to a probation report read in court, his involvement in drugs and dealing was steep. He started with marijuana and alcohol when he was eighteen and then got into the prescription painkillers Percocet and Oxycontin. He progressed to heroin and cocaine and was in drug rehab at age twenty.

"I liked being the rich kid in that area and having my own high-status life," Garrett Reid told a probation officer. "I could go anywhere in the 'hood. They all knew who I was. I enjoyed it. I liked being a drug dealer."

Andy Reid took a leave of absence from the Eagles on February 12, 2007. He was gone until March 23. Later that year, his sons were sentenced to prison. The judge said the Reid home, in Villanova, Pennsylvania, was a "drug emporium."

"There isn't any structure there that this court can depend upon," Montgomery County Judge Steven O'Neill said. He added, "I'm saying this is a family in crisis."

The judge said that Andy and Tammy Reid loved and supported their children and had tried to get them help. During Reid's time away from football, he accompanied Garrett to a drug rehabilitation center.

It is now more than five years since his sons' arrests and Reid is running training camp, his fourteenth with the Eagles, in the summer of 2012. Britt had just gotten married and was working as a graduate assistant in Philadelphia with the Temple University football team. His youngest son, Spencer, was a redshirt freshman running back for Temple. Garrett, the oldest, was at training camp with his father, working with the Eagles strength and conditioning staff. That kept him close to Andy and around football. You never stop worrying about a recovering drug addict. Garrett was set to begin classes in sports management in the fall.

On the morning of August 5, Garrett Reid was found dead in his dormitory room at Lehigh at 7:20 a.m. He was residing in Sayre Park, the campus housing the team uses during training camp. Police received a 911 call and efforts to revive Garrett were not successful.

"Garrett's road through life was not always an easy one," the Reids said in a statement. "He faced tremendous personal challenges with bravery and spirit. As a family, we stood by him and were inspired as he worked to overcome those challenges. Even though he lost the battle that has been ongoing for the last eight years, we will always remember him as a fighter who had a huge, loving heart."

The funeral was held two days later. More than nine hundred people paid their respects, including commissioner Roger Goodell, Cleveland Browns president Mike Holmgren, who was

Reid's boss in Green Bay, the entire Eagles team, Ravens coach John Harbaugh and Saints defensive coordinator Steve Spagnuolo, who were former Reid assistants, Colts general manager Ryan Grigson and Browns general manager Tom Heckert, who had worked for Reid in the Eagles front office.

One day after the funeral, Reid was back at training camp. He had already spoken with Dungy. If there was a coach in the NFL who understood the heartache of Andy Reid, it was Tony Dungy. It was surprising that Reid elected to return to work so quickly, but he gave a simple explanation: "I'm a football coach, that's what I do, and I know my son wouldn't want it any other way. I can't put it to you any more frank than that. He loved the Philadelphia Eagles. I know what he would want me to do."

Reid could relate to the emptiness felt by Dungy. Their jobs were high profile and paid extraordinarily well, but that didn't make them immune to family tragedy. Dolphins coach Joe Philbin understood. In January of 2012, when Philbin was the offensive coordinator of the Packers, his twenty-one-year-old son fell through the ice on a Wisconsin river and drowned. He had marijuana and twice the legal limit of alcohol in his system. The fourteen-year-old son of Ray Sherman, the Packers receiver coach at the time, died of an accidental gunshot to the head in the family's garage in 2003 as he played with a gun that had been a gift to his father.

Reid's players rallied around him. The Eagles fans, who have been tough on Reid for losing four NFL championship games and a Super Bowl, embraced him with chants of "Andy, Andy, Andy."

"I've watched Andy try so hard with his family over the years," Eagles owner Jeffrey Lurie said. "He cares so much about his family that it's a hard one."

He had football to distract him. But none of that would make up for what he lost in Garrett. "Friendship," he said. "You get these kids and they grow up. You get to the teens, the higher teens, and then the twenties and thirties. They become more than your son—they're your friend. You're going to miss that. But at the same time, you gain strength from it. He taught me a lot of lessons in life that I'll use down the road. You'll always remember his smile and the jokester that he was. Those help you get through the good and the bad times."

Reid is known to be part of the fraternity that works endlessly, spending long hours poring over tape and game plans and turning his office at the Eagles' headquarters into a studio apartment several nights a week. His five children were born in five different states as he kept moving around to find better coaching jobs. In Philadelphia, he lives only twenty-three minutes from the Eagles' offices off Broad Street but sleeps in his office four or five nights a week.

When he worked for the Packers, Reid arrived at his office at Lambeau Field by 4:30 a.m. Gruden, another rising star on Holmgren's staff, would be there with him. Holmgren felt they competed to see who could arrive first. Reid is a big man. He was twelve pounds when he was born. Between the 2008 and 2009 seasons, he lost eighty pounds and then gained half of it back. He said he was so "huge" that he had trouble walking from the dressing room to the sideline when the Eagles played the Cardinals in the 2008 NFC championship game in Glendale, Arizona. He then lost another twenty pounds. "I tell my wife there is something wrong here. You had the five kids, and it ruined my body," Reid said.

Every minute his eyes are open during the season, he's working. "Do I think this is the healthiest business in the world? The way we go about it? No, I don't," Reid said. "You try to do the best you can. Some people do it better."

Owners don't require their coaches to work around the clock, but they want results. No coach wants to be outworked, so they live with that fear and paranoia. "It's a sick life," Patriots owner Robert Kraft said. "I'm not sure if I had a daughter I would want her to marry a head football coach. It's a very demanding job."

Reid had two excellent reasons to cut back on his hours and spend more time at home: his health and his five kids. If he had a family in crisis, as the judge said, couldn't that be attributed partly to his not being home enough? If his house was a drug emporium, wouldn't a father who was around the house more have been more in tune with what was going on?

"I looked into that quite a bit," Reid said. "I'm not sure there was a correlation there. People can argue that back and forth."

He went through periods of guilt after his sons were arrested. He questioned himself. Was it his fault? Was he doing enough for his children? Was he around enough? "Then you talk to enough people, you receive enough letters, you go talk to counselors," Reid said. "You find out that you're not the only one; there have been plenty of dads that have spent every minute at home and work nine-to-five jobs with the same issues. Teachers that spend the whole summer at home and work nine to five during the year. It affects a lot of people," he said. "I don't mean to be cold. People can question it. Your house caused it. It's more than that. There's just more to it than that. That's not the primary cause. The best thing my wife and I did is we never turned our back on it; we hit it head on and didn't shy away from anything. We were real with the boys. We had a lot of support from people at the league, we all supported each other as a family, we had support from fans, people who had gone through things. It's a pretty big epidemic out there that touches a lot of people. At that moment, you think you are the only one, but you find out very quickly that you are not."

Reid finds peace and solitude during the hours when most people are sleeping. There is rush hour traffic outside his office door starting at 7 a.m. during the season. There are problems, situations, he must deal with every day. The personnel department has an issue. One of his player's kids is sick. One of his coaches has a question about a play in the game plan. There's an unexpected injury. That's why Reid says he starts work at 4:30 in the morning. "I am cranking," he said. "It's good, condensed, not interrupted work done at that period of time." It gives him two and a half hours until "people start knocking on that door," he said.

By the time things quiet down, it's 7 p.m. after twelve hours of mayhem. Reid has been through a day of practice and meetings and media obligations, just like every other coach. By 8 p.m., the players are home and the coaches are in their offices, and Reid works until 1 a.m. before he shuts his eyes and gets a little sleep on a bed he positions next to a window in his office. "I still delegate," he said. "But at the same time, you are paid to know what is going on. This is the reality of it. I treat it like I did finals. I am going to exhaust myself for that test on Sunday. I want that same feeling I had when I was in grad school and I was cranking. When you go into a game, they can throw anything they want and I got it."

Tom Coughlin won Super Bowls XLII and XLVI for the Giants, and he sleeps in his office once a week. "My heart goes out to Andy," Coughlin said after his sons were arrested. Reid is in the same division facing many of the same issues as Coughlin but has taken a different approach. Reid did not change his routine after his sons veered off the tracks.

"There are coaches today who go home. This is what works best for me," Reid said. "I don't really care what works for the other person. This is what I do. I try to get my family to come down here, which they do. They come visit. We got a nice place here we can eat if we need to eat. The door is always open for my family to come down. I don't golf or anything else. So when I go home, I am home. That's what I am there for. I wear them out with text messages and phone calls."

He has a nice study in his house and does personnel work there in the off-season, but that's about it. "If you are going to stay involved with offense, personnel, and the defense and have a grasp of what is going on, you need a condensed period of time when nobody is bugging on you," he said. "I do. I need that. Other people don't."

Tony Dungy was one of the coaches who didn't let the stress of the job affect his quality time at home. "I don't think it is harder for coaches than it is for anybody else," Dungy says. "Most people that are good at what they do work a lot of hours. We can't have a built-in excuse and say we are never going to have balance."

Dungy had balance in his coaching life, and Reid has struggled to find the right blend of coaching life and family life. Dungy's son committed suicide, and Reid's sons were arrested and jailed, and then his oldest son died at the age of twenty-nine. They took different approaches with results no father ever thinks can happen to him. "Anybody as a parent in America could feel for Andy," Dungy said, even before Garrett's death. "There is not a whole lot you can say or do other than just be there to support him and say, 'You know, I know a little bit about what you are going through.' "

Tony Dungy and Andy Reid forged a bond after the tragedy of James Dungy and the nightmare of Garrett and Britt Reid. That bond was strengthened by Michael Vick.

Connecting the dots from Indianapolis, to Tampa, to Philadelphia, to the U.S. penitentiary in Leavenworth, Kansas, it was Vick who brought Dungy and Reid together. They had competed against each other on the big stage when Reid's Eagles twice beat Dungy's Bucs in the playoffs. There wasn't much else they had in common. Reid was hired as a head coach by the first team that interviewed him after seven years as an NFL assistant coach, all with one team. He did not play in the NFL. Dungy was an assistant in the league for fifteen years with three teams and had four head coaching interviews before the fifth time was the charm with the Bucs. He was a defensive back for three years with the Steelers and 49ers. San Francisco traded him in 1980 to the New York Giants for wide receiver turned cornerback Ray Rhodes, but he didn't make it out of training camp and retired and went into coaching the next season. Ironically, Rhodes beat out Dungy for the Eagles' head coaching job in 1995.

"I didn't get frustrated necessarily with the interviews," Dungy said. "The worst year for me was '93, when we had seven openings and the Vikings were the number one defense in the NFL and I didn't get one phone call."

He initially thought it was a racial issue, but obviously that wasn't the case with the Eagles in 1995: Rhodes is also African American. But the more he analyzed it, the more he thought it had to do with his personality, not his color. He didn't curse. He didn't yell at the players. He didn't stay all night in the office. He didn't show up for work at five in the morning.

"Time spent in the office doesn't always reflect how the game is going to turn out," he said.

When Dungy left the Colts after the 2008 season, it was apparent he didn't plan to coach again. He was not going to catch his breath for a year and come back. He left the game as the most popular executive in the league. There weren't many who didn't like Dungy. Having his endorsement was considered just short of getting the Good Housekeeping Seal of Approval.

Vick was the most dynamic player in the NFL as he prepared for his seventh season in 2007. He had a rocket arm and explosive legs. Around the time of the draft, word started to leak about a dog-fighting operation that Vick was running out of his fifteen-acre property on Moonlight Road in Surry County, Virginia, in the name of the Bad Newz Kennels. Vick was invited to the draft to honor those who died in the mass shooting that recently had taken place at Virginia Tech, his alma mater. Roger Goodell asked Vick at the draft about the dog-fighting reports, and he denied any involvement. He lied to the commissioner's face.

Three months later, Vick and three other men were indicted on federal and state charges of running a dog-fighting ring for six years. The story disgusted football fans and shocked the Atlanta Falcons, Vick's team. The stories of the brutal killing of dogs in the ring and the execution of those who didn't perform well were stomach-turning. Goodell indefinitely suspended Vick before he could report to training camp. Unlike in the Saints bounty scandal, he did not hold the team accountable for not knowing Vick was into dog fighting. It was outside the confines of the team. It was not being talked about in team meetings with coaches present. The Falcons' punishment was losing their franchise quarterback. Vick was thrown in jail around Thanksgiving 2007 in the prime of his career. Vick paid the price with eighteen months in federal prison, losing two years of his career and the bulk of his $130 million contract.

The issue became which team was going to have the courage to sign him when he was released. It was going to take a coach who felt secure with his owner and in the community, because the owner was going to be criticized and portions of the community were going to be outraged. Atlanta suffered through a 4–12 season without Vick, but that set the team up to draft Boston College quarterback Matt Ryan with the third overall pick in 2008.

Dungy visited Vick at Leavenworth in May 2009, a couple of weeks before he was released from prison and before the Falcons officially cut ties with him. Dungy's visit came at the request of Vick's attorney, Billy Martin, who was from the same hometown as Dungy's wife. This was nothing new for Dungy. He had made prison visits to troubled young men convicted of crimes. "I asked him what I had asked most of those guys when I go in and visit prisons or I talk to youth offenders: Where do you want to go from here and why? What's important to you?" Dungy said. "Those are the questions I asked Mike, and it really seemed to me that he wanted to make things right and he wanted to be there for his kids. That's what I saw and what I sensed."

Vick needed a role model and mentor. Dungy was perfect. Goodell asked him to be both for Vick as the NFL considered reinstatement. As Vick tried to rehabilitate his image, he was convincing Dungy that he was a changed man. Dungy had met Vick when the Colts played the Falcons in a preseason game in Japan in the summer of 2005. They talked about getting together for a fishing trip when they had time after they returned home. Dungy always wondered what might have been if that trip had materialized. Maybe Vick would have opened up about the dog fighting. But who knows? He never told Dan Reeves, his first coach with the Falcons, and they had a good relationship. "I always kind of regretted not being able to spend the day with him," Dungy said.

Goodell reinstated Vick before NFL teams opened training camp in the summer of 2009.

Dungy and Reid were brought together by their mutual interest in Vick. Dungy was there to help Vick transition back into society and help him find the right team and city to continue his career. Vick could never replace James Dungy, but Dungy had a chance to influence Vick's life positively. Reid had seen with his sons the importance of giving young men a second chance. Of course, it helped that when Vick last played, he was the most dangerous offensive weapon in the league.

The Eagles still seemed an unlikely destination. They had McNabb, who had taken the team to the NFC championship game the previous season, and they had the promising backup Kevin Kolb. Reid was creative with quarterbacks and at the very least could work Vick in as a Wildcat quarterback, a formation that had been made popular in 2008 by the Miami Dolphins. But was Philly the right spot? Was Vick going to be more of a negative as a distraction than any positive he could be on the field? And how would McNabb handle it?

McNabb was Vick's host on his recruiting trip to Syracuse University. Vick eventually chose Virginia Tech, but he and McNabb remained friends. McNabb, who considered himself a big brother to Vick, lobbied the Eagles to sign him. Dungy wanted Vick to find a coach who had compassion, who perhaps could relate to the trouble young men go through until they find themselves and can differentiate what is right from what is terribly wrong.

If there was a coach in the NFL who would embrace taking a chance on Vick, it was Reid. He knew from the experience with his sons the importance of a helping hand. "They get out of prison, and it's like a deer in the headlights," Reid said. "Where do I turn? Nobody is going to trust me. The self-esteem level is down. They need a hand. So somebody has got to reach out and say, 'Hey, let's go. You can do it.' Like a coach. My boys were lucky enough that they met a family that reached out and said, 'Come on in, work for me.' "

One of Reid's sons worked at a restaurant. The other worked at an auto body shop. "They were sweating going in to interview for jobs. They thought nobody was going to hire them," Reid said. "Some of them just don't get that hand that reaches out . . . and boom"—Reid slaps his desk—"they fall right back into doing the drugs. Some of them latch on to that hand and don't let go. They got to build that résumé. How long can you stay clean? Are you really willing to change? You get a little money, are you going to fall back? Only time tells that."

Dungy knew he had a compassionate soul in Reid. "I think he was intrigued by helping someone," Dungy said. "It was going to help the Eagles, too. It's not a charity. I think he had a strong sense that this is a guy that deserves a chance, and I've got a job and I can give him a job, and so many employers today are afraid to take that step with ex-offenders."

Unless he was not interested for football reasons, which was entirely possible, Reid would be a hypocrite if he didn't at least consider Vick for his football team. Vick needed the same hand his sons reached out to grab.

"I really didn't steer Mike anywhere," Dungy said. "I just said, as he would ask me questions, that the thing you got to remember is you can't put your football career first. You can't say this is the best place for me to play or this is who is going to pay me the most money because it's going to be important for you to put your life back together. I really thought with the support system Philadelphia had in place, with Andy Reid being there, with Donovan McNabb being there, that it was really a good, good place for him."

Reid monitored any stories he could find out about Vick while he was in prison. It was about the same time his sons were locked up. He would go visit his boys every Thursday night, and the reception from the inmates could be a little rough if the Eagles had lost that Sunday. The Reid boys started prison life together at Montgomery County Correctional Facility, although they were not housed near each other. Andy Reid talked with different inmates and guards over a two-year period. He learned there were three phases the inmates could go through when they were locked up. Reaching stage three was the tough part. "The phase where it's everybody else's fault," Reid said, explaining the progression. "Then they realize, I messed up, I goofed. Then some reach the third stage when they admit they goofed and they are going to get it right and 'I ain't ever coming back.' Not all of them reach that phase. You look at certain guys, and you know he's going to struggle."

The transition from the sanctuary of the Eagles' practice field to the prisons was not easy. The surroundings were not pleasant. It was not like walking into the locker room. "They are human beings, and they goofed," Reid said. "Some of them goof real big and might never get out."

He continued to keep an eye on Vick when he was released from prison. He spoke with Goodell. He consulted with Dungy. Then he met with Vick. He wanted to be certain Vick would not "fall off the edge" and could function in the NFL. He wanted to see if he had reached stage three.

Reid, of course, doesn't own the Eagles. He didn't run into owner Jeffrey Lurie's office immediately after Vick was released and present a case for why the Eagles should be the team that would subject itself to ridicule. They didn't even need a quarterback. He waited to see how Vick behaved now that he was back home and out of prison. He wanted to see how he would build his résumé. Besides, the Bengals were the only other team that had shown interest, and they were on the periphery.

Lurie called himself an "extreme dog lover" who was still mourning the death of his two dogs in the two years before signing Vick. He brought in two new dogs, one rescued from abuse. He spoke at the news conference announcing Vick's signing after Vick left the room. He didn't look like a happy man. He used some pretty strong descriptive language to illustrate his feelings about what Vick had done to dogs: cruelty, torture, horrific, complete disregard for any definition of common decency, despicable. He called signing Vick an "impossibly difficult decision to approve."

Lurie believed in Reid. Reid believed in Dungy. Dungy believed in Vick. "He will never be able to recover from what he did criminally and murderously took part in, but he has an opportunity to create a legend where maybe he can be a force in stopping the horrendous cruelty to animals," Lurie said.

After Vick's first season in Philadelphia, in which he played sparingly and ended with a disappointing wild-card loss to the Cowboys on the road, Reid traded McNabb to the Redskins. Reid had been determined to trade one of his three quarterbacks, and he admitted he would have traded Vick if the right offer came along. He believed Vick deserved the right to start and that was not the plan in Philadelphia for 2010. Kolb was named the starter after McNabb was sent to the Redskins, but he suffered a concussion in the season opener against the Packers, creating a path for Vick to take the job. Vick helped the Eagles win the NFC East and get to the playoffs, but they lost to the Packers in their opening game in the divisional round. Kolb was then traded to the Cardinals following the season.

Reid and the Eagles had a lot invested in Vick. They had absorbed a tremendous amount of backlash after signing him, but if Reid could turn that investment into a trade that would benefit the Eagles, then he would have been traded instead of McNabb.

"If the opportunity came up where we could have been compensated and Michael could have had a good team to go to and it was right for him, then we do the deal," Reid said. "That didn't happen, but I would have looked at that. I would have looked at that to help him out, too."

Vick failed to get the Eagles into the playoffs in 2011, but he and Reid developed a close relationship in their first three seasons together. Reid was there for Vick when he was looking for a compassionate soul to assist him in reviving his career. When Garrett Reid died, Vick expressed strong feelings for his coach. "This is a very difficult situation for us all to deal with," Vick said. "Coach has always been a great supporter of us, as a team, as an organization. He's been a rock for us and a big teddy bear for us, so we're going to lean on him, and we're going to be there for him, and we're going to stay strong for him until he comes back and can lead us on."

Dungy trusted that Reid would be the perfect coach for Vick. Reid trusted Dungy that Vick was rehabilitated and in stage three. They both had their hearts broken by their own children and in their own way were looking for the same second chance as Vick.

THE DEAL OF THE CENTURY

On a February night in 1989, Jerry Jones made a ridiculous statement.

"What Jimmy Johnson will bring to us is worth more than if we had five first-round draft choices and five Heisman Trophy winners," Jones said. "History will show that one of the finest things that ever happened to the Cowboys is Jimmy Johnson."

It was hard to blame Jones for being a little giddy even though he had just flown back from Austin, where he had pulled Tom Landry off the golf course to let him know that the only coach the Cowboys had ever had was now the only coach the Cowboys had ever fired. Jones had purchased the Cowboys, America's Team, and the lease to operate Texas Stadium, the stadium that had a hole in the roof so God could watch his team, from the financially beleaguered Bum Bright for $140 million. He and Johnson had been teammates at Arkansas, and Johnson was the hottest college coach in the country after winning a national championship in 1987 at the University of Miami.

They were not great friends, but they were a package deal. Johnson might not have been worth five first-round draft picks, but he knew how to maximize his assets and turn them into valuable draft picks. He didn't have many assets with the roster he inherited from Landry, but he knew he had at least one: Herschel

Walker. History will show that Johnson's trade of Walker not even two months into his first season was one of the finest things to ever happen to the Dallas Cowboys.

Jones was being vilified for firing Landry. How dare an out-of-towner from across the Red River in archrival Arkansas of all places come into Big D and fire the legend? The truth was that the Dallas fans and media were hypocrites. For years, the talk shows had been filled with Landry must go chatter, and even Tex Schramm, the Cowboys' president who had hired Landry in the 1960 expansion year, was looking for a graceful way to ease Landry into retirement. His number one candidate was Jimmy Johnson. There was even speculation that Schramm had asked Johnson to come to Dallas and serve as Landry's defensive coordinator with the guarantee that he would be promoted when Landry retired.

"I don't know if that even came up in the conversation, but that was never even a factor for me," Johnson said. "In our conversation when he was talking about me becoming the head coach of the Cowboys, he might have brought up something like that. I immediately dismissed it. The only way I was going to leave Miami was to be the head coach."

Johnson was a guest in the Cowboys' suite at Super Bowl XXIII in Miami between the 49ers and Bengals and sat with Schramm, Landry, and team vice president Gil Brandt. In another month, Johnson would have Landry's job and Brandt's, too, because he would be in control of the Cowboys' personnel decisions: the draft, trades, and free agency. A few months after that, Schramm would also be gone. In Schramm's perfect world, he would have found another absentee owner like Bright and Clint Murchison before him, Landry would have exited to spend time on his charitable and religious endeavors, and then Schramm would have set the Cowboys up for the foreseeable future by hiring Johnson. Schramm and Johnson would have been great together. They liked to take chances. They were not afraid of failing.

After the 49ers beat the Bengals, Bill Walsh retired as San Francisco's coach. Johnson was rumored to be a candidate to replace him, but the 49ers ultimately went for continuity and promoted defensive coordinator George Seifert, which had been the direction Walsh steered the organization. That meant Johnson was still available for the Cowboys, although at the time it seemed that if he went to Dallas, he would be working for Schramm.

"Tex approached me," Johnson said. "At one time there were rumors about me going to the Philadelphia Eagles. Tex said just keep it in mind, whenever Tom retires, we've got thoughts about you coming to the Dallas Cowboys. He said keep that in mind as you are talking to these other teams. And that was the first time that he talked to me. Then he had me as his guest, with Tom Landry, at the Super Bowl when San Francisco played Cincinnati in Miami. That was the next encounter. And then the third encounter was at the Davey O'Brien Award in Fort Worth. Tex was there. Jerry wanted me to talk to Tex, make sure Tex knew that he was a legitimate buyer because Tex was brokering the deal. Then Jerry figured out that he wanted to bypass Tex and go straight to Bum Bright. That's when Jerry and I went and met with Bum Bright."

Schramm had come to realize that if Jones or any other hands-on candidate emerged as the new owner, he would be out. Bright realized that Schramm was interfering to protect himself and decided that the only way to finish off a deal was to keep Schramm out of the loop. Two days before Jones closed the deal, a Dallas television station broke the news that Jones was going to be the new owner and Johnson would be the new coach. The reporter was on camera from the campus of the University of Miami. Schramm knew nothing about it and warned the reporter that he would be committing career suicide by going with a story that had no basis in fact. The next day Schramm found out the report was true, and the day after that—a Saturday—he accompanied Jones on the new owner's private plane to Austin to break the news to Landry that he was out.

Jones and Schramm flew back to Dallas for the blockbuster press conference. It was not so much that Jones was buying the team as that he was going to be running the team and Landry was out. Murchison, the original owner, had given Schramm complete autonomy. Bright didn't get involved either except for an occasional dig at Landry as the team's fortunes slipped worse than his finances. But Schramm was still in charge. At the news conference that became known as the Saturday Night Massacre, a teary-eyed Schramm stood off to the side as Jones announced that he would control everything right down to the "jocks and socks."

Johnson was not at the news conference. Jones had sent him back to Miami to avoid the uprising that was going on in Dallas. He would be back that Tuesday for a news conference that was even more contentious than the grilling Jones had been put through three days earlier. Johnson had done nothing wrong other than dining in Mia's with Jones the night before the sale was official. Unfortunately for Johnson and Jones, a reporter from the *Dallas Morning News* was also at the Mexican restaurant, which was Landry's favorite. The picture of Jones and Johnson made the front cover of the *Morning News* the next day. The image was cruel: Jones and Johnson celebrating their hostile takeover of the Cowboys before the ink was dry on the sale agreement and before Landry was even told. And at the favorite spot of Tom and his wife, Alicia, no less.

Johnson was not intimidated by taking over for a legend. Jones gave him the security of a ten-year contract and total control of personnel even if Jones had the empty title of general manager. He was too busy trying to make money to worry about third-round draft choices. This was not the same pressure that George Seifert faced in taking over for Bill Walsh with the 49ers. Seifert inherited a team in 1989 that had just won the Super Bowl, a game Johnson viewed from the Cowboys' private box. Seifert had to maintain excellence. And he did: the 49ers won the Super Bowl again in his first season. Johnson's job was to rebuild the NFL's most visible and important franchise. The Cowboys had fallen apart. How much of it was due to the game passing Landry by? How much of it was a result of Brandt's drafts? How much was a result of Schramm not caring enough about the bottom line on the business side and letting Brandt have carte blanche on the personnel side?

Once Landry got over the indignity of having his team taken away from him, getting fired was the best thing for him. Instead of the fans picketing Texas Stadium or buying billboards demanding that he be fired, Landry turned into a martyr. They even threw a parade for him in downtown Dallas: "Hats Off to Tom Landry," which attracted a hundred thousand people. Many of them surely were the same fans who wanted Landry fired and then lamented when Jones did the dirty work.

Johnson took over a team that had the least talent and the worst record at 3–13 and the lowest expectations in the league. As long as the owner was patient and willing to spend to win—this was five years before the salary cap—it was an ideal situation. Johnson couldn't make it worse, and he was confident he would make it better. He just needed time. He won one game in his first season.

"Taking over for Tom Landry, as much respect as I had for him, that wasn't a concern because they had struggled so much before I got there. And people were ready for a change," Johnson said. "They were last in the league. What was stressful for me is I had been accustomed to winning football games. We lost two regular season games in my last four years at Miami. So to go there and all of a sudden lose fifteen—that was hard. It wasn't taking over for Landry and being the head coach of the Cowboys. It was being so unaccustomed to losing. The only thing that kept me going was my supreme confidence that we were going to get it done."

It was not a stretch to think that Johnson's teams at Miami had more talent and might have defeated the Cowboys. The Landry shadow didn't exist for Johnson. Landry had left him a big mess to clean up.

"Again, had they been coming off a playoff year or Super Bowl, it would have been different," Johnson said. "But they were so bad. People don't realize how bad they were. I realized it at our first minicamp. Plus, just the way they were operating back then. The players didn't even work out at the facility. Remember, they didn't even have an enclosed weight room. So the players, once the season was over with, that's the last they saw of them. Even the one minicamp they had, [conditioning coach] Bob Ward is the one that ran the minicamp; the coaches weren't really involved. I had gone around and visited pro camps for three or four years prior to going to Dallas. I had seen how other pro teams operated. The Cowboys weren't operating that way."

The first piece of the rebuilding project was a present from Landry: the first pick in the 1989 NFL draft. The Cowboys had clinched the valuable leadoff spot in the draft on the final day of the 1988 season when they lost to the Eagles and the Packers won in Arizona. UCLA quarterback Troy Aikman was going to be the first pick by either the Cowboys or the Packers and Aikman watched his fate unfold from the stands in Sun Devil Stadium as Green Bay beat the Cardinals. Johnson's first decision was an easy one: he drafted Aikman. The Packers selected tackle Tony Mandarich, who became one of the all-time draft busts, leaving Barry Sanders, Deion Sanders, and Derrick Thomas on the board. Aikman went on to win three Super Bowls, and he and the two Sanderses and Thomas are in the Pro Football Hall of Fame.

Johnson may have taken the chalk pick in Aikman, but by nature he was a risk taker when it came to football. He shocked the NFL when Steve Walsh, his quarterback at the University of Miami, applied for the supplemental draft held that summer and he took him. Why? It made no sense. Johnson had just drafted Aikman. There was no way Johnson could rationalize taking Walsh and forfeiting the Cowboys' number one pick in 1990. Johnson looked at Walsh as a valuable trading chip. He drafted Walsh, and his intent was to trade him immediately. There was no doubt who his quarterback was going to be. Aikman had a dynamic arm. Walsh, although he was a winner and was smart, wasn't going to be able to squeeze the ball between defenders or throw the tough sideline pass. His strength was managing games. Walsh's presence caused friction with Aikman, but Johnson figured it was only temporary. He would find a trade partner for Walsh before the season started. Johnson wasn't concerned about Aikman's feelings. He was trying to put the Cowboys back together again. Alienating Aikman before they even got to training camp wasn't on his mind.

"I didn't care. I knew that was value," he said. "And I did not anticipate keeping Steve. But I felt like he was a good enough player. We had the opportunity because we were at the top of the draft in the supplemental draft—to get a player of value and then make a trade down the road. I wasn't concerned about the competition at quarterback. I felt like Troy was going to be our guy, but I wanted to get another valued player, and I knew down the road it would pay dividends for us."

The Cowboys finished 1–15 in 1989, and Walsh was the quarterback for the only victory when Aikman was injured. After the season, Johnson's gamble paid off. The Saints gave him first-, second-, and third-round picks for Walsh.

"I tried to flip it right away, and I couldn't flip it right away," Johnson said. "As it turned out, Troy hurt his thumb and Steve played some, and so we were able to showcase him a little bit, and that helped us on the trade."

🏈 🏈 🏈

When Jones declared that Johnson was worth more than five first-round picks and five Heisman Trophy winners, Johnson took that as a challenge. Of course, if any team agreed with Jones, he would have traded them Johnson in a heartbeat to speed up the rebuilding process. Although Johnson was highly thought of in the NFL community and Jones was a complete unknown, they were an effective team. Jones, despite bragging that he held the general manager's title, deferred to Johnson on personnel decisions. The owner concentrated on turning the Cowboys, who had surprisingly never been a big moneymaker, into a cash cow. Johnson had never worked in any capacity for an NFL team before joining the Cowboys, but he was prepared. He knew he would be a head coach on the biggest stage sooner rather than later, and the transition was seamless. He quickly familiarized himself with the rules and the personnel around the league and was up to speed by the time he started having to make decisions in the draft. It took him no time to figure out the obvious—his team stank.

In training camp, he had one star in Herschel Walker. He had two rookie quarterbacks in Troy Aikman and Steve Walsh. His former Miami receiver Michael Irvin, the Cowboys' first-round pick in 1988, was on the team, but he had caught only thirty-two passes as a rookie without showing any indication that he would go on to have a Hall of Fame career. There was even talk that Johnson might trade him. In addition to Aikman, the first draft produced fullback Daryl Johnston, center Mark Stepnoski, and defensive end Tony Tolbert, who all became Pro Bowl players.

Johnson was not about to embark on a five-year rebuilding plan. The fans in Dallas were already skeptical about the Jones-Johnson regime, so they were going to receive a one-year grace period and then needed to show that they had the smarts to turn around America's Team. Johnson went into his rookie season knowing he didn't have much talent but was determined to find out which players he could win with while building the team around Aikman.

Johnson liked to jog with his coaches. They were brainstorming sessions. He was running players on and off the team and barely had time to learn their names. There was a lot to talk about with his "crew," as Johnson called his coaches. The jog he went on the first week of the 1989 season turned around the franchise. Johnson already had convinced himself that the only way to get better before the turn of the century was to trade Walker, the former Heisman winner and his only marketable commodity. Now he wanted to hear what his crew had to say about it.

Landry, Schramm, and Brandt invested a fifth-round choice in Walker in the 1985 draft. He was playing in the United States Football League, and the Cowboys retained his rights and would try to sign him either when his deal with the New Jersey Generals expired or when the USFL folded. Dallas had shown similar foresight in 1964 when it used a tenth-round pick on Navy quarterback Roger Staubach and then waited five years for him while he served his military commitment. That worked out pretty well for the Cowboys when Staubach led the team to its first two Super Bowl championships.

In the summer of 1986, the USFL was awarded $1—it was tripled to $3—in its $1.69 billion antitrust lawsuit against the NFL. The three-year-old league was counting on a huge settlement to bankroll its move to a fall season to compete against the NFL or on the award being so high that it forced the NFL into a merger. Instead, the USFL went out of business.

Dallas had Tony Dorsett, a future Hall of Famer, at running back, and he was coming off one of his best seasons, having rushed for 1,307 yards in 1985. Training camp began the next summer with Dorsett still the focal point of the offense. That changed the day the USFL folded. The Cowboys were falling over themselves trying to get Walker into training camp in Thousand Oaks, California. Walker was home in New Jersey insisting that he would flip a coin to decide whether to sign with the Cowboys or retire. Walker was a bit eccentric. He eventually signed a five-year

$5 million contract, the biggest contract in Cowboys history, and an NFL record for a running back. That angered Dorsett, who was making considerably less, and then Walker scored the winning touchdown in the season opener at Texas Stadium on a 10-yard run with 1:16 left against the Giants, who would lose only one more game the rest of the season on their way to winning the Super Bowl. Landry could never figure out a way to get the most out of Dorsett and Walker. Dorsett had a career-low 748 yards rushing in his first season sharing time with Walker. He and Walker played one more year together before the Cowboys gave in to Dorsett's trade demands and sent him to Denver.

In his first season with the job to himself in '88, Walker rushed for 1,514 yards for a 3–13 team. It would be the best season of his career. Landry was gone six weeks after the season ended, and Johnson took over. He was going to be true to his personality, which meant he was going to be a wheeler-dealer; in the world of the NFL, where executives are concerned about being second-guessed, Johnson just didn't care. He was going to do what he thought was right and live with the consequences.

He told his coaches on that jog that Walker had to go. "The way this process is, number one, you build your team through the draft, and I understand that. But that's a long process the way the system is now. And we're the worst team in the league, by far. We were the worst team before I got there, and we were the worst team my first year," Johnson said.

Here is what he told his coaches: "We've got to look for a way to speed up the process. Only way you could speed up the process is to get more picks. And the only thing we've got that anybody wants is Herschel Walker. Nobody wants any of our other players. What are your thoughts about trading Herschel Walker?"

Johnson's coaches were shocked. Was he nuts? Walker was all the Cowboys had going for them.

"The defensive coaches, they were lukewarm. Our offensive coaches were vehemently against it. They said, 'Hey, we won't score a point if we don't have Herschel,' " Johnson said. "David Shula and Jerry Rhome, they were all against it. They said no way, don't trade him. But I told them there was no way we can improve our football team two years down the road just by going through the draft. I said I've got to do something to speed up the process."

Fortunately for Johnson, two teams were interested. Browns general manager Ernie Accorsi would set the market, and Johnson planned to use Cleveland's interest to drive up the price on Vikings general manager Mike Lynn, who had casually mentioned being interested in Walker over the summer. Johnson had dismissed it at the time, saying Walker was his only Pro Bowl player. Now, with the regular season having arrived, he realized that dealing Walker would be taking a step back in the short term but could lead to big long-term gains.

Johnson would go on to win Super Bowls in his fourth season and fifth and final season with the Cowboys, and if he hadn't pulled off the deal of the century with the Vikings that fast tracked the Cowboys' ability to compete for a championship by at least three years, he said, "I'd have found a way. I'd have done something."

Landry planned to draft Aikman first overall in 1989, but there is no way he ever would have approved trading Walker. He loved Walker's skill set, admired him as a person, and considered him the foundation of the Cowboys' future. Johnson turned him into the draft picks that became the Cowboys' foundation.

The Walker trade turned out to be the most lopsided trade in NFL history. How did it happen?

"It actually came about when Ernie Accorsi called me. They wanted Herschel Walker," Johnson said. "They felt like that was the missing piece for them. I just told them what I wanted. I wanted three ones, three twos, and three threes. He said that's awful steep. He was our only Pro Bowl player on a horrible team."

Accorsi was the general manager in Baltimore in 1983 when

the Colts drafted John Elway even though Elway said he would never play for them. Accorsi fielded numerous trade offers before the draft but turned them all down. He was a big believer that you always take the franchise quarterback. One week after the draft, Colts owner Robert Irsay traded Elway to the Broncos behind Accorsi's back. Throughout his front office career, Accorsi was always enamored with big names.

Johnson was now intent on dealing Walker and continued to negotiate with Accorsi. "They didn't have a one the next year," Johnson said. "They had an outside linebacker that they had drafted from Florida, Clifford Charlton. What they would do is they would give us him and a one the following year and a one the following year and then the twos and threes. I said let me give that some thought. I said I think we could probably pull the trigger on it, so let's talk tonight. He said I got to get Art Modell to talk to you before it's a finalized deal anyway. He said let me have Art call you tonight. I said fine."

Johnson felt he had the parameters for a trade that he could now shop around the league. He went to Jones, and they elected to see if they could do better. Jones called Falcons owner Rankin Smith. Walker had played at Georgia and was still a big name in Atlanta. Walker would help sell tickets. Johnson called Lynn, who had reached out in the preseason about Walker. The October 17 trade deadline was one week away. The Cowboys were 0–5, and the only intrigue left was whether they would be the first 0–16 team in NFL history. That honor eventually went to the Detroit Lions in 2008. The Vikings were 3–2 but felt Walker would make them instant Super Bowl contenders.

Johnson got on the phone with Lynn. He put a 6:30 p.m. deadline on Lynn to top Cleveland's offer.

"Here's what I've got on the table. If you can get something better, maybe we can pull this thing off," Johnson told Lynn.

He outlined the Browns' proposal. "Well, when I got in from practice, he had faxed me his proposal," Johnson said. "His thinking was, he was going to unload some players who were better than anything we had, but a couple of them were injured, a couple of them were toward the end of their career. They were expendable for the Vikings, but again, they were better than anything we had.

"He said we would tie a draft pick to each player, and if I kept the player, I wouldn't get the pick. But if I cut the player or released him, then I'd get the pick. Well, when I looked at it, I could see that as the year would go on, if I didn't fall in love with these players, I could get the picks and I could have leverage on him to keep the player and the pick."

Lynn offered his first-round pick in the 1992 draft and linebackers Jesse Solomon and David Howard, cornerback Isaac Holt, running back Darrin Nelson, defensive end Alex Stewart, and six conditional draft picks. Each of the picks was tied to one of the players Minnesota traded to Dallas. The players could help Johnson during the 1989 season, and then he would decide between the player and the draft pick. It sounded like a game show.

Solomon was attached to the Vikings' first-round pick in 1990. If he was on the roster on February 1, the Vikings would keep the pick. If Johnson cut him, Dallas would get the pick. Howard was attached to a 1991 first-round pick, Holt to a second- and a third-round pick in 1992, Nelson to a second-round pick in 1991, and Stewart to a second-round pick in 1990.

Johnson liked the Vikings' offer better than Cleveland's. He called Accorsi after getting the Minnesota proposal and told him he was making the trade with the Vikings. The deciding factor was Cleveland not having a first-round pick in 1990. "That was an important pick for us," Johnson said.

He called Lynn and told him they had a deal. Johnson knew from the moment Lynn made the proposal that he would release all the Vikings' players and take all the draft picks. There was no reason to tell Lynn.

"If I cut them all, he would get nothing and I'd just get all these picks," Johnson said. "So I didn't say anything about it, but I knew what I was going to do. For that reason, even though the players were the best players we had, like David Howard and Jesse Solomon, I wouldn't let our defensive coaches start them because if they started for us, the fans would fall in love with them, our coaches would fall in love with them, and I wouldn't be able to pull off the deal. So I told them they have to be second teamers, so don't put them in until the second quarter even though they are our best players."

Lynn visited Walker's home in Dallas to ease any concerns he had about coming to Minnesota. The Cowboys kicked in $1.25 million as a going-away present. "I'm out of here, but I got a lot of good memories," Walker said as he was packing his bags in the Cowboys' locker room.

The Vikings had nine Pro Bowl players in 1988, and they judged Walker to be the piece to put them over the top. "When I went to Herschel's house in Dallas, I told him if we don't win the Super Bowl in the next two years, this deal has failed," Lynn told the *Boston Globe* a few days after the trade. "This was all done to win a Super Bowl. Our coaches told me this is what we needed, a back that could really produce, so that's what we got for them."

As part of the trade agreement, the Vikings could not sign any of the players they traded to Dallas if Johnson released them, and Dallas would not receive the corresponding Vikings draft choices if it traded one of the players. When Nelson refused to report, Johnson wanted to trade him. The Chargers were offering a fifth-round pick. Johnson was not going to trade Nelson and forfeit the second-round pick he was attached to in the trade. Cutting Nelson would not benefit the Vikings, either, because they couldn't sign him. Johnson had Lynn backed into a corner. In exchange for Minnesota waiving the no-trade agreement regarding Nelson, San Diego's fifth-round pick was sent to the Vikings. In return, the Vikings sent their sixth-round pick to Dallas. The Cowboys still received the second-round pick for Nelson. The

Walker trade just kept getting better. Johnson thus squeezed another draft pick out of the deal for a player he had no intention of keeping.

Walker got off to a fast start for the Vikings, rushing for 148 yards on 18 carries in his debut against Green Bay at home. On his first rushing attempt late in the first quarter, he ran for 47 yards. Minnesota defeated the Packers. Lynn was looking good. That turned out to be the highlight of Walker's season and his short Vikings career. He rushed for just 669 yards in eleven games in 1989. The Vikings finished 10–6 and won the NFC Central in a tiebreaker over the Packers, giving them a bye in the first round of the playoffs. But they lost in the divisional round to the 49ers. Walker obviously was not all that was missing in the Super Bowl puzzle for Minnesota.

Dallas finished the season with one victory. If Johnson had not taken Walsh in the supplemental draft, he would have owned the first pick in the 1990 draft and could have drafted Southern Cal linebacker Junior Seau or defensive tackle Cortez Kennedy, who had played for Johnson at the University of Miami. But he wasn't complaining. He soon would trade Walsh to the Saints for three premium picks, and he had the incredible haul from the Walker trade. Lynn was counting on the Cowboys keeping the players, but the reason Johnson traded Walker was to speed up the rebuilding process through the draft. He liked the Vikings players, but not enough to keep them instead of the picks he would receive by cutting them.

"At the end of the year, I told Mike, 'Hey, you're not going to get anything; let me give you a couple of late picks and let us keep these players,'" Johnson said. "He said they were just getting beat up for the trade already and he said, 'Jimmy, I'm getting just killed up here.' He said, 'I can't do it. You just got to keep the players.' I said, 'Well, I'm not going to keep the players.' So he wouldn't answer my phone calls, and I sent a certified letter to him and the commissioner, saying all these players were released as of this date and the only person that could stop that release of those players was Mike Lynn of the Minnesota Vikings. It was right at the end of the season.

"After I sent the certified letter to the commissioner and to him, Mike called me; he said, 'just help me out,' " Johnson said.

Johnson had cut Stewart in November but now had Lynn in a bind once again. If he released the players, Lynn would lose all the draft picks. Johnson gave him a chance to save face, but barely. One month after the season, Johnson and Lynn came to an agreement: Dallas sent its third-round picks in 1990 and 1991 and its tenth-round pick in 1990 to the Vikings and kept Solomon, Howard, and Holt and all the conditional picks from the original trade.

Advantage: Dallas

Big advantage: Dallas

"I thought of the players that we sent them; they would keep a number of those players," Lynn, who died in July 2012, once told the *Minneapolis Star Tribune*. "So I thought the number of draft choices would not be as great as it was."

The Vikings finished just 6–10 in 1990 and 8–8 in 1991. Walker rushed for 770 yards in his first full season in Minnesota and 825 yards in 1991. The 1,595 yards was barely more than he'd had in 1988 for a very bad Cowboys team. Incredibly, the Vikings cut Walker in May 1992, less than three full years after making the worst trade in NFL history. They were 21–22 with him. Lynn lost his power in Minnesota on January 1, 1991, when Roger Headrick became the team's president and CEO.

On the twenty-year anniversary of the trade, Lynn told the *Star Tribune* that he had "no regrets" about making the Walker deal. "I did what I thought was the right thing at the time," he said. He still hadn't figured out why the trade went so badly for the Vikings. "It's been a mystery to me all along what happened," he said. "All that we lacked on that team was a big back. Herschel was the best big back in the league. He gained 1,500 yards the previous year. He was in marvelous shape when he got here. It would have worked out." He went on to say, "Everybody sure thought it was a great trade that day. But something happened. I don't know what it was, but whatever he had, he didn't have it any longer. It was like a great horse not having it. Just gone overnight or in a week."

After he was released by the Vikings, Walker signed with the Eagles and rushed for 1,070 yards in his first season in Philadelphia. He played three years with the Eagles and then spent one year with the Giants before returning to finish his career with the Cowboys in 1996 and 1997. By then, Johnson was no longer with the Cowboys. He had only sixteen carries in those two years; his primary job was returning kickoffs.

Were the Vikings better off without Walker? They were 11–5 and won the NFC Central in 1992. Terry Allen took over at running back and rushed for 1,201 yards. He was a ninth-round draft pick in 1991 who rushed for 563 yards backing up Walker in his rookie year.

All those picks burned a hole in Johnson's pocket. He turned the Walker trade into a cottage industry, making fourteen trades with the assets he'd picked up from Minnesota. In some form, almost sixty players were affected by the Walker trade. It usually takes a few years to evaluate a trade fully. Because the Vikings didn't even have Walker for three full seasons—that still seems unimaginable considering how much they gave up to get him— the trade was completely lopsided.

By the '92 season, all the Vikings had left to show for the deal was wide receiver Jake Reed. The Cowboys had running back Emmitt Smith, safety Darren Woodson, defensive tackle Russell Maryland, wide receiver and cornerback Kevin Smith, and cornerback Clayton Holmes. Johnson used picks from the Vikings to maneuver into position to draft those players. He traded every one of the Vikings' picks to move up or move down. Smith, of course, was the biggest addition. Johnson, who didn't have his own number one in 1990, used the Vikings' pick, the twenty-first overall, in a trade to move up four spots to the Steelers' slot at number seventeen to take Smith, who retired as the NFL's all-time leading rusher.

"There's no way that you could actually say here's what we got for those players for Herschel because I made half a dozen other trades with those picks that I got," Johnson said.

By 1991, the Cowboys were in the playoffs. The next year they won their first Super Bowl since the 1977 season. And then they repeated in 1993, Johnson's fifth year in Dallas. Johnson and Jones had built a minidynasty. Despite major free agent losses, the Cowboys were incredibly deep and young with Aikman, Smith, and Irvin—the Triplets—along with Woodson and a defense that was fast and quick. All Jones and Johnson had to do was keep the core intact and happy and they might have won another two or three Super Bowls in a row. They were that good. They were that much better than anybody else. As it turned out, the most unhappy person was Johnson.

Dallas wasn't big enough for Johnson and Jones to coexist after they had all that success. There wasn't enough credit to satisfy both of their Super Bowl–size egos. At the league meetings in Orlando in March 1994, Jones minimized Johnson's contributions, claiming that "five hundred coaches" could have won those Super Bowls with the Cowboys' talent. Of course, it was Johnson, not Jones, who had accumulated all that talent. He was talking at 3 a.m. in a hotel bar and might have been better off going to bed. He revealed in that chat with two reporters from the *Dallas Morning News* that he was thinking about firing Johnson and hiring Barry Switzer, the former Oklahoma coach. Earlier in the evening, Jones felt he was snubbed by Johnson at a league party. No rich man likes to be shown up by one of his employees.

Considering that at that point only Vince Lombardi, Don

Shula, and Chuck Noll (twice) had repeated as Super Bowl champions, it appeared that Jones was letting his heart do the speaking instead of his head do the thinking. Just five years earlier, he had declared that Johnson was worth more than five first-round picks and five Heisman Trophy winners, and now, after Johnson had helped resurrect a dormant franchise and put a lot of money in Jones's pocket, all of a sudden five hundred coaches could have done the same thing. Once again, he had made a ridiculous statement.

Obviously, when Jones's comments were relayed to Johnson in the morning, his well-coiffed hair started doing backflips. He stormed out of the meetings in Orlando, got in his car, and headed south to his home in Tavernier in the Florida Keys. One week later, he demanded that Jones settle the final five years of his ten-year contract and walked away with a check for $2 million. Jones hired Switzer just as he'd promised. Johnson gave up the chance to be the first coach to win three consecutive Super Bowls.

That summer, Johnson was sitting on his boat docked 30 feet from his back door loving life. The sun was shining, the wave runners were humming, and the fish were sure to be biting. The Heinekens were cold.

He was stung by Jones's words four months earlier. How could he possibly think five hundred coaches could have done what he did? Take over a 1–15 team and win the Super Bowl in his fourth and fifth years? Make the greatest trade in NFL history by dealing off his only star player? Was he kidding?

"I really feel like I had accomplished a tremendous amount in five years. I was very proud of it. To be sloughed off like I was, it hurt," Johnson said that day. "Just tossing out that he could hire anybody to coach this team to win the Super Bowl bothered me. It bothered my ego. I put together a team that won two Super Bowls. Evidently, he doesn't appreciate that. What else could I do for the guy?

"I was hurt when Jerry said five hundred coaches could've taken that team to the Super Bowl. Are there five hundred coaches out there who could have made the personnel decisions and put together a team that won two Super Bowls starting from scratch?"

Jones's perspective then was, "He knew that I knew other people could be successful coaching the football team. I feel some of his enthusiasm had diminished, and our differences were going to be magnified and very visible. The minute I saw we weren't working together, I wanted to make a change. I didn't want to invest any more time with him."

Switzer took the Cowboys to the NFC title game in his first season, but after having beaten the 49ers the previous two years in the championship game, the Cowboys lost this time. Switzer did win the Super Bowl the next season when Dallas beat the Steelers, giving the Cowboys three titles in four years. If Johnson had remained, who knows how many they would have won? It wasn't simply that Johnson was a better coach than Switzer, but with Johnson gone, Jones was no longer the general manager in title only. He was really the general manager. That was not good for the Cowboys.

"There is nothing you can trade me for having those five years we had together and what we went through together and how it worked out," Jones once said. "There is nothing you can give me to have one more day of it."

If time heals all wounds, it also changes perceptions. Nearly twenty years after their painful and public divorce, Jimmy and Jerry are buddies again. Jones sends his private plane to Florida to pick up Johnson so that they can meet in Las Vegas for big boxing events, one of Johnson's passions. It's just that they couldn't stand the sight of each other after working together for five years.

"It wasn't really a me and Jerry thing," Johnson now insists.

When Jones bought the Cowboys, in addition to saying how valuable Johnson was to the franchise, he insisted he would not have bought the team if Johnson was not going to be his coach. Maybe he wouldn't have bought the team if Bright had insisted that he keep Landry, but there was no way Bright was going to make that a condition of the sale. He disliked Landry. But the idea that Jones was going to give up his dream of owning America's Team if his former teammate and casual friend from Arkansas was not going to be the coach was never put to the test. We will never find out. But it's hard to fathom Jones walking away from the deal if he couldn't get Johnson. As he said, there were five hundred coaches out there who could have had the same success.

Two decades later, Johnson says he was going to leave the Cowboys before the 1994 draft even before the blowup with Jones. Is that revisionist history? Johnson saving face? There was never any indication he was going to leave until Jones insulted him that night in Orlando.

"I've always been kind of a gypsy. I never stayed anywhere longer than five years. I was ready to move to south Florida," Johnson said. "I'd already bought a place in the Florida Keys."

He said he had his Corvette driven from Dallas to Atlanta for the Super Bowl so that it was closer to its final destination in the Keys. The driver was William Wesley, who years later became known as World Wide Wes. He became close to many NBA stars, including LeBron James. "I put him on our sideline. Look at the picture when they are throwing the Gatorade on me in the Super Bowl in Atlanta," Johnson said. "He's got a coat and tie on. He's right there next to me on the sideline."

That was Johnson's way of saying he was gone from the Cowboys. If the Corvette was headed to his home in Tavernier, so was he. At the time, the thought was that Johnson would get antsy after making a run at a third consecutive title. But now he says he was planning to leave even before that night in Orlando. What would have happened if Jones hadn't said some silly stuff in the bar at 3 a.m.?

"I'd have left," Johnson said. "I already had it marked on the calendar when I was leaving before that even happened. I was going to give them time to prepare before the draft. And I think that probably had a little bit to do with Jerry's attitude. Kind of like a jilted lover. I don't think he knew it. He might have sensed it."

The Cowboys' headquarters is a sprawling one-level building. Jones occupied Tex Schramm's old office on the management side of the building. Johnson had Landry's old office in the football operations side of the building. The place was not big enough for the two of them to coexist.

If Johnson was indeed not planning to come back in 1994, it would have made more sense for him to walk away right after the Super Bowl the way Bill Walsh did with the 49ers after beating the Bengals in January 1989. "The only thing I hate about it is I think it really put a bad taste in the mouths of all the players," Johnson said. "Troy and I have talked about it. Michael and all of them. They felt not only did I leave Jerry, I left them. So with the players, I think it really strained the relationship. Troy comes down here to the house on occasion. We spend a lot of time together. One night he even got almost angry talking about it. That's the only thing that I regret."

Ultimately, the egos of Jerry Jones and Jimmy Johnson tore the Cowboys apart. Switzer won a Super Bowl, but Dallas won despite the coach, who was just a caretaker. Jones and Johnson had a great thing going. The Cowboys of the '90s might have been remembered as the best team of all time if they had been able to keep the management infrastructure in place.

"I was ready to leave," Johnson said. "I had done my deal. I was ready for something else."

He had done his deal. The Herschel Walker deal. The greatest trade in NFL history. The deal of the century.

TRICK OR TREAT

Mike Shanahan had nowhere to turn. He was stuck right in the middle of one of the most bitter coach-quarterback feuds in NFL history: Dan Reeves versus John Elway.

It's virtually impossible to succeed if the coach and the quarterback have little use for each other. You can have the creative tension that existed between Bill Walsh and Joe Montana and still win because of the respect they had for each other. Bill Belichick and Tom Brady don't have to spend their summer weekends sailing on the waters off picturesque Cape Cod to win three Super Bowls, but no coach and quarterback think more alike. Jimmy Johnson and Troy Aikman were sparring partners until Johnson, who has an affinity for fish tanks, realized that Aikman was becoming interested in having his own aquarium. "I have a saltwater fish tank Jimmy helped me put together," Aikman said. They bonded over goldfish and guppies and won two Super Bowls together.

It's not necessary for the coach and the quarterback to find a hobby that each enjoys so that they have something to discuss while dissecting the game plan, but they can't be stabbing each other in the back. Few situations have been as contentious as Reeves and Elway. One of the great achievements in the 1980s was Denver getting to three Super Bowls with Elway and Reeves barely being able to stand the sight of each other. Of course, they lost all three of those Super Bowls over a four-year period to the Giants, Redskins, and 49ers by the combined score of 136–40. That was humiliating and an unsightly blotch on Elway's record that was not erased until the final two years of his career.

Elway once described his relationship with Reeves as "the worst." He didn't like his offense. He didn't like him. Reeves's conservative style would keep Elway handcuffed until the fourth quarter, when he would let him loose and tell him to go win the game. Elway invariably responded to the pressure by bailing out Reeves and rallying Denver to a victory. A story in *Sports Illustrated* during training camp in the summer of 1993, the Broncos' first after Reeves was fired, said Elway had rallied the Broncos to thirty-one game-saving drives in the fourth quarter in the ten years he played for Reeves. "That was our philosophy," Elway said.

Elway, who had the greatest arm the NFL has ever seen, was naturally frustrated. His statistics were dwarfed by those of Miami's Dan Marino and Buffalo's Jim Kelly, the other two future Hall of Fame quarterbacks from the quarterback class of 1983, and that bugged him. If Reeves had let Elway be Elway, he could have been setting all those passing records instead of Marino. Then again, Marino made it to the Super Bowl in his second season and lost, and that was his only appearance during his sensational seventeen-year career. And he played for Don Shula, the all-time winningest coach in NFL history.

"The last three years have been hell," Elway told *Sports Illustrated* that summer. "I know that I would not have been back here if Dan Reeves had been here. It wasn't worth it to me. I didn't enjoy it. It wasn't any fun, and I got tired of working with him."

When Reeves was informed at the Giants' training camp of Elway's remarks, he responded, "Just tell him it wasn't exactly heaven for me, either. One of these days, I hope he grows up. Maybe he'll mature sometime."

Shanahan was the offensive coordinator at the University of Florida when Reeves hired him to be his quarterback coach in 1984, Elway's second year in the league. The Broncos had pulled off a spectacular trade one week after the 1983 draft to acquire Elway, considered the greatest quarterback prospect of all time. The Colts had the first overall pick, but Elway was adamant that he wouldn't play in Baltimore. It had nothing to do with the city or the team. He didn't want to play for volatile coach Frank Kush.

Elway's father, Jack, the head coach at San Jose State at the time, steered his son away from Kush. Colts general manager Ernie Accorsi knew his team needed an elite quarterback to have any chance of winning a championship and didn't want to trade Elway, whose only viable recourse would be to sit out the year and wait for the 1984 draft. Elway became an outfielder in the New York Yankees system—he spent six weeks playing minor league ball for the Yankees after his junior year at Stanford—and threatened to play baseball that summer and take the year off from football. That was not what Elway wanted—he knew his future was not in baseball—but he had no desire to play for the Colts. Accorsi was prepared to call his bluff.

"I had made up my mind unless I got the greatest compensation in the history of the league—three number ones, with two in one year, and two number twos—I wasn't going to make the trade," Accorsi said.

Elway put together a wish list of ten teams. The Cowboys were on the list, but Accorsi asked Tom Landry, Tex Schramm, and Gil Brandt for future Hall of Fame defensive tackle Randy White, a local Baltimore favorite who had played at the University of Maryland; quarterback Danny White, who had guided Dallas to consecutive NFC championship games in his first two years after taking over for Roger Staubach; and two number one picks. It couldn't hurt to ask. Dallas thought about it but ultimately refused to part with Randy White, and that ended the talks.

The Chargers and Raiders put together impressive offers. San

Diego owned three number one picks (the fifth, twentieth, and twenty-second) but would not give up the best of the three. Deal killer. The Raiders, selecting twenty-sixth, needed a higher pick to satisfy the Colts. They thought they had a deal completed to acquire the Bears' pick at number six, which they would have sent to Baltimore along with their other choice. But when the Bears demanded defensive end Howie Long in return, the Raiders dropped out. If Accorsi had gotten Chicago's pick, he was going to draft Marino.

The 1983 draft started at seven in the morning. Before things got under way, Colts owner Robert Irsay came to Accorsi with a trade proposal he had just received from New England: All Pro guard John Hannah and a swap of first-round picks. The Patriots were picking fifteenth. "I told him there would be two press conferences: one to announce the trade, one to announce my resignation," Accorsi said.

Five minutes before the draft started, Accorsi told Irsay his plan.

"I'm going to take Elway one second after seven," he said.

"Go do what you want to do," Irsay replied.

Accorsi picked Elway and was willing to wait him out. Nothing against the kid, but Accorsi was protecting the franchise. That became irrelevant one week later. Accorsi was sitting on his couch watching an NBA playoff game on television when it was announced that Irsay had traded Elway to Denver. "I called Frank Kush and asked if he was watching because I think they just traded the quarterback," Accorsi said.

In return, the Colts received tackle Chris Hinton, who had been picked three spots behind Elway, veteran quarterback Mark Herrmann, and a number one pick in 1984, which the Colts used on guard Ron Solt. In addition, Denver owner Edgar Kaiser agreed that the Broncos would play the Colts in preseason games at Mile High Stadium in 1984 and 1985. That meant a lot to Irsay. His fifty–fifty share of the gate receipts was worth $800,000.

Sean Payton, Roger Goodell, and Drew Brees were all smiles the morning after the Saints defeated the Colts in Super Bowl XLIV in Miami following the 2009 season. Just two years later, Goodell suspended Payton for the entire 2012 season after a league investigation determined the Saints had been setting bounties on opposing players for three seasons and Payton didn't stop it. *Getty Images*

Joe Gibbs might have done the best coaching job of his Hall of Fame career late in the 2007 season after Sean Taylor, his best defensive player, was murdered in a home invasion. Gibbs prevented his players from emotionally falling apart, and they honored the memory of their teammate by making a run that earned them a playoff spot. *Courtesy of the Washington Redskins*

Robert Kraft thought he hit the lottery when he bought his hometown Patriots in 1994 and inherited iconic coach Bill Parcells. He soon found out the view of Parcells up close was much different from what he saw from a distance as a Patriots fan.
John Iacono/Sports Illustrated/Getty Images

Kraft really wanted to promote Bill Belichick when Parcells left for the Jets in 1997, but felt he needed a clean break from the Parcells regime, so he hired former Jets coach Pete Carroll, at the time the defensive coordinator of the 49ers. Kraft was very fond of Carroll, but the team regressed in each of his three seasons and Kraft fired him and finally hired Belichick.
Sporting News via Getty Images

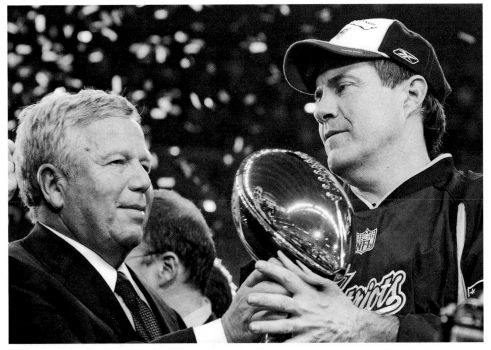

Kraft and Belichick lifted three Super Bowl trophies together as New England dominated the early part of the new millennium. But the Spygate scandal in 2007 rocked the Patriots and led to Kraft calling Belichick a "real schmuck," when Belichick told Kraft the surveillance was not much help to New England. *Jeff Haynes/AFP/Getty Images*

Lawrence Taylor tested the patience of Bill Parcells with his drug issues, but the greatest defensive player in NFL history and one of the best coaches of his era were quite a team. Parcells would not have won two Super Bowls without LT, and Taylor might have only been great instead of incredible if he didn't have the Tuna pushing him. *Getty Images*

It was a proud day for Tampa coach Tony Dungy when President Bill Clinton visited the Bucs in 2000. Dungy and his thirteen-year-old son, James, presented Clinton with a Bucs T-shirt when he stopped by training camp for a surprise visit. Five years later, not far from where he met the president, James Dungy committed suicide by hanging himself in his apartment. *Getty Images*

Eagles coach Andy Reid and former Bucs and Colts coach Tony Dungy shared an interest in Michael Vick after he was released from prison on 2009. The problems Reid and Dungy had with their own sons helped lead them to Vick. They knew Vick needed a second chance. And Vick eventually led Dungy and Reid to each other. *Courtesy of the Philadelphia Eagles*

Broncos quarterback John Elway and coach Mike Shanahan celebrate the Broncos' victory over the Packers in Super Bowl XXIII. The next year, they would beat the Falcons and their nemesis, Dan Reeves, in the Super Bowl in the final game of Elway's career. *Copyright © Eric Lars Bakke/ Denver Broncos*

When Jimmy Johnson was hired to coach the Cowboys in 1989, his only assets were Herschel Walker and the first pick in the draft. He selected Troy Aikman in the draft, but a little over one month into the season he traded Walker to the Vikings in a cleverly constructed one-sided deal that helped turn the Cowboys into Super Bowl champs. Johnson used one of the picks to move up in the 1990 draft to take Emmitt Smith, who finished his career as the NFL's all-time leading rusher. *Getty Images*

Broncos coach John Fox was thrilled to ride the wave of Tebowmania into the 2011 playoffs with a series of incredible last-minute victories. But John Elway and Fox acted quickly to trade Tebow to the Jets after they signed Peyton Manning, who had been released by the Colts. *Copyright © Eric Lars Bakke/Denver Broncos*

Fox jumped around Elway's office as Manning was telling Elway he had decided to sign with the Broncos after the Colts released him. Fox knew the pressure was now on him to make it work with one of the best quarterbacks in NFL history, but it was a challenge he was eager to accept. *Copyright © Eric Lars Bakke/ Denver Broncos*

Dick Vermeil turned around a moribund program in Philadelphia, but burned himself out doing it. He quit the Eagles after the 1982 season to regroup, which took much longer than anticipated. After turning down several opportunities, he accepted the Rams job in 1997 and won the Super Bowl in his third season. *Courtesy of the Philadelphia Eagles*

Jets coach Rex Ryan and Mark Sanchez have enjoyed a father-son relationship, but Pops wasn't too happy when his quarterback was caught eating a hot dog on the bench during a 2009 game in Oakland, which Ryan considered a sign of disrespect to the Raiders. Sanchez had to be a little confused when Ryan traded for Tim Tebow in 2012, less than two weeks after Sanchez signed a contract extension. *Boston Globe via Getty Images*

Giants coach Tom Coughlin puckers up and plants a kiss on the Vince Lombardi Trophy after New York defeated the Patriots in Super Bowl XLVI, the second time in five seasons Coughlin defeated Bill Belichick in the Super Bowl. After the game, Coughlin was hugging Flava Flav, a hip-hop star he had never heard of before wrapping his arms around him. *Getty Images*

"God, it was a slam dunk as far as I was concerned," Reeves said.

Reeves had spoken to the Colts before the draft, but the asking price was much too high. Kaiser once tried to buy the Colts franchise from Irsay, and he had a relationship with him. The Broncos knew the Colts were interested in Hinton before the draft, and so it helped that they drafted him. Kaiser stayed in touch with Irsay after the draft and then called Reeves when he had the parameters worked out.

"You got a pencil?" Kaiser said.

He gave Reeves the terms.

"I would do that in a heartbeat," Reeves said.

Elway was traded to Denver. Accorsi quit after the 1983 season and was hired by Art Modell in Cleveland in 1985 as the Browns' general manager. The Mayflower trucks showed up at the Colts' offices at 2 a.m. on March 29, 1984, and the Colts were off to Indianapolis.

The Elway deal never stopped haunting Accorsi. Elway prevented Accorsi's Browns from getting to the Super Bowl with victories in the AFC championship game after the 1986, 1987, and 1989 seasons. The football gods made it up to Accorsi in 2004 when Eli Manning refused to play for the Chargers, who had the first pick, and traded him to the Giants, whose general manager at the time was Accorsi. Even though Accorsi retired one year before Manning won the first of his Super Bowl titles, he was the architect of the trade that brought Peyton's little brother to New York. Here's the irony: when Elway was hired to run the Broncos, he reached out to Accorsi to help him as a consultant.

Shanahan's career path changed once he teamed up with Elway in 1984. Elway had a difficult rookie year and needed a mentor. Reeves named Elway the starter for the 1983 season opener in Pittsburgh, and it looked like it was the first time he'd ever stepped on a football field. He had played so well in the preseason, but the defenses he saw in the practice games were just the appetizer. The

Steelers served up a five-course dinner at Three Rivers Stadium and had Elway thoroughly confused. He threw for 14 yards and was sacked four times.

"I remember it didn't last very long because I got benched at halftime. I was one for eight with a pick," Elway said. "I wanted to click my heels together, and say, 'Auntie Em, bring me home. You can have your signing bonus back; I don't want to stare at Jack Lambert spitting and drooling at me anymore. What the hell have I gotten myself into?'"

It was the days before the NFL introduced radio helmets that allow the coach to communicate with the quarterback from the sidelines to send in the plays. Elway received the plays by hand signal or messenger. "He was just lucky to get a play off, much less look over and anticipate what the defense might do," Reeves said.

Even though Elway showed only flashes of greatness his rookie year and was benched for a stretch in the middle of the season, the Broncos made the playoffs as a wild-card team with him as the starter. "By then, you knew you had something special," Reeves said. "He was unbelievable."

Shanahan struck gold in getting this job. It would be the starting point on his journey to being a head coach. He had spent nine years in college football and considered it a dream come true to work with Elway. They became close friends. They played a lot of golf together. Shanahan introduced Elway to lifting weights for the first time in his life. His father never had him lift weights in the football off-season because it would interfere with baseball. "He started off in the weight room as a complete novice," Shanahan said.

Elway worked under the guidance of the Broncos' conditioning coach, but Shanahan was constantly by his side. They started to build a relationship. Elway trusted Shanahan, and Shanahan became the buffer between Elway and Reeves. "He knew I was going to work him hard and do everything I could to make him better," Shanahan said. "He knew I cared about him, and he was willing to do the little things the right way."

As Elway's career took off, so did Shanahan's. After the second of the Broncos' three Super Bowl losses, Shanahan was offered the Los Angeles Raiders' head coaching job by Al Davis in 1988. Davis rarely went outside the organization for key management hires. This certified Shanahan as special. He lasted four games into his second season before Davis fired him. He coached only twenty games for the Raiders and won eight. Davis didn't give him much of a chance. "I think the first time I knew it wasn't going to work is when he would come to practice and he would substitute guys," Shanahan said. "He would come out and say, 'You guys don't have to practice.' He took them out of a drill. That's when I knew, OK, I won't last long here. It was early—like the first five or six days of summer camp."

As soon as Davis fired Shanahan early in the 1989 season, Reeves offered him the opportunity to come back to Denver to work with Elway again. He left the Raiders on bad terms—to the day Davis died in 2011, Shanahan claimed he still owed him money—and returning to Denver gave Shanahan an opportunity to restore his reputation and get some measure of revenge against Davis in the AFC West. The Broncos made it back to the Super Bowl in the season Shanahan returned but again were not competitive, losing 55–10 to the 49ers, the largest losing margin in Super Bowl history.

Shanahan's relationship with Reeves had begun to deteriorate. Reeves felt Shanahan and Elway were scheming behind his back and tinkering with the game plan and suspected that too much of what was being said in staff meetings was being relayed to Elway through Shanahan. Newspaper stories detailing Elway's dislike for Reeves caught Reeves by surprise, and he believed Shanahan knew but didn't tell him. He felt Shanahan's loyalty should have been to him, not to Elway. Shanahan was incredulous that Reeves claimed to be oblivious to what seemed obvious: his quarterback despised him.

After the 1991 season, Reeves fired Shanahan, citing "insubordination."

Reeves admitted he had no proof. Shanahan was stunned that Reeves questioned his integrity. "I got tired of hearing about it," Shanahan said. "I thought I was close to Dan. I was probably Dan's best friend. We played golf together. We did all those things. I am the one that got Dan and John together when they were having the problem. I said, 'Hey, you don't like him, he doesn't like you. You are two grown men; let's try to solve this problem.' I was kind of the buffer. When you are the buffer as an assistant coach, especially as a coordinator, it doesn't always work out well between the head coach and the coordinator."

The years have not softened the hard feelings. "I've been fired a few times, and it's hard for me to have the same feeling for people who fired me, and I fired him," Reeves said. "That's never going to change."

Shanahan had been fired by Davis, then fired by Reeves. He needed a gentle landing spot. Mike Holmgren had just accepted the job as the Packers' head coach, and so his job as the 49ers' offensive coordinator was open. Montana was still recovering from elbow surgery, but Steve Young was establishing himself as one of the best quarterbacks in the NFL. The 49ers were going to be a Super Bowl contender in 1992, and Shanahan knew the 49ers were a classy organization that did things the right way. After his experience with Davis and then having his relationship with Reeves blow up over Elway, he needed less drama and more football. George Seifert offered him the job. San Francisco was the perfect place at the perfect time.

His departure meant that Reeves and Elway were left to settle their problems on their own. In Shanahan's last season as an assistant in Denver, the Broncos were 12–4 and lost to the Bills in the AFC championship game. They dropped to 8–8 in 1992 and didn't make the playoffs. Broncos owner Pat Bowlen stunned Reeves by firing him. He had been there twelve seasons and had gone to three Super Bowls but had a lousy relationship with the franchise quarterback—he once was rumored to have considered trading him to the Redskins—and angered him even further when he selected twenty-year-old UCLA quarterback Tommy Maddox in the first round of what turned out to be his final draft in Denver.

In Shanahan's first season in San Francisco, Young was voted the most valuable player in the NFL and the 49ers went to the NFC championship game, where they were upset by the Cowboys at Candlestick Park. Shanahan had hardly settled into the Bay Area when Bowlen called. He had fired Reeves and wanted Shanahan to return to Denver as the head coach. Finally, Shanahan could work with Elway without having Reeves's paranoia get in the way. Bowlen and Shanahan had an excellent relationship. Shanahan and Elway were close, probably too close for a player and a coach, but it was better than the alternative of not talking.

There was a problem. Shanahan didn't want the job. Not yet, anyway. He was bitter about the way things had ended for him with Reeves. He didn't like the perception that he'd undermined the head coach. He didn't share Bowlen's belief that the Broncos were close to winning a Super Bowl. He wasn't happy with the budget Bowlen had given him for assistant coaches. Plus, he had just gotten to San Francisco and wasn't ready to pack up. He felt he had made more than a one-year commitment to the 49ers.

He rejected Bowlen's offer. Bowlen then promoted defensive coordinator Wade Phillips. Shanahan didn't want anybody saying he was targeting Reeves's job all along. "I got so tired of listening to that crap," Shanahan said. "I just didn't like what went on with Dan, the rumors about me wanting to come back and my relationship with John. I didn't feel comfortable going back."

Elway was angry. How could Shanahan do this to him? He was finally free of Reeves and thought his good friend was on his way back to Denver. It wasn't easy for Shanahan to break the news to Elway. He felt he couldn't give Elway the real reason he was staying in San Francisco—he was still bitter. He didn't think it would be fair to the organization. So he made something up. "This is an interesting story," Shanahan said. "I never really told this story to anybody."

He leaned back in his chair in the head coach's office at Redskins Park—he was hired by Washington in 2010—and relayed the conversation he'd had with Elway.

"Hey, John," Shanahan said.

"Why aren't you coming?" Elway said.

"John, it's a little bit financial, and they are not willing to make that commitment," Shanahan said.

"Well, what is it?" Elway said.

"I don't want to go down there," Shanahan said.

"No, I want to know what it is," Elway said.

Shanahan lied. He told Elway that Bowlen's financial package was insufficient and he wanted a couple more courtesy cars than Bowlen was offering.

"We're probably $300,000 off on the total package," Shanahan said.

"How many years?" Elway said.

"Three or four years," Shanahan said.

"That's no problem. I will take care of that," Elway said.

Elway was prepared to write a $300,000 check to Mike Shanahan.

Twenty years later, as the executive vice president of football operations for the Broncos, Elway remembers trying to buy Shanahan's way back to Denver by offering to pay the difference between Bowlen's offer and what Shanahan said he wanted. "When he turned that down, I knew it was something else," Elway said.

Elway could afford the $300,000. He was about to sign a four-year $20 million contract. But paying part of the salary of the head coach not only would have been unprecedented, it would have caused friction in the locker room when his teammates found out. And they would find out. "He was going to pay me out of his salary what I was short," Shanahan said. "That kind of gave you an idea how much he wanted to win. I had totally made up the financial stuff, thinking he would back off. He said, 'No, no, I'll take care of that. I got enough money. Money is done. Car is done.' He didn't blink."

Elway was not concerned about any backlash in the locker room. "That's how much I believed in him at the time. I thought he was the right guy," he said. "I was running out of time. That was my eleventh year. I wasn't a young buck at the time. I wasn't too concerned as long as we went out and won, which I thought we would do. My selfish feeling is I wanted him to come back. I was in a little bit more of a hurry than he was."

Elway was so upset that he didn't talk to Shanahan for an entire year. "He was mad at me for obvious reasons," Shanahan said. "We were very close friends. I had a chance to come back to be the head coach and didn't."

Phillips lasted just two seasons with the Broncos. By that time, the 49ers had lost another NFC championship game to the Cowboys, but then they beat them in 1994 in the title game and went on to win the Super Bowl with a lopsided victory over the San Diego Chargers. This time when Bowlen called, enough time had passed and Shanahan accepted. But things didn't get better right away. The Broncos were 8–8 in 1995 and missed the playoffs and were the AFC's number one seed with a 13–3 record in 1996 but lost in the divisional round to the Jacksonville Jaguars, a second-year expansion team. Maybe it wasn't Reeves's fault. Maybe it was Elway.

Maybe not.

Elway ended his career in style by winning the Super Bowl the next two years, his final two years in the NFL. He beat the heavily favored Packers and Brett Favre after the 1997 season when he was the sentimental favorite. When he stood on the podium with Bowlen and Shanahan after the game, Bowlen held up the Vince Lombardi Trophy and declared, "This one's for John."

The Broncos won their first fourteen games in 1998 and made it back to the Super Bowl, this time against the Falcons, who were now coached by Reeves. He had lasted four seasons in New York, had been fired, and was hired by the Falcons in a homecoming—he was born in Rome, Georgia, and grew up in Americus, Georgia—and had the Falcons in the Super Bowl in his second season against Elway and Shanahan. That was when a lot of the old wounds from the Denver days were pried open.

"I don't think (Shanahan) had my best interest in mind at the time," Reeves said. "If John Elway had a problem with me, and you're coaching that position, why did I not know prior to reading it in the paper? If you were the position coach and you're that close to the quarterback, why didn't I know that?"

Shanahan insists Reeves already knew that Elway had no use for him and didn't need Shanahan to tell him. "Dan Reeves knew his relationship with John," he said. "There's no ifs, ands, or buts about that. They know it was a tough relationship from the second year, from the first year."

The Broncos beat the Falcons, and months later Elway retired. Shanahan lasted another ten years in Denver and was fired by Bowlen after missing the playoffs three straight seasons. He sat out one year, the 2009 season, and then was hired by the Redskins. Reeves was fired by the Falcons with three games remaining in the 2003 season. Elway and Shanahan see each other occasionally, primarily at league meetings, and Reeves and Elway have decided life is too short to stay mad at each other.

"You lose three Super Bowls, and the two people who get blamed are the head coach and the quarterback. That will certainly strain anybody's relationship. Believe me, I had the utmost respect for John," Reeves said. "People talk about I tried to trade him. That's the biggest lie in the world. The only time it was ever mentioned was Joe Gibbs called me and asked what it would take to get John Elway. That was right after Wayne Gretzky was traded. That was an unbelievable deal they made. I said it's going to have to be something like that. And it isn't going to be me. It's going to have to be through the owner. I would never have traded John Elway. Hell, they would have run me out of Denver. No way."

When Elway was inducted into the Pro Football Hall of Fame in 2004, he invited Reeves to attend the weekend in Canton. Reeves accepted and sat next to Elway's mother at the ceremony. "It never crossed my mind not to invite him," Elway said. "Time heals everything. There are absolutely no ill feelings on my part toward Dan."

Their relationship had come full circle. "I was thrilled, to say the least," Reeves said.

Reeves had a contentious relationship with Elway in the decade during which he coached him. It wasn't until Elway wasn't playing anymore and Reeves was no longer coaching that they finally found common ground. They still managed to get to three Super Bowls together. Maybe instead of losing all three, they could have won a Super Bowl ring or two if they had just gotten along.

In 2011, John Fox enjoyed Tebow Mania while it lasted, which wasn't very long. The Broncos thought Tim Tebow was a great person and Elway even said he was the kind of guy you want your daughter to marry, but he clearly wasn't a quarterback Fox and Elway thought could win a Super Bowl. Tebow became the most popular player in the NFL during his incredible playoff run, but when the Colts cut Peyton Manning the next March, the Broncos jumped right into the cross-country chase. Eventually, Manning chose the Broncos over the 49ers and Titans, and then Denver immediately traded Tebow to the Jets.

This is a cold business that is based strictly on results. Tebow won enough games for the Broncos in 2011 to deserve a chance to build on that success, and Fox was planning for him to be his starting quarterback in 2012. But the Broncos couldn't push him out the door fast enough once Manning became available. He was the most popular player on the team, but it was just business. "They went a way that they thought was best for the organization. I'll never blame them for that," Tebow said. "There's no ill will toward the Broncos, Peyton Manning, or anybody. I wish them nothing but the best."

Manning missed the entire 2011 season after starting every game in the first thirteen years of his career. He had four surgical procedures on his neck in a two-year period. From a football standpoint, it was worth the gamble for the Broncos. They were getting Peyton Manning, a future Hall of Famer. They elected to trade Tebow not so much because it would have required them to reinstall the unconventional Read Option offense for the unconventional Tebow if Manning was injured but because Tebow was such a fan favorite and it was not worth taking the chance that the fans would turn on Manning and demand Tebow if Manning got off to a slow start.

That doesn't mean it was easy for Fox to say good-bye to Tebow. As the Broncos were deciding between offers from the Jets and the Jaguars, Tebow's hometown team, Fox was in constant communication with Tebow, who was working out in Los Angeles. The Broncos, as a thank-you to Tebow for helping to revive the franchise, allowed him to choose between the two teams. The Jets presented Tebow with a better opportunity to get onto the field running a Wildcat package. His value to the Jaguars would have been his immense popularity and his ability to sell tickets. Tebow chose the Jets.

The Broncos drafted Tebow in the first round in 2010 when Josh McDaniels was the head coach and before Elway returned to run the team he had led to five Super Bowl appearances. Fox and Elway inherited Tebow and had no obligation to make it work. He was not their draft choice. McDaniels was fired late in Tebow's rookie season. Bowlen hired Elway to run the team, and Elway then hired Fox, who had been fired after nine seasons as head coach of the Carolina Panthers. If things had worked according to plan in 2011, Tebow wouldn't have been on the field much. Kyle Orton easily won the starting job coming out of training camp once a trade sending him to the Miami Dolphins fell through, and it was only after Denver started 1–4 that Fox and Elway realized that they had nothing to lose by playing Tebow. The fans basically demanded the move. Tebow responded by winning his first start in an overtime game in Miami and seven of his first eight with a variety of improbable last-minute victories. The Broncos lost their final three games but still won the AFC West with an 8–8 record and then beat the Steelers in the wild-card round on Tebow's 80-yard touchdown pass to Demaryius Thomas on the first play of overtime before they were crushed by the Patriots in the divisional round in New England.

"I thanked Tim for all the memories," Fox said. "He sparked our football team. I'll be forever grateful for that. I really will. We shared some great moments together."

Fox first met Tebow the night before his pro day at Florida as Tebow was preparing for the draft. The Panthers had traded their 2010 first-round draft pick, but felt they had a chance to get Tebow in the second round. Tebow might have been one of the best college players of all time, but most scouts didn't believe he projected well as an NFL quarterback. He ran the ball better than he threw it. His accuracy was a major concern. Nobody questioned his character or leadership ability, but it takes more than that to be a successful professional quarterback.

Fox made a reservation at Mark's Prime Steakhouse in downtown Gainesville and arranged to meet Tebow for dinner along with Panthers offensive coordinator Jeff Davidson and quarterback coach Rip Scherer.

"He was definitely unique. You could see the intangibles," Fox said. "They just oozed out of him. It was easy to see what kind of leadership skills he had. He had a notepad and took notes. He was real respectful, willing to learn; he had passion for the game."

They enjoyed a nice dinner. Fox came away impressed, and

although he wasn't sure the Panthers would take him when their pick came up in the sixteenth spot in the second round, he thought there was a good chance he would be available. "Early in the process, it would be fair to say some people weren't expecting him to go in the first round," Fox said.

As dinner ended, Fox asked the waiter for the check. Tebow said he already had taken care of it.

"It wasn't one of those last minute things, 'Oh here, I got it,' " Fox said. "He had it paid for. Obviously, he had a little juice in Gainesville and the guy that waited on us; Tim already gave him his card."

Of course, Fox didn't let Tebow pay. But if Tebow was looking to make an impression, he got the job done. "I never had a prospective player do that," Fox said.

He estimated that in all his years as a college coach and in the NFL, he's taken way more than two hundred players out for a meal and Tebow was the first who tried to pick up the check. "There weren't any holes in him as far as the intangible part," Fox said. "We spent more time on his football knowledge, how he would fit in, his delivery. It was more football stuff."

The scouting reports on Tebow raised a lot of questions about his ability to make it in the NFL as an every-down quarterback. The scouting report by the general manager of one team raised a lot of issues:

STRONG POINTS: size, rare intangibles, production, running strength, toughness, level of comp., game day history.

CONCERNS: mechanics, intermediate accuracy, style of offense he's played in.

A big strong overachieving athlete at position. He has a strong arm, but mechanically flawed with marginal intermediate accuracy, particularly hitting moving targets. Where QBs make their living in our league. They run mostly from the shotgun in their spread offense, that employs many future pros at all the skill positions, along with a NFL looking line. Everything is built around him and he delivers. There is no player in college sport who can impose his will to win and have such an emotional impact on his peers and get the results he has over a career. He's a rare competitor and what he brings can't be measured statistically. That said many of his throws are errant of his receivers and his best plays aren't necessarily drawn up in any playbook. The best thing he does as a passer is get it down field with surprisingly good accuracy, not much air under it, but finds the mark. You love the kid, but there is no pro offense featuring his strengths and if you adopt what he does best in all probability he'll have a short career given the pounding he's going to take. You have to be careful not to let his character bleed into the tape. He has a better downside as a good serviceable back up, than he does upside as a starter. He would be enticing in the third round, because he wouldn't get the unfair scrutiny a top pick incurs at position.

SUMMARY: Again see him more like a Joe Kapp type of starter, one you win with not because of, or at worst a serviceable backup. There is one last point that needs to be considered. Alex Smith the #1 overall pick played in the same system with similar results under the same head coach. There is a lot of buyer beware with Tebow.

Fox never had the chance to make a decision on Tebow in the draft. The Broncos selected him in the first round, the twenty-fifth pick overall. That shocked draft rooms around the league. The Panthers were in the market for a quarterback and selected Notre Dame's Jimmy Clausen with their second-round pick. The next year, after Fox left the Panthers following a 2–14 season, they drafted Auburn's Cam Newton with the first overall pick.

When Fox was hired in Denver, it didn't take long for Tebow to seek him out. "He was one of the first guys in my office," Fox said. "It didn't surprise me because that's the kind of guy he is."

Fox and Tebow had a connection from the previous year when they'd had dinner. The lockout prevented Fox from having an opportunity to work with Tebow until training camp in 2011. The off-season conditioning program, minicamps, and OTAs were canceled. That put Tebow at a disadvantage. He needed the work. Once Orton failed and Tebow had a chance to get on the field, he began winning games in the most unusual ways. His following, not only in Denver but around the league, was unprecedented. He was a little too open with his religious beliefs for some people, but nobody questioned his heart and desire. He became a polarizing figure: fans either loved or hated him. Judging by the sales of Tebow merchandise, more fans loved him.

"I'm not a sociology major. I'm a football coach. I evaluate him as a quarterback," Fox said. "Can he lead the team? I respect him tremendously. It upset me at times, when here's a guy doing everything you want a guy to be, I don't care what his religious beliefs are or what neighborhood he came from—we ought to be celebrating this guy. He's doing things the way you are supposed to do them. I'm not saying it's always pretty as a football player. You're playing against the best in the world."

Fox was convinced Tebow would be the Broncos' starting quarterback when they opened training camp in 2012, but with each event in the NFL, there is a domino effect. Peyton Manning had spinal fusion surgery on his neck a few days before the 2011 season, and although the Colts didn't place him on injured reserve, his chances of returning during the season were minimal. The Colts cut Manning in March 2012 before he was due a $28 million option bonus, having made up their mind to gut the franchise and start over by drafting Stanford quarterback Andrew Luck with the first overall pick. Luck was considered the best quarterback prospect since Manning in 1998.

Manning might have been the most valuable player in the NFL in 2011 despite not playing one down. The Colts won only two games without him after making the playoffs nine years in a row with him. Shortly after the Colts released him, Elway and Fox acted immediately. They sent a private plane to Miami, where Manning has an off-season home in South Beach, to bring him to Denver. The plane stopped off in Stillwater, Oklahoma, to pick up Fox and Elway, who were attending workouts at Oklahoma State. It was Manning's first free agent visit, and he was going to be thorough. He went from Denver to Arizona to meet with the Cardinals. He didn't seem anxious to meet with the Dolphins but did so in Indianapolis after a personal request from Marino, the former Dolphins quarterback and one of Manning's heroes. Manning had made his NFL debut in the first game of the '98 season at home against Marino and the Dolphins. He then visited the Titans in Nashville. Manning had gone to school at the University of Tennessee in Knoxville and was still an icon in the state.

Manning held private workouts at Duke University in Durham, North Carolina, for the Broncos, 49ers, and Titans. He was working out with Duke coach David Cutcliffe, who had been an assistant coach when Manning was at Tennessee and later was his brother Eli's head coach at Ole Miss. Manning eliminated the Cardinals and Dolphins before the workouts and never gave the Chiefs or Jets a chance to get into the race. The 49ers were the secret team pursuing Manning, and he was intrigued. San Francisco was coached by Jim Harbaugh, who had been the last quarterback to start a game for the Colts before Manning arrived in Indianapolis. Fox and Elway traveled from Denver to Durham to watch Manning throw and came away convinced that he would make it all the way back from his neck injury.

A few days later, as Elway and Fox were nervously anticipating Manning's decision on an otherwise quiet Monday morning, the phone rang in Elway's office. It was Manning. Fox and Elway froze.

"How are you doing?" Elway said.

"It has kind of been a rough morning because I have had to call these other teams and say I'm not going to go to work for them," Manning said.

Elway wondered where the Broncos stood. Were they on the list of teams being rejected? Or had they won the Manning Derby?

"I just wanted to tell you that I want to come play for the Denver Broncos," Manning said.

Elway made a thumbs-up motion to Fox. Elway continued the conversation as Fox started jumping around the office. Manning soon signed a five-year $96 million contract.

It's easier for a coach to establish a relationship with his quarterback if he gets him right out of college than if he gets him in the middle of his career or, in Fox's situation with Manning, the end of his career. That was why Walsh and Montana were so successful and why Belichick and Brady have always been on the same page. The young quarterbacks were slighted in the draft—Montana went in the third round, Brady in the sixth—and came in looking to soak up all the football knowledge they could from their head coaches. It was Walsh's first year with the 49ers, but he already had developed a reputation as one of the best quarterback coaches in football. It was Belichick's first draft with the Patriots, although he previously had been the head coach in Cleveland for five years. Brady came in with a chip on his shoulder, looking to prove he was much better than the 199th player in the draft and certainly better than the seventh quarterback selected.

Manning's first coach with the Colts was Jim Mora, who had been the Saints' coach in Manning's hometown of New Orleans for many years. It was up to Fox to develop a good working relationship with Manning, who had played for Mora, Tony Dungy, and Jim Caldwell, in Indianapolis. Manning was set in his ways, and Fox knew that the best way to make it work was to defer to

Manning and let him have major input into the way the offensive playbook was written. "Welcomed input," Fox said.

Fox is a smart, experienced coach. In his nine seasons with the Panthers, they reached two NFC championship games and one Super Bowl. Carolina owner Jerry Richardson let his contract run out after the 2010 season and then fired him. It's unusual when owners let a coach enter the final year of his contract without either extending him or firing him. When Richardson didn't offer Fox a new deal after the Panthers were 12–4 in 2008, Fox knew his time was just about up in Carolina. "It's their team. I was hired to do a job," Fox said. "I had a contract through the 2010 season, and I honored that contract. It's the business. There are two parts of football. There is football, and then there's the business. They are both part of the game."

By the time Manning joined the Broncos, Fox had ten years of head coaching experience in the NFL. He knew he just needed to let Manning do what he'd always done and pretty much just get out of the way. "He raises all boats," Fox said.

Fox made his name in the NFL as a defensive coach. He was the defensive coordinator with the Giants when they went to the Super Bowl in 2000. The offensive coordinator was Sean Payton. Jim Fassel, the head coach, was an offensive coach. Fox had the run of the defense, and the success of the Giants helped him get his first head coaching job with the Panthers. Carolina had elite offensive players in wide receiver Steve Smith and running backs DeAngelo Williams and Jonathan Stewart, and Fox squeezed some excellent seasons out of the journeyman quarterback Jake Delhomme. But those Panthers teams were not known for their creativity on offense. Fox didn't want his offense to put his defense in a vulnerable position.

When Tony Dungy was hired by the Colts in 2002, Manning

already had played four years in the NFL. In Dungy's six seasons in Tampa, the Bucs were known as a defensive team with an anemic and antiquated offense. Their scheme was more suited for the leather helmet days. Dungy made the playoffs four times and had a 1–4 record. In the five games, the Bucs scored a total of 39 points on six field goals and three touchdowns. They didn't score a touchdown in any of the last three losses. Scoring 39 points was considered a good single game for Manning.

"He was kind of apprehensive because of how we played in Tampa and my reputation as a defensive coach," Dungy said.

"Probably similar to my reputation," Fox said.

Dungy took the job with the Colts knowing he was going to have to sell himself to Manning to win his confidence. Although Manning had yet to win a playoff game, he was one of the most prolific quarterbacks in the NFL. He didn't want to play conservative, which was the mandate for Dungy's quarterbacks in Tampa. Dungy had Warren Sapp, Derrick Brooks, and John Lynch, and so the goal was for his offense not to put his defense in bad spots by turning the ball over and creating a short field. He wasn't looking for his quarterback to win the game, just not to lose it. That was not the way Manning played. It was not the way he wanted to play. Dungy had no intention of putting handcuffs on Manning. After going through too many years of Trent Dilfer and Shaun King with the Bucs, he finally had a quarterback who could win games.

"I think he felt early on that we might pull back and change the way we were going to do things," Dungy said. "So I had to make that clear to him that I ran this offense in college. I understand how it works. We've got a lot of money spent on offense. This is an offensive team. We're not going to change what we do. We just want to change how we do it a little bit. We're still going to attack, but we want to get to the point where we got enough confidence we don't have to take unnecessary chances, we can still be explosive, but some things that I believe in, protecting the football and winning the turnover battle, that is how we are going to win."

Dungy retained Tom Moore as the offensive coordinator. When Dungy was a quarterback at the University of Minnesota, Moore was on the staff. "It was really convincing Peyton that our offense has enough weapons if we get eighty plays in a game, we're going to score forty points," Dungy said. "But if we only get sixty plays or forty plays because we are turning the ball over or taking chances or our defense is not playing well enough to get us the ball back, that's going to be difficult. So that's how we are going to try to improve the team and not change what we do. I think having that conversation with him was good and that was the beginning of it. Then he had to kind of grow to trust me that we'd put the team together that way, and as we went on, I think he really started believing it."

Dungy and Manning had no history together. They had met only once before Dungy was hired by the Colts. It was after the 1997 season at the Maxwell Club Awards in Philadelphia. Manning, who had just finished his career at Tennessee, was being honored as the college player of the year. Dungy had just guided the Bucs to the playoffs in his second year as head coach. It was Tampa's first trip to the postseason since 1982, the strike year when the season was reduced to nine games and eight teams from each conference qualified for the playoffs.

"We rode in a limo together from the hotel to the affair: he and his mom and dad and my wife and I," Dungy said. "So we're riding in the limo and talking about the draft upcoming, his career, and everything. I said, 'I'd love to have you, but you're going to be the first or second pick in the draft.' So, four years later, it's January of '02 and I get the job, and he comes to the press conference and he approaches me. He comes into my office and we're talking, and I say you may not remember this conversation, and he repeated everything to me verbatim: the hotel we stayed at, the limo ride over, my wife's name, different guys who got awards, and what a nice evening it was."

Dungy was blown away by Manning's memory. They had not seen each other since that night in Philadelphia. "I just said, 'Wow, I felt like I have a good memory. I remember the night and the conversation, but I certainly didn't remember the hotel and all of that,' " he said. "I said, I see why this guy is special, just his ability to process information and remember things."

Then came the money line from Manning. "I'm looking forward to being coached; we want to win, whatever it takes," he said.

The Colts made the playoffs in 2002 but were embarrassed in the wild-card round by the Jets 41–0. It was the fourth straight playoff game in which Dungy's team failed to score a touchdown. That was not a shutdown Jets defense, either. It was a tough time for Dungy. Jon Gruden had been hired to replace him in Tampa, and just a few weeks after the Colts' season ended, the Bucs won the Super Bowl. It was the team Dungy helped build, but it was Gruden's system. The change helped the Bucs. But the change for the Colts and Manning was not paying off yet.

Manning's numbers improved only slightly in Dungy's first season. His touchdowns went from twenty-six to twenty-seven, and he cut his interceptions from twenty-three to nineteen. That was not what Dungy had in mind. Manning was still giving the ball away too much. By their second year together, the message started to get through. In the opening game of the 2003 season, the Colts beat the Browns 9–6 in Cleveland. "We didn't play lights out, but we won," Dungy said.

He thought that was the game when Manning bought into his philosophy. He did not have a great game, throwing two interceptions, but the Colts' defense kept the Browns out of the end zone. It was 6–6 when the Colts got the ball at their own 24 with 2:39 remaining. The Colts called ten consecutive pass plays as Dungy put the game in Manning's hands. He completed eight for 65 yards, setting up Mike Vanderjagt's game-winning 45-yard field goal with one second remaining. The Colts went on to win twelve games and finish first in the AFC South. Manning finally won his first two playoff games but then lost to the Patriots in the conference championship game. The Colts lost again to the Patriots, this time in the divisional round, in 2004.

The Colts had a huge disappointment in 2005. They were the AFC's number one seed, finishing with a 14–2 record after they opened the season with thirteen consecutive victories. But they lost to the number six seed Steelers at home in a heartbreaker in the AFC championship game. It was a very difficult time for Dungy. Just a few weeks earlier, his son James had committed suicide in Florida. There was a feeling that Dungy might walk away after that season, but he elected to return in 2006.

That turned out to be a very good decision for the Colts. Dungy didn't have his best team, but he had a resilient team. They finished 12–4 and were the AFC's number three seed. Dungy, who had lost his first playoff game as the Colts coach to his good friend Herm Edwards when he was the Jets' coach in 2002, beat Edwards in the wild-card round in his first season coaching the Chiefs. In the next round, the Colts beat the Ravens in Baltimore 15–6. Neither team was able to score a touchdown, but Dungy had built Manning a defense. Even though he had a bad game, throwing for only 170 yards with two interceptions, the Colts' defense shut down the Baltimore offense. Maybe this was going to be the Colts' year.

They caught a big break when the Patriots beat the Chargers in San Diego in the divisional round. The Chargers had been the number one seed. But with New England beating them and the Colts beating the number two seed Ravens, Indianapolis would host the AFC championship game against the Patriots.

Dungy and Manning had lost to Belichick and Brady twice in the playoffs. They beat them this time, 38–34. Two weeks later, the Colts beat the Bears to capture Super Bowl XLI.

"I just have to say how sweet this is," Dungy said.

He had the obligatory Gatorade bucket dumped on his head by his players. They carried him off the field on their shoulders. On the podium Dungy had passed the Vince Lombardi Trophy to Manning. Their relationship began in a limo ride and picked up four years later with the coach feeling the need to win the trust of his quarterback, whereas it's usually the quarterback who needs to win the trust of his coach. Now they had achieved the ultimate together, which forges a lifelong bond.

"I'm certainly proud to be a part of his team," Manning said. "I'm proud Tony is our head coach."

Dungy took a deep breath after the game. "It's tough to win," he said. "It's tough to win the Super Bowl."

Now the pressure shifted to Fox. He knew he needed to create a system that eliminated the transition time for Manning to adapt to Denver. He could go to school on how Dungy handled Manning after he inherited him. Dungy let him run the offense from the line of scrimmage, building a solid defense around him so that the Colts didn't have to score 40 points every week. Dungy had the benefit of time. He arrived in Indianapolis just as Manning was hitting the peak years of his career. Fox got him at the tail end, hoping to squeeze a few more years of greatness out of him.

Eight p.m., Halloween night, 1995, Green Bay, Wisconsin, Mike Holmgren's house.

Don Beebe was wearing Brett Favre's number 4 jersey. Brett Favre was wearing Don Beebe's number 82 jersey. As they walked toward Holmgren's front door in a residential area of Green Bay, Beebe said to Favre, "Put it on, baby."

Beebe slipped a mask with a pink helmet over his head. Favre pulled a rubber mask over his face. They were accompanied by Frank Winters, the Packers' center. He was wearing a mask, too.

"We're going to coach Mike Holmgren's house to get a little candy from the big boss," Beebe said.

Four little girls were in front of them. Holmgren, the Packers coach, had just arrived home after a Tuesday night working up the game plan for that Sunday's game against the Vikings. The Packers had lost at Detroit two days earlier, and their record was 5–3.

The girls and Beebe knocked on Holmgren's door. They rang the doorbell. Holmgren told his wife, Kathy, he would get this one. She and Holmgren's daughters had been passing out candy all night.

"Trick or treat," the girls said.

"You are not going to believe this, but we just gave out our last piece of candy," Holmgren said. "I am sorry, kids. I am so sorry."

He had no idea Favre, Beebe, and Winters were also standing in front of him.

Holmgren looked down at the girls. He patted one of them on the head. "I like your outfits," he said. "You are all so beautiful."

Then, looking at Beebe dressed in the Favre jersey, he said, "Not you, necessarily." Beebe said, "You don't like me?"

Beebe then stuck his head inside the front door to see if Holmgren was telling the truth. There was no candy. Holmgren gave him one of those "what the hell are you doing?" looks. "I put my hand on his chest. I shoved him out," Holmgren recalled.

Holmgren still had no idea it was Favre, Beebe, and Winters. He was thinking, "Big guys wearing masks."

The kids were still asking for candy.

"What if I say that was Don Beebe or Brett Favre?" Favre said from under his mask.

"I'm sorry. We have none left," Holmgren said.

"What about Mr. Gil?" Beebe said.

That gave it away. Beebe was referring to Gil Haskell, Holmgren's longtime friend and offensive coordinator, who happened to be at Holmgren's house that evening.

"Oh, gee whiz," Holmgren said as he pulled off Beebe's mask. They all had a good laugh.

Roger Staubach never went trick-or-treating at Tom Landry's house. Surely, Elway never went knocking on Reeves's door, although in his rookie year in Denver, Elway was such a big story that the aggressive Denver newspapers did report on what kind of candy he was giving out to the kids on Halloween. Phil Simms never trick-or-treated at Bill Parcells's house, and it would be hard to imagine Bart Starr coming in full costume to Vince Lombardi's house or Tom Brady asking Bill Belichick for a treat. That would be a treat to watch.

Favre, Beebe, and Winters arranged to have their field trip to Holmgren's house taped, and it was shown at the Saturday night team meeting at the hotel in Minneapolis a few days later. "That's Brett," Holmgren said. "He's a knucklehead."

Holmgren was a longtime high school history teacher before he made coaching his full-time profession. Teachers must have a lot of patience, and that quality helped Holmgren in his relationship with Favre. He had worked with Joe Montana and Steve Young in San Francisco—he also coached Young at Brigham Young University—and that provided him with invaluable experience when he was hired by the Packers in 1992. Montana was a coach's dream, the perfect West Coast quarterback. Young was an incredible athlete who liked to run at the first sign of trouble. Holmgren helped him become a Hall of Fame quarterback. Favre would be a much bigger challenge.

Near the end of the 1991 season, the Packers hired Ron Wolf as their general manager. He had been an assistant to Jets general manager Dick Steinberg. When Wolf was preparing for the 1991 draft, he had Favre, the quarterback from Southern Mississippi, ranked first on the Jets' board. The Jets didn't own a first-round pick, having used it the previous year in the supplemental draft to take Syracuse wide receiver Rob Moore.

The Jets didn't pick until early in the second round, number thirty-four overall. When Favre began to slip toward the end of the first round, Steinberg began dialing around the league, frantically trying to trade up. Favre kept slipping. It was not a great year for quarterbacks. Dan McGwire, the brother of baseball slugger Mark McGwire, went to the Seahawks at number sixteen. Todd Marinovich was selected by the Raiders at number twenty-four. Steinberg and Wolf were close friends with the Falcons' general manager, Ken Herock. They knew the Falcons really liked Favre, but they had not selected him with either of their first-round picks. Instead they took cornerback Bruce Pickens at number three and wide receiver Mike Pritchard at number thirteen. The Falcons' next pick came one spot before the Jets' pick in the second round. Steinberg and Wolf were cetain Herock would take Favre in the second round. Steinberg finally was able to find a trade partner, working out a deal with the Cardinals, who were picking number thirty-two, one spot ahead of the Falcons and two spots ahead of the Jets.

The Cardinals were intent on taking defensive end Mike Jones, so this was a no-lose situation for them. If they flipped spots, New York would take Favre, the Falcons would take Louisville quarterback Browning Nagle, and the Cardinals still would be able to draft Jones. At the last minute, for a reason Steinberg never knew, the Cardinals pulled out. They stayed put and drafted Jones. The Falcons then took Favre, and the Jets took Nagle. That didn't work out well for the Jets. Nagle lasted just three years in New York before spending a year with the Colts and then finishing his career with one season in Atlanta; that was ironic considering what happened in the 1991 draft.

Favre barely played as a rookie with the Falcons and fell out of favor with the coach, Jerry Glanville. There were rumors that Favre was enjoying himself too much off the field and that his drinking had become a concern. He even missed the team picture his rookie year. Herock and Glanville have argued publicly for years over who ordered Favre to be traded after the season, but the Packers were the beneficiaries. Just two days after Wolf hired Holmgren, he told him he was thinking about trading one of Green Bay's two first-round picks to Atlanta for Favre. Wolf still liked him very much despite his forgettable rookie season.

"Let me get my reports," Holmgren said.

Holmgren conducted Favre's workout at Southern Miss leading up to the draft in front of a dozen teams. Wolf dug up his draft report on Favre to compare to Holmgren's. "Very talented guy. Could be special," Holmgren wrote.

He told Wolf that in his version of the West Coast offense Favre would have to learn to make different types of throws. "He threw the ball so hard all the time," Holmgren said. "He's strong, and he threw it hard. He had to get serious about how he handled himself off the field as well. But as a talent, this guy is special."

One week later, Wolf made the trade. "It was two guys who had seen him from different teams the year before coming together and agreeing on the fact that this is a talented, talented man," Holmgren said. "I was cocky enough to think all that other stuff I could take care of. I could mold him a little bit."

He knew that would be a challenge. After he conducted the predraft workout for Favre, he remembers sitting down with him for a little talk. The workout went very well, and Holmgren was impressed.

"How are you going to spend the rest of the day?" Holmgren asked him.

"I'm going to do a little catfishing, a little beer drinking," Favre said.

Holmgren was surprised to hear Favre talk about drinking beer so openly. He was an offensive coordinator for one of the best teams in the NFL, and Favre didn't seem to be watching his words. "I just registered that a little bit," Holmgren said. "Of course, he did have a certain reputation. We did our homework. He had a little bit of a reputation down in Atlanta. The quarterback position is so important to everybody, particularly in our offense. We're as good as the quarterback, basically. I thought I might have to work on this a little bit."

Holmgren was willing to give Favre the benefit of the doubt for his rookie year in Atlanta. "It's not unlike a lot of guys coming into the league their first year and not playing," he said. "You got money in your pocket, you're single, you're in the city for the first time, you're a professional football player. I don't think it's unusual for these guys to go out and cut it up a little bit."

Favre did more than just cut it up later in his career. In May 1996, he checked into the Menninger Clinic in Topeka, Kansas, for a six-week stay after he became addicted to the painkiller Vicodin. He said at the time that the doctors at the clinic stated that he did not have an alcohol problem. It became part of Favre's legend that when he faced adversity, he played his best. The Packers went on to win the Super Bowl less than seven months after Favre left the rehab center. He threw for four touchdowns and 399 yards in Oakland the day after his father died unexpectedly in 2003.

Early in his Packers career, Favre would infuriate Holmgren with his schoolyard brand of football. Favre probably would have been happy drawing the plays up in the dirt and winging it. "Here I have this thoroughbred quarterback who is used to winning games by playing a certain way," Holmgren said.

The coach believed in a more disciplined approach. He worked hard to get Favre to trust the system, but it didn't happen right away. "You got those old *National Geographic*s with those two rams on the mountainside banging into each other," Holmgren said.

One was Holmgren. One was Favre. Holmgren was trying to break him down and build him up.

Favre got his break in Green Bay when Don Majkowski was injured in the third game of the 1992 season. Favre took over as the starter the next week, beginning a streak of 297 consecutive regular season starts that didn't end until late in the 2010 season when he was in the final year of his career with the Vikings.

The streak was almost over before it had a chance to really get started. During the 1994 season, Favre's third in Green Bay, Holmgren revealed that there was sentiment in a staff meeting that Holmgren should give the job to backup Mark Brunell. He had played well after Favre was injured against the Vikings in the season's seventh game, and some of Holmgren's coaches were lobbying for him to start the next game in Chicago.

"I went around and asked my coaches. I went around the room and got their feelings," Holmgren said.

Enough hands went up for Brunell that Holmgren didn't immediately dismiss it. He trusted his coaches. He decided to sleep on it. Favre still had the wild streak. Brunell played under control. The next day, Holmgren called Favre into his office. He had decided to stick with him but never told him that he had considered benching him. Holmgren felt that putting fear into Favre was not the way to motivate him. Some coaches want their players on edge all the time. Bill Parcells always used intimidation as his way to get through to his players.

Holmgren sat Favre down. He didn't threaten him. Just the opposite. He wanted Favre to know he was completely supportive. He believed that was the way to get the best out of him.

"You are my guy, and we are joined at the hip," Holmgren said. "We are either going to get to the top of the mountain together or we are going to wind up in the dumpster together. But we are going to be together."

He stuck with Favre and never second-guessed himself. "Sometimes you just have to commit," Holmgren said. "You are not always right. But it did happen to work out for us in Green Bay."

Favre never lost his boyish enthusiasm for the game even if by the end of his career he turned people off with his on-again off-again retirements from the Packers, the Jets, and finally the Vikings. Favre and Holmgren had an interesting relationship. The coach liked to follow a script. The quarterback liked to ad lib. Somehow they made it work.

"He had a great ability to make me laugh even in the tightest situation," Holmgren said. "It tied in with his great leadership. He was remarkable that way. Teammates loved him. They played hard for him. But it's fair to say he drove me a little crazy. When he and I talk about it now, we start laughing so hard. I was hard on him, but for the right reasons. I recognized he was a supertalent, and I was going to get the most out of him. I'd hold him to a very high standard. Maybe at times it was somewhat unreasonable."

Nearly twenty years later, Holmgren still has fun telling the story of Favre coming to the sidelines in the final game of the 1995 season against Pittsburgh.

"It's an important, important football game for us. It's cold; it's really cold in Green Bay," he said. "We got a big third-down play coming up, and I got a couple of plays I want to call. I call time-out. He comes over. It's third and short."

He started talking to Favre. "Okay, I got two plays. Which one do you like best? He's kind of looking at me. Which one do you like the best? He's just staring at me. He doesn't say anything. Hey, are you listening to me? Which play you like the best? He still just stares at me. So I banged him on the chest. Boom. I hit him on the chest. Hey, pay attention. Which play do you like the best?"

Finally, Holmgren got a response from Favre.

"Mike, you ought to see your mustache," he said.

"What?" Holmgren said.

It had frozen over, and Favre thought it was hilarious. "He broke me," Holmgren said. "I'm just laughing. It's a crucial part of the game. Ty Detmer and Brunell are on each side of me. They don't know whether to laugh. They don't know what I'm going to do. I just go, okay, all right, do I have your attention?"

Favre smiled at Holmgren. They picked a play. It was third and goal from the Steelers' 1. Favre ran back on the field and threw a touchdown pass to Mark Chmura. The Packers won the game. Holmgren's mustache began to thaw out.

THE KING OF BURNOUT

Dick Vermeil is giving a tour of his log cabin house that sits on 180 acres in rural East Fallowfield, Pennsylvania. It's the dream house he and his wife, Carol, had built to their specifications and have been living in for over a quarter of a century.

"One hundred percent pine log," he says proudly.

The deck overlooks a breathtakingly beautiful backyard with acres of countryside that go on forever. It is as peaceful a setting as you can find sandwiched between the tumult of New York City to the north and Philadelphia to the east. The driveway off a side street is so long that you need a GPS to find the house once you turn in. The first half leading from the street is an unpaved dirt road; the second half is blacktopped. When a winter storm hits, it takes days for the snowplow company to dig out the Vermeils. The basement is filled with enough keepsakes from his coaching days with UCLA and the Eagles, Rams, and Chiefs to fill a sports memorabilia museum. There are plenty of pictures on the wall of Vermeil with a who's who of the NFL. He is tanned and relaxed and loving life. The only immediate appointments on his schedule are motivational speaking engagements, although the market is not what it used to be. His main business concern is the production of the next batch of wine with the Vermeil label from his California vineyard. The quality is excellent. The market is competitive.

The wine business is a passion, but it does not keep Vermeil up nights.

Is this the same man who at the age of forty-six was so completely burned out and "emotionally frozen," as he puts it, that he could not summon the inner strength to get out of his car as he sat in front of Veterans Stadium to go to work on a Monday morning? Is this the same man who became the face of coaching burnout to the extent that all coaches who have had enough and walk away are compared to Vermeil?

"It doesn't bother me," Vermeil said. "First, it's the truth. I think if a person has a hard time dealing with the truth, then they are going to have a hard time dealing with themselves. It doesn't bother me because I understand the kind of pressure you can put on yourself. The pressure I felt in coaching was not put on me by Leonard Tose or Georgia Frontiere or Lamar Hunt. It was put on by me, myself, my own pride. My own evaluation of myself and the kind of commitment I was making to do the job and do it right."

He believed he owed it to his players to work them hard and work them beyond the limits they had set for themselves. His two-a-day practices with the Eagles were legendary and often stretched out to three-a-days. "I really believe that sometimes you got to push people to do things they didn't know they could do," he said. "It's so easy for a professional athlete to think, I've arrived. I'm making all this money. Sometimes, to make them as good as they can be, you got to push them beyond what they think they already are."

Vermeil could push his players. He could not push himself. He was collapsing under the burden of his own expectations. After seven years as head coach of the Eagles, he decided to take one season off and get refreshed.

He took fourteen.

So much of who he tried to be as a coach came from the great John Wooden. Vermeil was an assistant at UCLA in 1970 and then went to the Rams as an assistant for three seasons before returning as the UCLA head coach in 1974 and 1975. Wooden always told him that he didn't coach basketball, he coached kids who play basketball. His office was right next door to Wooden's, and he tried to absorb as much as he could from the Wizard of Westwood.

"He used to come and sit and have breakfast with us every morning during football season at our training table. He'd then go walk the track in the morning," Vermeil said. "John Wooden was a guy that never talked about winning. He felt your obligation as a coach was just to make the players you have the best they can be, each and every one of them. From the third-string guard to the starting guard. Make them the best they can be, and that will handle all the other things. He said to me, I remember this vividly, don't worry about being better than those guys across town. That was USC. He said you're never going to be as physically as good as they are. But just make sure your players are as good as they can be. He said if you work that way, eventually you will find a way to beat them. I have never forgotten that."

Wooden was a basketball coach. Vermeil was a football coach. But that didn't mean their issues didn't overlap. Wooden had so much talent on those basketball teams—he won ten NCAA championships in a twelve-year period, including seven in a row—that players who could be starting at just about any other program were sitting on his bench.

"John, I got three running backs; it's a problem. You can't keep them all happy," Vermeil said.

"Pick out who you think is the best one and make him happy," Wooden said.

Vermeil felt that was good advice. It's also a nice problem to have. "I have audiotapes in my desk downstairs of meetings with him," he said. "He was a real plus for me. I leaned on him. In the off-season, he would talk to my whole staff. We had ten coaches, and we'd all sit there and ask him questions. I used to watch them practice and how important it was to practice fast tempo. You want practice to be game tempo. Maybe not in intensity but tempo. I bought into that and learned that. Practice fast, practice fast. And fundamentals. Nobody is so good that they can't improve their fundamentals.

"He had a great way of coaching value systems that carried over into your work ethic and carried over into how you lived your life. That didn't mean he didn't get on their ass, because I've seen him do it. But if they believe you, they will follow you even if they are mad at you. He was a leader of people."

Vermeil carried Wooden's philosophies and concepts into his first NFL head coaching job when he was hired by the Eagles. He was just thirty-nine years old. "I wasn't really qualified to be the head coach of the Philadelphia Eagles, but I was, so you learn," he said.

Vermeil ran a brutal training camp in the summer of 1976, his rookie year in Philadelphia. He had the players sucking air. The Eagles had been just 4–10 the season before he arrived, and he was trying to find out which players would still be part of his team when he got the program turned around. It was a relief when the season arrived: Vermeil could no longer run two-a-days. Or three-a-days.

Philly lost its season opener and was 2–2 after the first month. Maybe this college guy knew what he was doing. But then the Eagles lost three in a row, beat the Giants for the second time, and lost five in a row. The record was now 3–10.

It was 9 a.m. on the Monday after the latest loss. It was 6 a.m. in Los Angeles.

Suzette Cox, who was his administrative assistant, knocked on Vermeil's door.

"Coach wants to talk to you," she said.

"Coach who?" Vermeil said.

"Coach Wooden," she said.

Vermeil picked up the phone.

"I've been following, and I know it's tough. You know what you are doing. You've done it before. Stick with your principles. You will get it done."

The conversation lasted two minutes. "The most meaningful well-timed conversation I've ever had on the phone," Vermeil said.

The Eagles won their final game of the season to finish 4–10. There was no quick fix in the NFL back then. Free agency was nearly twenty years away. Teams had to build through the draft or make trades. The previous regime left Vermeil without a full complement of draft picks. He didn't have a first-round or second-round pick until his fourth draft in 1979. But the Eagles were getting better. They won five games in Vermeil's second season.

The next year, 1978, the NFL expanded the regular season to sixteen games and added a second wild-card team for each conference. Philadelphia finished 9–7 and made the playoffs but lost to the Falcons in the opening round. Incredibly, it was the first time the Eagles had been in the playoffs since 1960, when they'd won the NFL championship. The Eagles were 11–5 in 1979 but had to settle for a wild-card spot after losing the NFC East tiebreaker to the Cowboys. They beat the Bears in the wild-card round before losing to the Bucs. By 1980, Vermeil really had it going. The Eagles finished 12–4, once again tying the Cowboys for the NFC East's best record. But this time the Eagles won the tiebreaker, received the first-round bye, and then wound up beating Dallas in the NFC championship game to get to their first Super Bowl.

They lost to the Raiders 27–10 in Super Bowl XV in New Orleans, and the story of that game was not what happened on the field but what happened off the field. While the Raiders were tearing up Bourbon Street night after night, Vermeil had the Eagles tucked in bed with a strict curfew before the Raiders were downing their first hurricane of the evening. The Raiders' victory was a victory for all those players who believed the Animal House approach wins. All they had to do was show up on Sunday ready to play. It didn't matter how late they staggered in from Pat O'Brien's in the middle of the week. Vermeil was tight during Super Bowl week, and his players were tight in the Super Bowl.

Still, Vermeil had become one of the NFL's best coaches. He had transformed the Eagles into perennial playoff contenders. That was an impressive accomplishment considering that the Eagles had not once finished over .500 in the nine seasons before he arrived.

Everybody seemed happy in Philadelphia except Vermeil. He was driving himself crazy. He was miserable. He didn't have an off switch. Tom Landry was making sure he was home for dinner every night with his wife, Alicia. He might bring some film home to watch in the evening, but he never slept in his office. Vermeil didn't know when enough was enough, couldn't figure out when he had reached the point of diminishing returns or understand that a relaxing night with his wife and three kids would benefit the Eagles more in the long run than watching one more tape of the Giants' kickoff coverage team.

He was setting the standard for the next generation of coaches who would put more into their jobs than they were getting out. It was a form of paranoia: How can I go home and watch television when Joe Gibbs is in his office grinding away? He didn't believe in reaching a point of diminishing returns.

"I didn't feel comfortable unless I was in the office working," Vermeil said. "I can remember after a game I would come home and get back in the car and turn around and go back to the stadium. If we lost, I would blame myself. What could I have done to prevent it? That's what beats you up from the inside. These are all things that are not good if you are a head football coach."

Vermeil tried to help himself when he was with the Eagles. He traveled from Philadelphia to New York to meet with Dr. Herbert Freudenberger, a psychologist who was the author of the book

Burnout: The High Cost of High Achievement, published in 1974. Freudenberger is credited with coming up with the term "burnout," which he defined as "the extinction of motivation or incentive, especially where one's devotion to a cause or relationship fails to produce the desired results."

The ends were not justifying the means for Vermeil. He was working hard but was not pleased with the results. He said meeting with Freudenberger was "really helpful," as he was clearly on a path toward burnout.

At the time, it was thought of as a badge of honor that Vermeil slept in his office more than he slept in his own bed. Look at how hard this guy works. Marvel at the commitment he has made to turning the Eagles into Super Bowl contenders. In reality, he was forcing himself into retirement. He lived in Bryn Mawr, Pennsylvania, just eighteen miles from the Eagles' offices at Veterans Stadium. That was close enough for Vermeil to sleep in his own bed every night, but he chose the hideaway bed in the head coach's office on the first floor of the stadium.

"You are driving to work on the Schuylkill Expressway," he said. "It gets backed up. It's like a parking lot. The hour I wasted—sometimes longer—to drive to work, I could be in my office already working or I could get one or two more hours of sleep."

And in that extra time, he might find a new wrinkle in the Redskins' punt protection. Of course, he might have found it during normal working hours. He just didn't see it that way. At the end of the strike-shortened 1982 season, when the Eagles were 3–6, Vermeil quit. He was fine physically. He was running five miles a day in the off-season. Mentally, he was spent. He burned himself out. "I was my own worst enemy, that's all," he said. "I was a mess."

*   *   *

Rex Ryan lives in Summit, New Jersey, a mere twenty minutes from the Jets' offices in Florham Park. He fell right into the trap in his first year as the Jets head coach in 2009 of sleeping in his office on Monday and Tuesday nights, the busiest nights of the week, when the coaches are preparing the game plan to present to the players on Wednesday. As Ryan became more familiar with the demands of the job after his rookie season, he scaled back the overnight stays in the office. He stays until he feels the work for the day is done. "I've never been a guy that has punched a clock," he said. "And I don't want our coaches doing that either."

It's not as if Ryan is staying over for the luxury accommodations. His office is on the ground floor of the Jets' sprawling complex. When you exit the main door of the coaching suite, it empties right into the Jets' indoor practice facility. There are no windows to the outside world where the coaches work. It's dreary. No turndown service or chocolates on the pillow, either. But the team cafeteria is about forty yards away, so securing food is not a problem.

There are enough hours in the day to drive home, but there are times Ryan finds that it takes some of the pressure off when he is able to work at his own pace without then having to drive home. "That's just me because I'm slow," he said. He has come up with creative ways to help him deal with dyslexia. It may take him longer, but that has never stopped him. "There are other coaches who can leave at nine o'clock or ten o'clock. That's fine. There's other coaches who are here later than me on other days," Ryan said. "Sometimes I will leave and come back. I hate that. My deal is I want our coaches out of here by midnight because I want them fresh for the next day. For the most part, that is the way it is."

The wives become conditioned to not seeing their husbands much during the season. Joe Gibbs picked up a lifetime supply of Redskins Park points for all the times he slept in his office, especially in his first stint with the Redskins. He spent the early part of the week staying over in his office and would make it home late in the week. As he walked out the door, his wife, Pat, would hand him a tape of all the latest news and updates on what was going on with their two young sons. He would play the tape in his car. When Pat started yelling at one of the boys, Gibbs would hit the eject button and put on some music instead.

"My wife one time got on me when I came home early. It was eleven at night," Ryan said.

"What are you doing?" Michelle Ryan asked.

"I feel good. We've already played these guys. We are ready. We got them dialed in," Ryan said.

There was no need to stay in the office any longer. Ryan was convinced that his preparation was complete. But his wife had become so used to the routine of his staying late, sleeping in his office Monday and Tuesday nights every week even though he lived so close to the Jets' facility, that it surprised her when he came home at a reasonable hour.

John Fox, who coached nine years with the Panthers and made it to one Super Bowl and then was hired by the Broncos, says that he slept in his office maybe once or twice in his years in Carolina.

"With today's technology, if you can't get it done between 7 a.m. and 11 p.m., you are doing something wrong," Fox said. "Looking at cutups on film, you just have to touch a button. Back in the day, we were splicing 16-millimeter film. You can practice your team all hours of the night, too. At some point, there are diminishing returns. You are standing before the team, and you can hardly stay awake. You are not making good decisions. And with the players, you can work them until they are half dead."

Fox has managed to keep his job in perspective. There is only so much you can do to prepare the players, and then they must go out and play. Not all coaches see it that way. "Everybody has got their own personality. Some have addictive personalities," Fox said. "I don't think any of us are finding a cure for cancer. It's not like we are doing something that is really hard. Coaches get upset if you leave too soon. I'm not one of those guys."

Coaches know they make the job much tougher than it needs to be. But they also know that the margin for error has been reduced drastically in the free agent era. Owners are paying so much for players in a system designed to create parity that coaches have no more than three years to get a team into the playoffs or they are gone. In prior eras, a team would introduce its new coach, who would announce a five-year plan to turn things around. Early in the development period, he would draft a quarterback and then tutor him for two or three years before putting him on the field.

That doesn't happen anymore. Elite college quarterbacks start right away. The owner expects the quarterback to be playing at a high level by his second year. He expects the coach to be in the playoffs by his third year or he will find another coach.

"No doubt, it's a hard way to make a living," Fox said.

There are thirty-two of these jobs, and the pressure to win and avoid getting fired leads to awfully long hours. But it's also a glamorous life, and coaches are well compensated. Jeff Fisher made it to one Super Bowl and lost in his sixteen full seasons as the head coach of the Houston Oilers/Tennessee Titans. Including the playoffs, he was twenty-six games over .500. He is a very good coach. After the Titans fired him following the 2010 season, he sat out one season. He was the most accomplished candidate in a weak pool of available coaches after the 2011 season. The Dolphins wanted Fisher. So did the Rams, the team coached by Vermeil that beat his Titans in Super Bowl XXXIV after the 1999 season. Fisher had leverage and turned it into a five-year $35 million contract, making him one of the highest paid coaches in the league.

Mike Shanahan, who won two Super Bowls in Denver before moving to Washington, has never been a sleep-in-his-office coach. He does work fourteen hours a day during the off-season to prepare for the season and believes coaches who work until 2 a.m. haven't done a good job setting things up. "Now, does that mean we don't get in early?" Shanahan said in his Redskins Park office in Ashburn, Virginia. "I've had the same hours since I've been in the NFL. I'll go from six o'clock in the morning until ten o'clock at night," he said. "I only live ten minutes from here, so the chances of me staying over are very slim."

Vermeil was an extreme case. But it takes all kinds. One prominent player once complained that his head coach was not a hard worker. He said the coach used to park one of his cars in the front of the team's offices in the spot that had his name tag on it. He parked another car in the back of the building in a spot with no name tag. The coach had a routine of leaving early in the car that was parked in the back but giving the impression that he was in the building because the car out front was still there. He was the anti-Vermeil, and he survived longer than he deserved to as a head coach.

❡ ❡ ❡

Dick Vermeil's sabbatical from football lasted quite a few more years than he first intended. The plan was to sit out one year, get reenergized, maybe reevaluate the way he did things, and get right back into the grind. He had job offers every year he was out except for one year. Many years he had more than one offer. The Falcons wanted him. The Bucs wanted him. The Chiefs wanted him. The Rams wanted him. It's nice to feel wanted.

Once when Vermeil's father was dying of pancreatic cancer, he was sitting by his side when Tampa Bay owner Hugh Culverhouse called.

"You can write your own check," Culverhouse said.

"Give me a day to think about it," Vermeil said.

He turned to his dying father.

"Dad, that was Hugh Culverhouse."

"Who's that?"

"He owns the Tampa Bay Bucs. He's a nice man. He just offered me an unbelievable situation."

"Do you need the aggravation?"

"No."

"Then don't do it."

Vermeil called Culverhouse back and turned down the job.

"I never went into coaching because of money," Vermeil said. "I coached in this league for a long time and made nothing. I'm not going to go back into coaching because of money, but I'm not going to go into coaching without good money."

The Rams kept calling every time they had an opening. Vermeil kept saying no.

Vermeil regretted not taking his good friend Carl Peterson up on his offer in 1989 to be the Chiefs' coach. They had worked together at UCLA and in Philadelphia and had remained close. When Vermeil turned him down, Peterson hired Marty Schottenheimer.

"I just didn't trust myself," he said. "They are going to pay a lot of money; they deserve the best they can get."

He was tempted when new Eagles owner Jeffrey Lurie wanted him in 1995. Lurie had inherited Rich Kotite and fired him after one season. Vermeil came close but got cold feet.

"When I spoke to Jeffrey, it was the thing that really convinced me that I wanted to do it again," Vermeil said. "It was not anybody's fault but my own because he offered me a job. I can remember saying, Jeffrey, I'm not your guy. I'd been away from coaching at that time for twelve years. And here's an entirely new management staff. None of them had been in pro football. When I went to New York and met with them and the lawyers and I looked at it, and none of these guys have been in football and I haven't for twelve years, I don't think I'm the right guy for the job."

That would have been an incredible story. Vermeil had remained popular with Eagles fans, and they would have embraced his return. Gibbs left the Redskins after the 1992 season and returned in 2004. Gibbs had said he would never coach again and then changed his mind. Vermeil never said that. Clearly, he wanted to coach again. But he found a reason every time to stay away.

After Vermeil decided not to return to the Eagles, Lurie was at the East-West Shrine Game in Palo Alto, California, where he ran into Bill Walsh, one of Vermeil's closest friends.

"Why in the hell didn't you hire him? Get it done," Walsh said.

That prompted Vermeil and Lurie to start talking again. But Lurie elected to hire Ray Rhodes. He would have been better off with Vermeil. Even so, with so little experience in the Eagles' front office and so much time away from the game, Vermeil said, "I didn't feel confident enough that I could do it."

He was becoming a big tease to NFL owners. That could not continue forever, of course. By the time the Rams called again in 1997, Vermeil was sixty-one years old. He was still fighting the inner turmoil. Could he coach again in the NFL and not star in the sequel to *The Burnout*? He couldn't pledge to the Rams that he would stay long enough to guide them through a rebuilding period. What happens if he wants to leave after one year? That wouldn't be fair. He had been away so long, and the game had changed so much and the attitude of the players had changed so much. Was it too late? Vermeil had kept up with the game in his media work because that's who he is. He knew personnel. He knew how to structure an organization. The scary part was that he also knew himself.

"I wasn't sure within myself that I was capable of going back and keeping the game in proper perspective," he said. "I met with a psychologist, probably ten times, and really studied myself. I just wanted to correct some faults within my own personality. It was good for me. It was really good for me. I just never was sure I could control my own drive."

Vermeil worked for the Los Angeles Rams for three years before UCLA hired him as its head coach. The Rams played in St. Louis now. Vermeil was reluctant when the Rams called after the 1996 season, and so they started to interview other candidates. They came back to Vermeil, and he finally said yes. "I just figured if I didn't do it now, I would be too old," he said. "No one is going to offer me the president of football operations and head football coach when I had been out of it fourteen years."

He signed a five-year $9 million contract. The money had changed since he'd last coached. In Philadelphia, he made $50,000 per year when he was hired. It was important to get paid market value, but Vermeil returned because his passion had returned. "Fourteen years ago, I left coaching. I left coaching because I had to. And I'm not embarrassed to say it," Vermeil said when he was introduced by the Rams. "Today I'm back, because I have to. I'm excited about being able to say it."

Finally, Vermeil was back. "I promised my wife I would never sleep in my office," he said. On the nights he was sleeping in his office in Philadelphia, he wouldn't get to bed until four or five in the morning and then be up for a staff meeting at 7:50 a.m. "Sometimes I was so driven that I drove myself into a hole," he said. "It's my personality type. It's predictable."

He lived twenty minutes away when he coached in St. Louis and left the office no later than 1 a.m. At least he was sleeping in his own bed. He and Carol were married when they were nineteen, so by now nothing came as a surprise. Vermeil had been away from coaching a long time. He was the little general in Philadelphia. In St. Louis, he was a tyrant. "I was forty-six when I walked away, and I just felt I wasn't as good a football coach as I should be with the responsibilities I had in the frame of mind that I was in," he said. "You become blind. You are so driven that you don't see some of the obvious things."

Now he was doing it again. He was working the players so hard that he was losing the locker room. The mind-set of players had changed in all the years Vermeil was gone. They were making so much money now that they didn't live in fear of the head coach. If the team didn't win, the coach would be gone, but the big-money players would remain. The balance of power had shifted. Vermeil was 5–11 in his first year in St. Louis. The Rams regressed to 4–12 in his second year. He had a built-in excuse if he wanted it: Tony Banks was his quarterback. Vermeil faced a team mutiny early in his second season when the players called him into a meeting and complained about the long meetings and practices. After the season, Vermeil admitted that he had drained the enthusiasm out of his team.

Vermeil said it was not a revolt, just a serious discussion. "I'm old-fashioned," he said. "The only way you can make somebody better is to work them. The only way to work them is to keep them on the field. Then, in the third year, we said we are going to move the program in a little different direction. We backed off them a little bit, not a lot."

He was trying to change the culture of a franchise that last had had a winning season in 1989 back in Los Angeles. The time away from the game didn't appear to have given him a new perspective. Maybe he'd been right all those years when he kept turning down opportunities to coach.

There was speculation that he would be fired after the 1998 season. This just wasn't working. Vermeil went into the '99 season coaching for his job. At least he didn't have to deal with Banks anymore. At Vermeil's first training camp, Banks showed up with his Rottweiler puppy, Felony. Vermeil was not happy. Felony was sent home. The Rams signed free agent quarterback Trent Green for the 1999 season. Vermeil told team officials he thought he had a playoff team. Then San Diego safety Rodney Harrison ran into Green's left knee in the third preseason game. Torn ACL. Out for the year. Vermeil had reached the point in his life where he was not afraid to display his emotions in public, and two days later, in announcing that the team was going with Kurt Warner at quarterback, Vermeil lost it. He started crying.

"That's just my makeup," he said. "It used to embarrass me. I would be at a team banquet talking about one of my players, then all of a sudden I'd get emotional. My wife said, Hell, you don't get that emotional about me. That's just me. I've embarrassed myself many times, but I learned to just piss on it. They don't like it. I could give a damn. A lot of people don't get that close to their players. They don't really care. They don't give a shit."

As it turned out, Green's misfortune gave birth to one of the great stories in NFL history. After the 1998 season Warner was included among the five Rams exposed on the expansion list for the new Cleveland Browns. The Browns passed on Warner, an unknown with virtually no playing experience outside of the Arena Football League and NFL Europe. They selected Kentucky quarterback Tim Couch with the first overall pick in the 1999 college draft. It was hard to fault the Browns. Who was Kurt Warner?

Warner, of course, came out of nowhere in 1999 to be named the season MVP and the Super Bowl MVP. Rams linebacker Mike Jones prevented the Titans from sending the Super Bowl into overtime when he stopped Tennessee receiver Kevin Dyson on the 1-yard line on the final play of the game. In his third year back in the game after taking off for fourteen years, Vermeil was a Super Bowl champion.

He then made the biggest mistake of his career. He had put everything he had into building the Rams. He had a shooting star in Warner. He had a dynamic back in Marshall Faulk. And he quit. Two days after the Super Bowl, he was gone. Frontiere had asked him to take two weeks before deciding. The ability to leave on his own terms and on top was too appealing. He saw Tom Landry get fired in Dallas. He watched as Don Shula was pushed aside for Jimmy Johnson. He had his ring and was at peace. He knew if he waited two weeks and then elected to leave, it would set the Rams back in their planning for the 2000 season.

His three children were on the East Coast and wanted him to come home. "I was really exhausted," he said. "In three years, we put six years of work into that program because it was a mess. I had a son tell me, Dad, you've gotten what you've always wanted to get done, now come on home. He was right."

It didn't take long for Vermeil to realize he had made the wrong decision. His job was handed to offensive coordinator Mike Martz, who had distinguished himself with the work he had done with Warner in his first year coaching with the Rams. He had come to the Rams from the Redskins, where he had worked with Trent Green. He was a natural fit for Vermeil. But now Martz was a hot commodity, and St. Louis could have lost him to another team if Vermeil had waited weeks to decide his own future and then left. Maybe he should have done that because if Martz had left, it might have compelled Vermeil to stay.

Vermeil was handing out the Super Bowl rings in May when he knew he should still be coaching this team. His team. Sure, he had won the Super Bowl ring he'd always wanted, but this team was good enough to get him another. And another. It was a feeling of emptiness. He had turned over his team and all his hard work to benefit someone else.

"When I started handing those rings out, God, I've got tears in my eyes and hugging these guys as I'm giving them their world championships rings, and I say, 'I spent three years of my life and my whole career getting to a point where I can do this. What a stupid thing to do,' " he said. "I have taught myself never to regret or look back. I don't allow myself to do that. You move on."

Vermeil's emotional ride as a head coach took a strange turn. He knew he should still be coaching in St. Louis, but Martz had that job. He sat out the 2000 season, and then Peterson finally persuaded him to coach the Chiefs. "I realized I missed it," he said.

Of course, he first told Peterson he wouldn't do it, so Peterson hopped on a plane to Philadelphia and wouldn't leave until Vermeil accepted the job at $4 million per year.

He stayed five years in Kansas City, and just as in St. Louis, his team peaked in the third year. Kansas City started 9–0, finished the season as the number two seed with a 13–3 record, but lost its first playoff game to Peyton Manning and the Colts. It was the only time Vermeil's Chiefs made the playoffs, although they did finish 10–6 in his final season.

The time in Kansas City was rewarding. The Chiefs traded for Green after Vermeil arrived. He'd never played a regular season game for Vermeil in St. Louis after he was Vermeil's big off-season free agent signing in 1999. But in Vermeil's five seasons, Green started every game for the Chiefs. Vermeil and Green became close friends. In the spring of 2010, Vermeil and his sons Rick and David, both in their fifties, and Green went on a dove hunting trip to South America. Vermeil once had confided in Green that he felt that he had cheated Rick and David and his daughter Nancy. "I see you with your kids and I see my sons with their kids, and I cheated my own by not always being there for them like you guys are," he told him.

On the hunting trip, Green discussed with Rick and David what their father had said. Vermeil had never discussed this with his boys. "They told Trent they really understood it and a lot of their friends had dads who were working and traveling all over the country all the time," Vermeil said. "So I wasn't that unique to them. So they didn't feel like they were being deprived. Plus, they enjoyed the involvement. They enjoyed being on the sidelines of games. I did feel good about that. I never felt real guilt because the kids have turned out well and Carol has done a good job with them."

Vermeil has eleven grandchildren. He is a very attentive grandpa. "I think I'm pretty good," he said.

This time, when he left Kansas City, he walked away from coaching for good. He wasn't burned out. He wasn't emotionally frozen. It was time to go back to the log cabin in the woods of Pennsylvania and wait for the next shipment of Vermeil wine to arrive.

THANKS FOR EVERYTHING. YOU'RE FIRED.

Brian Billick was enjoying himself at the Ravens' all-night victory party in Tampa after they crushed the Giants in Super Bowl XXXV. It doesn't get better than the euphoria in the hours after winning the Super Bowl. It doesn't last long, but when everybody is giddy and the champagne is flowing, the perils of the job seem distant; you can forget that even the great ones get fired.

"When you get into coaching, you acknowledge it from the get-go. That's the nature of the life that you have," Billick said. "It very rarely ends well for coaches under any circumstances."

Bill Parcells put the thrill of winning in perspective for coaches at every level in every sport. After his second Super Bowl victory, he said, "Winning is better than anything. Better than sex. Better than Christmas morning."

Billick and the Ravens had been through a lot in the previous twelve months, and he finally had a chance to take a deep breath and enjoy what his team had accomplished even if the ride caused him to navigate potholes deeper than the ones in which cars have disappeared on the FDR Drive in Manhattan.

There had been the life-changing situation of Ray Lewis, his best player. Lewis had been indicted on murder charges the previous year after a fight outside an Atlanta nightclub in the early morning hours after the thrilling Rams-Titans Super Bowl game at the Georgia Dome. He was jailed for fifteen days before posting $1 million bond. Lewis eventually made a guilty plea to obstruction of justice. The murder charges were dropped. He avoided further jail time, and that was good news for the Ravens. Now Lewis was the Super Bowl MVP. Billick had managed him brilliantly during the season, trying to deflect attention and keep the focus on the team. He did the same thing at the Super Bowl, lecturing the media, which only fostered his arrogant image, but he was running interference for Lewis and doing what was best for his team.

Lewis addressed his teammates on the first night of training camp in the summer at McDaniel College in Westminster, Maryland, one month after his case was resolved. "I need to get to a Super Bowl," he told his teammates.

Lewis didn't want to be a distraction for his team. He didn't want to be a distraction all season with questions about a case in which there was not enough evidence to convict him of killing another man.

"Our method, once we got to training camp, we put Ray in front of the media, we're going to give you one shot at this, we're going to answer all the questions we possibly can, we want to be as transparent as we possibly can, but after that, that's it," Billick said. "We are not going to address this every day in camp or the season. Players rallied around it. Not to sound mercenary, but it did become a rallying focal point for the team in support of Ray and his circumstances. It did kind of bring the team together. That was a good by-product of a very tragic situation."

At his first news conference in Tampa at the Super Bowl, knowing that ESPN had rebroadcast a piece in which a relative of one of the victims called Lewis a murderer, Billick was proactive in addressing the media, telling them they were not qualified to retry the case. He was trying to avoid a circus but might have created one. At Lewis's podium at the Ravens' hotel, tight end Shannon Sharpe stood behind Lewis, intending to support him, but created a scene. It was a Super Bowl first. A player accused of murder after one Super Bowl playing in the next Super Bowl. That's a record nobody wants to match.

Sharpe interrupted Lewis's media session and began preaching the virtues of Lewis as a player and a person. He spoke for five minutes. Lewis was wearing a blue floppy hat that was low enough to cover his eyes as he looked straight ahead during Sharpe's lecture.

"He's been exonerated of all charges," Sharpe shouted. "All charges. You know why? Because they know he's not guilty. They're just probably not going to say it publicly that they made a mistake."

Then Sharpe scolded the media surrounding Lewis. "But you talked to the man, and not one time did you ask him any questions about the Giants or the Super Bowl or the Ravens. 'Well, Ray, what was it like when you were in jail?' What the hell do you think it was like? The man was fighting for his life, his livelihood, all the things that were going to be taken away from him. Imagine someone's going to take your life away from you."

The Ravens had lived through a season in which playing road games became a true test of Lewis's will.

"I would purposely go out for pregame warm-ups right after Ray came out," Billick said. "It's amazing to me the things people would say as he could come out on the field. On two fronts, you can't believe one human being would yell that out to another. And secondly, I used to almost half smirk, thinking these people had no idea what they were doing. The racial slurs, killer, you can imagine. The derogatory . . . many of them racially laced . . . but all the negative things you can imagine someone might say. I used to think, you're not helping your team much, folks, because all you're doing is stoking the fire here for a man who doesn't need it anyway. He played like a man possessed all year long."

Billick had also become one of the few coaches to win a Super Bowl by spending the season coaching around his quarterback.

He made the switch to journeyman Trent Dilfer during the season and won games with a productive running game and a dominating defense, the second best defense of the Super Bowl era behind the 1985 Chicago Bears. Billick was supposed to be a state-of-the-art offensive coach, but when the choices are Tony Banks and Dilfer, there is no other choice: run the ball and play defense. Billick switched to Dilfer in the ninth game, and the initial results were not encouraging. The Ravens lost 9–6 to the Steelers, and their only points came on long field goals by Matt Stover. It was the third straight game the Ravens didn't score a touchdown. They had a three-game losing streak and a 5–4 record, and all four of the losses came when the offense didn't get into the end zone. The Ravens were wasting a terrific defense led by future NFL head coaches Marvin Lewis and Rex Ryan.

But as so often happens during a season, a team gets hot out of nowhere. The Ravens won their last seven games to finish 12–4. Dilfer ended the season with twelve touchdowns and ten interceptions—barely adequate—but the Ravens' defense, led by Lewis, set an NFL record for a sixteen-game season by allowing just 165 points; that's just over 10 points per game.

All Billick needed was for Dilfer to manage the game, not screw it up.

"Trent understood his limitations and understood how we could win," Billick said. "It's not like I had to fight him on it."

In the Super Bowl, the Ravens forced New York quarterback Kerry Collins into four interceptions. The defense held the Giants without an offensive touchdown. The only Giants points came on a 97-yard kickoff return by Ron Dixon to make the score 17–7 in the third quarter, but Baltimore's Jermaine Lewis then took the New York kickoff back 84 yards for a touchdown to put the game away. It was a different formula for Billick. He was the offensive coordinator in Minnesota in 1998 when the Vikings set the record for the most points in a season, a record that was eclipsed by the 2007 New England Patriots. He checked his large ego at the locker room door and did what was required to win. A successful coach adapts his system to fit his personnel.

The plan worked. The Ravens won the Super Bowl, and the party was going all night. At 6 a.m., Billick left, went up to his suite to shower, and then tried to get a bit of sleep. It was just two and a half hours before the NFL would transport Billick to the media center in downtown Tampa for the morning-after news conference for the winning coach and most valuable player, which was Lewis. Billick had won the Super Bowl in just his second season as a head coach, faster than Tom Landry, Bill Walsh, Chuck Noll, or Bill Parcells. He was forty-seven years old.

"In the shower, I had a panic attack," Billick said.

He had just reached the mountaintop of his profession, but his thoughts were focused on tumbling right on down. "My God, what do I do now? This is just my second year," he said. "Where do you go from here? We may never get back here again. What if this is it?"

Coaches are judged by championships. Billick had his first, and that would give him job security for many years even if it was his last. But he didn't have a lifetime appointment. He knew that. By winning the ring in his second year, he had set the bar high. But how many times do you hear players say they will be back in the Super Bowl the next year and they never get back again? Dan Marino made it to the Super Bowl in his second season in 1984 and lost to the 49ers. He had to figure that with Don Shula as his coach there would be plenty more Super Bowls before he retired and was enshrined in Canton as a first-ballot Hall of Famer. But when Marino quit after the 1999 season, it was still the only Super Bowl in which he had played. As great as Shula was—and no coach in NFL history won more games—he had two humiliating blotches on his record.

Shula was the Baltimore Colts' coach when they lost to the Jets in Super Bowl III, the greatest upset in pro football history.

The Colts were a 17-point favorite on January 12, 1969, at the Orange Bowl in Miami but were dominated by Joe Namath and the Jets. Shula restored his credibility and built a legacy when he left Baltimore and was hired by the Dolphins in 1970. After losing to the Cowboys in the Super Bowl after the 1971 season, his second in Miami, he won back-to-back Super Bowls. Miami was a perfect 14–0 in 1972 and is still the only team to make it through the regular season and the playoffs undefeated in the modern era. Shula was an institution in southern Florida. He made it back to the Super Bowl in 1982 with David Woodley as his quarterback. The Dolphins lost to the Redskins, and a few months later, Shula couldn't believe how lucky he was when Marino was available in the first round of the draft after twenty-six other teams had made their choices. When Miami's pick at number twenty-seven came up, Shula hit the lottery. In one of the all-time cases of teams overanalyzing players, Marino almost slipped out of the first round and was the sixth quarterback selected.

But Shula made it to as many Super Bowls with Woodley as his quarterback as he did with Marino. That wasn't as bad as losing to the Jets, but it was pretty bad. By the mid-1990s, even Shula's icon status wasn't enough to protect him against the mounting criticism: he had one of the greatest quarterbacks in NFL history but couldn't get back to the Super Bowl. Meanwhile, the Robbie family had sold the team to Wayne Huizenga, and things were changing in Miami. After Shula took an average team to the playoffs in 1995, where the Dolphins lost in the wild-card round in Buffalo, Shula gave no indication that he wouldn't be back in 1996. He planned to fulfill the final year on his contract.

He had a problem, however. The big elephant in the room, or at least down at his home in the Florida Keys, was Jimmy Johnson. It had been two years since Jerry Jones had handed Johnson a $2 million check to leave Valley Ranch after the Cowboys had won the Super Bowl in 1992 and 1993. Johnson then went to work for HBO and Fox, but there was little doubt he would get back into coaching one day. And there was no doubt that Shula's job was the one he wanted. A couple of days after the loss to the Bills in the playoffs, Shula resigned. Huizenga knew better than to fire him as Jones did with Tom Landry in Dallas after he bought the team in 1989. If Shula wasn't technically fired, he at least left under pressure. Miami had started 4–0 but then dropped to 6–6. At that time, three southern Florida newspapers ran reader polls, and an alarming 10,000 of the 13,000 who responded wanted Shula gone. Shula wanted to make changes in his staff after the season, but after consulting with general manager friends George Young, Bobby Beathard, and Bill Polian, he knew it would be hard to attract quality assistants if he planned to coach just one more year. He had also been irritated by the Johnson-to-Miami rumors that had been going on for two years.

Billick knew nothing was forever, not even for greats such as Shula and Landry. Johnson was held accountable by Dallas fans for getting Landry fired, but that wasn't fair. His college teammate bought the team and offered him the security of a ten-year contract.

Now Johnson was looking over Shula's shoulder. He owned a home in Tavernier in the Florida Keys, an hour's drive to the Dolphins' headquarters in Davie. He was revered in southern Florida for the job he had done at the University of Miami.

Johnson had put himself in an enviable spot after he left Dallas. He was a free agent. He was red-hot. He could call his shot on his next job. The Eagles and Saints offered him huge deals. He turned them down. The Bucs wanted him before they failed to get Steve Spurrier and settled for Tony Dungy. The phone kept ringing, and Johnson kept saying no. There was just one reason: he wanted the Dolphins job. And he got it. He didn't have much success in the four years he coached the Dolphins, but in addition to his two Super Bowl titles in Dallas, he is known as the coach who shoved aside Landry and Shula.

Billick had been a Super Bowl champion for only a few hours and was already stressed out. "There is a chance, a recognition, strictly a business observation, that we may not get back here again," he said. "What do I do now, so early in my head coaching career? I knew going forward that was going to be the only benchmark that I was going to be measured by."

By the time he arrived at the press conference, Billick had calmed down. The fear of failure drives coaches. They all know that at some point they are going to be fired. It's the nature of the profession. Only the chosen few are allowed to leave on their own terms. "Bill Walsh said for years and years you can only do this for ten years in one place, even if you can last that long," Billick said. "Well, when you are in the middle of a coaching tenure, you don't want to believe that. Now, looking back, I think he's probably right. Typically, you don't last that long because you get fired in year two, three, or four because you are not good. But if you're good enough to last, it means you have been good enough early in your career. But you are going to take a dip; everybody does. There's going to be a couple years where you are going to struggle."

Billick had a grace period. The Ravens moved to Baltimore from Cleveland in 1996 in the most controversial franchise relocation in NFL history. The Browns were beloved in Cleveland, but Art Modell was bleeding profusely in the checkbook because he was playing in run-down Cleveland Stadium and couldn't get the city to help him build a new one. The Browns were a cornerstone franchise of the NFL but had never won the Super Bowl. Their history was tarnished by crushing playoff losses, once to the Raiders when Brian Sipe threw a last-minute end zone interception on "Red Right 88" when a short 30-yard field goal would have won the game, and three times to John Elway and the

Broncos in the AFC championship game, the first time on "The Drive." But they didn't carry that baggage with them to Baltimore, which had been without an NFL football team from the time Colts owner Robert Irsay loaded up the Mayflower trucks in the middle of the night in 1984 and moved to Indianapolis. Baltimore had been passed over by the NFL when it expanded by two teams in 1995, losing out to Carolina and Jacksonville. The city was thrilled to have the Browns, now called the Ravens, and the state of Maryland financed a $220 million stadium right next to Camden Yards, the home of the baseball Orioles.

Billick was the NFL's hottest assistant after the 1998 season, when the Vikings' offense was racking up points like it was a video game. The NFL had put an expansion team back in Cleveland for the 1999 season. They would play in a beautiful new stadium on the site of the old Cleveland Municipal Stadium. If the city had built that stadium for Modell instead of an expansion team, he never would have moved. It was ironic that the new Browns and the old Browns each wanted Billick. He chose the old Browns and went to Baltimore. The Browns hired Chris Palmer, who turned out to be the first of six head coaches they would have in their first thirteen years back in the league.

Billick's premonition about never winning the Super Bowl again turned out to be spot-on. He also never got to test Walsh's theory about being in one place ten years because he was fired after nine. The ramifications of getting fired stretch way beyond the head coach. It changes the life of his family. A new coach generally brings in his own staff of assistants, maybe keeping one or two from the previous regime to help in the transition. Those fired coaches have families, too. Now they are going to have to relocate. The wives have to find new jobs and make new friends. The kids have to go to new schools. Maybe some of their children have special needs and have found schools tailored to suit those needs. Now they have to leave all that behind.

It's a cutthroat business, a results business. Win and you stay.

Lose and you leave. The good ones get to pay down the mortgage for five or six years before moving on. The bad ones are better off if they rent.

Billick was one of the good ones. He made it nine years with the Ravens. He did make a mistake after the Super Bowl when Dilfer, a free agent, was not re-signed. Billick wanted more from his quarterback, but Dilfer was popular in the locker room and did a lot for team chemistry. Dilfer is the only quarterback to win the Super Bowl and then not be asked back. It was a flawed decision. Billick first wanted Brad Johnson—they had been together in Minnesota. But Johnson signed with Tampa and won a Super Bowl in 2002. Instead, Billick signed Elvis Grbac, which turned out to be a big mistake.

The Ravens' management team of Billick, Ozzie Newsome, and James Harris didn't think it was realistic to expect that the defense could have another historic season and that the Ravens would run the ball as well. "We needed productivity at the quarterback position," Billick said.

In 2001, Baltimore finished three games behind the Steelers in the AFC Central with a 10–6 record. They beat Miami in the wild-card round but then lost in Pittsburgh in the divisional round. Grbac retired after one season with the Ravens, which began a revolving door at quarterback for Billick from Jeff Blake to Kyle Boller, Anthony Wright, and Steve McNair. Baltimore made the playoffs again in 2003 and 2006 but didn't win a playoff game. The 2006 team was a huge disappointment. The Ravens were 13–3 and the AFC's number two seed. Billick hired his good friend Jim Fassel, the former Giants coach, as his offensive coordinator, but that relationship deteriorated and the Ravens' offense took off after Billick and Fassel had a falling out. Early in the season Fassel left the team, either on his own or he was fired, depending whether Billick or Fassel is telling the story. Billick started calling plays again, and he and Fassel have not spoken since.

In the Ravens' divisional-round game at home, they held Peyton Manning and the Colts without a touchdown but lost 15–13. It hurt even more the next day when the Patriots won in San Diego. If the Ravens had defeated the Colts, they would have hosted the AFC championship game. Baltimore football fans were not happy that the Ravens had been eliminated by the team that had abandoned their city. After the season, Ravens owner Steve Bisciotti, who had purchased 49 percent of the team from Modell in 2000 and in 2004 exercised his option to buy the remaining 51 percent, gave Billick a new four-year contract.

That gave him security even though he had yet to fulfill offensive expectations or find a quarterback. The new contract apparently provided Billick with another grace period. Bisciotti certainly wouldn't have committed to him for that long if he wasn't planning to stick with him for at least two years. But the Ravens fell apart in 2007. They started off 4–2 and then lost nine games in a row, including a crushing 27–24 loss to the Patriots when it looked like Baltimore was going to end New England's unbeaten string at 11–0. Two weeks after losing to an undefeated team, the Ravens lost to the winless Dolphins, who were 0–13. Even so, Billick looked safe.

One week before the end of the season, he said he met with Newsome and Bisciotti and the Ravens owner assured him he would return in 2008. They outlined what the Ravens needed to do to get better. The plan, according to Billick, did not include hiring a new head coach. The Ravens then ended their season by defeating the hated Steelers. Billick was convinced that Bisciotti was giving him another chance.

"Bill Cowher didn't go to the playoffs in year seven, eight, and nine, but his organization stuck with him," Billick said. "Then he came out of it, as typically will happen, and ended up being rewarded with a Super Bowl. That's very rare. Most organizations will bail on you at that point, and you recognize that."

Billick came to work at the Ravens' beautiful complex in

Owings Mills, Maryland, the Monday morning after the season ended. He was already making plans for the off-season. He knew he had to hire an offensive coordinator because Rick Neuheisel had accepted the head coaching job at UCLA. "I was ready to hit the road and hire a couple of staff members," Billick said.

Newsome, who'd had a great career as a tight end with the Browns and was inducted into Canton in 1999, accompanied Modell when he moved the team to Baltimore. He was the first African-American general manager in NFL history when he was promoted in 2002. He was very good at his job.

Billick had his morning cup of coffee in his hand when he walked into Newsome's office. He was about to detail his plans for the week and go over staff hirings.

"Brian," Newsome said. "Steve is going to come in. He's decided to make a change."

Billick was shocked and actually mad at himself for being surprised. "I was emotionally floored because I wasn't prepared for it," he said. "It caught me totally broadside."

He knew what kind of business this was. He knew he was coming off a horrible season. Yet firing a coach one year into a four-year contract? Not many owners would be willing to eat that kind of money. He had won thirteen games the previous year. He had won a Super Bowl. That should have been enough collateral, but he had run out of the benefit of the doubt. In a way, he had lasted longer than perhaps he could have expected. Bisciotti was not the man who hired him. Modell was. Coaches like to handpick their quarterbacks. Owners like to handpick their coaches. Billick was Modell's guy. Bisciotti inherited him.

Billick wasn't convinced that Newsome had endorsed Bisciotti's decision. In their conversations the previous week, Bisciotti told Billick and Newsome that he had faith that among the three of them, two of them were always going to be right in any given situation. Billick thought of that exchange when Newsome told him he was about to be fired.

"I was half joking with Ozzie that I know I don't think I should be fired and you don't think I should be fired and that our two-thirds majority doesn't seem to be holding water," he said.

Bisciotti kept Billick waiting a couple of hours. He didn't come into the office until early afternoon. Bisciotti's office was at the other end of the building. When Billick was summoned, he made the long walk alone, but he had company. He was not the first coach to win the Super Bowl and be fired. George Seifert won two Super Bowls with the 49ers after he took over for Bill Walsh but was let go two seasons after winning the second one. Mike Ditka, a legend in Chicago, won a Super Bowl but later was fired. It would happen to Jon Gruden after the 2008 season, just six years after Tampa had given up two first-round picks and $8 million to the Raiders to get him out of his contract and he won the Super Bowl in his first season with the Bucs.

The meeting between Billick and Bisciotti was over in five minutes. There was nothing to discuss. Bisciotti had made up his mind. It was time for a change.

"Steve made it very clear he had made his decision and this was what he was going to do," Billick said. "Here's your $18 million and now go away."

He remained on the Ravens' payroll for the next three years. "I just kept receiving my checks," he said.

Billick was in the process of building a house on the Chesapeake when he was fired. The house is now complete, and he's living in it. There's not a day that goes by that somebody in Baltimore doesn't thank Billick for winning that Super Bowl. It wasn't enough to give him lifetime immunity from the fate that brings down most coaches, but it allowed him to have the satisfaction of knowing he'd once reached the height of his profession.

"I have huge respect for Steve Bisciotti. It was a business decision," Billick said.

They've had several conversations since that day in Owings Mills when Bisciotti fired him. "He said at some point we will sit down and have a glass of wine in that new house of yours," Billick said.

Billick had the perfect response. "It's the least I can do, because you're paying for it."

Billick's résumé is impressive enough that he deserves another chance to be a head coach. Coaches who have accomplished a lot less have been given an opportunity to try to learn from their mistakes and get better the second time. Norv Turner is on his third job in San Diego after failing in Washington and Oakland. He is the most ridiculed head coach in the last fifteen years. But each year as coaches were getting fired and coaches were getting hired, Billick was not getting a serious nibble. He's had a couple of teams call, but it didn't go very far. He didn't like what he was hearing. He was never brought in for an interview.

"I guess having the ring gave me more latitude to more objectively size it up," he said. "When you are a coordinator and you desperately want to become a head coach, you say, well, if the right people and the right situation, and then Charles Manson could offer you a job and you'd take it. You convince yourself of that. Fortunately, because of my circumstance, because of the ring, because of the contract, I didn't need to convince myself of that. I could look at it with a much more objective set of eyes."

But not even Daniel Snyder or Al Davis offered him a head coaching job, and they changed coaches the way most people change their socks. Eric Mangini was fired by the Jets the day after the 2008 season, and by the end of the week he was hired by the Cleveland Browns. Chan Gailey got a second chance with the Bills. Romeo Crennel is on his second job in Kansas City. Jeff Fisher was given a new opportunity in St. Louis. Billick hasn't come close to a second head coaching job.

Billick is not for everyone. He's strong-willed and opinionated. He felt coaches who were on the bubble were threatened by his presence when he visited their facilities to prepare to do their games on network television. "I've been told that," he said. "Besides the fact that I am an arrogant asshole."

He might have been better off staying away from the game for a year like Fisher and Mike Shanahan, who each sat out one season and then had no trouble being hired. Billick believes his time to be an NFL head coach has passed. "I can't imagine the circumstances at this point," he said. "It's a general manager's league now. What they are looking for in the head coach is not what I represent, at least in their minds, in terms of that partnership. They are looking for the guru, the genius, go craft up the game plan, don't talk to me about personnel, don't ask about the cap."

Billick has his ring; he has his house. He was paid $18 million not to coach. He did well for himself.

Mike Shanahan had not been given much of a chance by Al Davis, which didn't necessarily make him unique, although it did make him bitter.

Davis, who always considered himself the smartest football man on the planet, reached outside the Raiders organization in 1988 to hire Shanahan, who was the most desirable coaching assistant in the NFL. He had made a name for himself for his work with John Elway, and the Broncos were coming off consecutive Super Bowl appearances. Okay, so the Broncos were outscored 39–20 by the Giants and 42–10 by the Redskins in those Super Bowls, but Shanahan, as Elway's mentor and offensive coordinator, had helped develop the immensely talented quarterback into the most dangerous offensive player in the league.

Davis had a reputation for interviewing candidates with the intention of picking their brains and no intention of hiring them. Davis, even as he lost his touch with personnel, which turned his "Commitment to Excellence" from a team motto into utter nonsense, still realized there was a lot to gain in the interview process with each candidate. Just about every coach worth a damn has at one time interviewed with Davis—Bill Belichick was nearly fitted for a silver and black hoodie before Davis hired Jon Gruden in 1998—or turned down the opportunity to interview with him or simply turned down a job offer from him, as Sean Payton did in 2004 before going to Hurricane Katrina–ravaged New Orleans two years later.

Davis had transformed the Raiders into such a mess that Payton decided to go to a team with no tradition and a city under water and undergoing a massive rebuilding job rather than become another statistic—coaches who have had their careers sidetracked or even destroyed working for Davis.

Shanahan was a rising star in the late '80s, and stealing him away from the Broncos, a hated rival in the AFC West, made him a perfect hire for Davis. It was also a rarity for Davis because Shanahan had no connection to the Raiders' once-proud legacy. "I was the first that hadn't been with the organization," Shanahan said. "So that was unique at that time. When I came in there, everybody had been a disciple of the Raiders. So that was quite a step for me."

He then added, "I only lasted a year and four games."

Shanahan was a few months short of his thirty-sixth birthday when he got the job and a few months past his thirty-seventh when he lost it. In between, he was 7–9 in his first season and had a 1–3 start in his second year. Hell, even Rich Kotite lasted longer with the Jets; he was 3–13 in his first year in 1995 and gone after going 1–15 in his second. Was it all Kotite's fault? Bill Parcells came in the next year and put together a 9–7 season with mostly the same personnel, losing out to the Dolphins on a tiebreaker for the final wild-card spot on the last day of the season.

If getting fired from his first NFL head coaching job wasn't bad enough for Shanahan, he contended that Davis never paid him $250,000 he was owed on his contract or even donated the money to Oakland's public schools as Shanahan requested when

Davis refused to write the check directly to him. Their parting was contentious.

That was not unusual when it came to Davis and his coaches. When he fired Lane Kiffin in 2008, it also came after just twenty games. It ended with Davis holding a bizarre press conference in which he blamed Kiffin for just about everything but the national debt. Kiffin was 5–15 in his short stay in Oakland. Shanahan was 8–12. At the time Kiffin was dumped, Shanahan couldn't help getting in a dig at Davis.

"I was a little disappointed, to be honest with you," he said. "When you take a look at it, I was there 582 days. Lane Kiffin was there 616 days. So what it really means is that Al Davis liked Lane more than he liked me. I really don't think it's fair. I won three more games, yet he got thirty-four more days of work. That just doesn't seem right."

After Davis decided that Shanahan was not for him early in the 1989 season, Shanahan went back to Denver right away to work for Dan Reeves and with Elway again for a few years. But he had a falling out with Reeves, who fired him after the 1991 season because he felt he was scheming behind his back with Elway. Shanahan was hired by the 49ers to be their offensive coordinator. Not a bad job. Steve Young, who was in his second season after taking over for Joe Montana, was on his way to a Hall of Fame career.

The 49ers won the Super Bowl in 1994, and contributing to the championship in San Francisco was sweet for Shanahan after those lopsided Broncos losses to the Giants and Redskins.

Still, the Vince Lombardi Trophy might not have been as satisfying to Shanahan as the mythical Al Davis Trophy he won on the opening Monday night of the 1994 season in San Francisco when the 49ers hosted the Raiders. That was the game in which Jerry Rice scored three touchdowns and broke the immortal Jim Brown's record for career touchdowns.

The 49ers were coming off back-to-back NFC championship game losses to the Cowboys and were considered a strong Super

Bowl contender once again. The Raiders were playoff contenders but not in the 49ers' class. The 49ers-Raiders games always had added intensity, even in 1994, the Raiders' last year in Los Angeles before they moved back to Oakland.

Shanahan had been gone from the Raiders for five years by then, but he was still burned by how Davis had treated him. And for one brief terrifying moment before the kickoff, he actually thought he had ordered Davis's execution. "So, before the game, we are warming up. Al has got a way of coming out to about the 30-, 35-yard line, out on the numbers," he said.

Davis was on the 49ers' side of the 50 in his trademark white sweat suit and black patent leather shoes. Sometimes you wondered if the man owned any clothes other than the business suits he wore in the courtroom and Raiders sweat suits he wore for every other occasion. Davis was looking over the 49ers' players during the warm-ups, trying to find an edge of any kind he could relay to his coaches. It might have been forty years since he was a coach, and a pretty good one, but he knew more football than any owner in the league. His presence was felt by the Niners' players during the warm-ups. They came up to Shanahan and said Davis shouldn't be allowed to stand so close to them. Young, in particular, was aggravated by Davis's presence.

"Guys, we'll win the game, don't worry about it. Don't let him bother you," Shanahan said.

He knew Davis was trying to distract his players. Davis, though not a big man, had an imposing presence. He was a legend of the game and a mysterious man at that. The end of the 49ers' pregame drill took them back to their own 5-yard line. Davis was standing 35 yards away. "We are running plays left and running plays to the right. All of a sudden everybody is chirping in my ear," Shanahan said.

"Hey, get him out of there," the players said to Shanahan.

"Guys, just concentrate on the game. We beat them, all that stuff will take care of itself," he said.

But Shanahan was pissed at Davis for disrupting his pregame routine. And surely he was still pissed at him for not paying him the $250,000.

"Now I started thinking. Okay, so we got one more play left," Shanahan said.

Shanahan is telling this story seated behind his desk at Redskins Park. It's a quiet spring day, but suddenly he's animated. On the sideline, Shanahan's face gets red, and it looks like the veins are about to pop out of his neck when he gets mad. But off the field, you rarely see his emotional side. He's mild-mannered. He doesn't raise his voice. He tries to not to show too much of himself. But he was talking about Davis now. He had no use for Davis. Davis had embarrassed him by firing him almost without giving him a chance, and during that pregame Shanahan wanted to put a scare into his nemesis.

Shanahan came up with the idea of how to send Davis back to his side of the field and needed one of his quarterbacks to be his accomplice. Young said he was more than happy to oblige. "Al was in the way," Young said. "It's our field."

Shanahan was reluctant to reveal the identity of the quarterback who threw the ball that sent Davis flying. First, he said it was Steve Bono, but by 1994, Bono was in Kansas City. Then he said it was Elvis Grbac, who was Young's backup. Shanahan went out of his way to say it wasn't Young. He didn't want to distract him, he said. Young admitted, somewhat sheepishly, that it indeed was him. Young said Shanahan was just trying to protect him. They are close friends.

"Throw a go route," Shanahan told Young. "If you happen to hit that guy in the white outfit with the ball, you won't make me mad."

The receiver was Rice. He ran the go route.

Shanahan didn't really want to drill Davis. But if it happened, maybe he would never stand on the 49ers' side of the field again. Of course, if he hit Davis, Shanahan would never get his $250,000.

Young dropped back to pass. He threw the ball in Davis's direction. Rice, whom Shanahan did not bring into the loop on this little bit of mischief, was running downfield, looking up for the ball. He was not looking at Davis. He didn't see Davis. Shanahan saw the ball. He saw the receiver. He saw Davis. All three were about to occupy the same spot. Shanahan thought Davis saw the ball coming. He did not. "He's looking at our offensive and defensive linemen," Shanahan said.

Young threw a perfect pass. Rice was going for it. Davis was oblivious.

"Oh, my God," Shanahan said. "I wanted to scare him. I didn't want to kill him."

The ball and the receiver were closing in on Davis. "Al realizes that the ball and everybody is coming at him about five yards before there is going to be contact," Shanahan said. "I think he's going to be run over. And he dives; he actually dives out of the way. Well, half of our players see what happens, and they are all laughing."

Young drilled Davis in the leg. It was not surprising that he found his target. Young completed 64.3 percent of his passes in his career and has the third highest passer rating in NFL history. "Ten years after this happened, I was walking out of a stadium on a Monday night, and Al came up to me," Young said. "He told me that he knew it was me."

Young told Davis that he was ashamed of himself, more so than with anything else he had ever done. He then sent him a letter of apology.

Shanahan is so fired up that he gets out of his seat to finish the story. He loves this story. It was revenge. He explains in great detail Davis diving on the grass at Candlestick Park, getting to his feet, his hair falling down in front of his face. Shanahan just can't stop laughing. Davis stared him down from 35 yards away and gave him the middle finger.

Fuck you.

"Our team goes crazy," Shanahan said. "Everybody is laughing. Al is looking right back at the huddle, knowing it's intentional."

Shanahan's only concern once he realized Davis was indeed alive was not letting his personal feelings about Davis interfere with the game. As it turned out, he had nothing to worry about. The 49ers won 44–14. After beating the Chargers 49–26 in Super Bowl XXIX, Shanahan was on his way back to Denver as the head coach to work with Elway. This time, he would last a lot longer than he did with the Raiders before he was fired. He won two Super Bowls, which did not impress Davis.

"Shanahan has an asterisk next to those two Super Bowls, because they were caught cheating," Davis said.

The Broncos indeed were fined in 2001 for reported infractions concerning deferred payments to Elway and Terrell Davis for circumventing the salary cap between 1996 and 1998, during which time the Broncos won their Super Bowls.

"I don't think I have to go down that road anymore," Shanahan said in response to Davis's comments.

The strength of the relationship between the millionaire and billionaire owners and their head coaches is often a direct reflection of wins and losses. When Shanahan was winning Super Bowls and getting the Broncos to the playoffs just about every year, you heard about his tight bond with Denver owner Pat Bowlen. But when things went bad in 2008 and Denver fell apart down the stretch, turning an 8–5 first-place record into an 8–8 nonplayoff year, Bowlen decided to fire his friend.

Shanahan's shelf life eventually expired in Denver. And his next stop was working for the mercurial Daniel Snyder.

On the opposite side of the table where the coach sits when he's told to pack his bags and take his playbook with him is the rich owner doing the firing. It's never a pleasant experience, but Daniel Snyder of the Redskins is really good at it. After buying the team in 1999, he fired Norv Turner, Marty Schottenheimer, and Jim Zorn; didn't bring back interim coach Terry Robiskie; and had Steve Spurrier quit after two years and Joe Gibbs go back into retirement after four years. By the time he hired Shanahan in 2010, it was his seventh head coach in twelve years. During exactly the same period, Andy Reid was the only coach of the division rival Eagles. The Giants had two. The Cowboys had five, but then again, Jerry Jones is Snyder's role model.

Finding common ground with his coaches has not been an easy thing for Snyder. He tortured Turner; ran off Schottenheimer; made a bad decision on Spurrier; revered Gibbs as a kid growing up in Silver Spring, Maryland; had no respect for Zorn; and allowed Shanahan to try to re-create the magic he had in Denver with Elway. Shanahan made a mistake trading for Donovan McNabb his first year, made a bigger mistake trying to get through the 2011 season with Rex Grossman and John Beck, and then traded three first-round picks and a second-round pick to move up four spots in the 2012 draft to position the Redskins to take Baylor's Robert Griffin III, the Heisman Trophy winner. Elway won two Super Bowls playing for Shanahan. Jay Cutler was starting to develop in Denver when Shanahan was fired. Griffin gives Snyder hope that the future is secure at the most important position.

Snyder has developed a reputation as a meddling owner to be avoided if longevity and continuity are high on the list of a coach's goals. Snyder pays well but has a reputation of being impossible to work with for any length of time before he sends his coach running for the exits.

He was just a baby when he bought the Redskins and Jack Kent Cooke Stadium in May 1999 for $800 million. Snyder is a college dropout and a self-made American success story. He was thirty-three years old when he joined the exclusive NFL ownership fraternity. He got his financial empire started by leasing jets to fly college students to spring break. He initially was to be the minority partner in the purchase of the Redskins after his group had won a bidding war. But majority owner Howard Milstein withdrew the bid, knowing NFL owners were going to turn him down on the basis of the debt structure. Snyder then put together his own group in which he had controlling interest, which was approved by the NFL. He never would have been satisfied as Milstein's minority partner. That's not his personality.

Snyder had a lot to learn when he bought the Redskins. He was a football fan but had no football background. But early on he was so involved in every aspect of the franchise that it seemed only a matter of time before he was coaching the team himself. He has learned how important it is for the owner to be supportive of his head coach rather than undermine him. "You trust him, he trusts you, you can accomplish a lot," he said.

It was too late in the off-season and too close to training camp when Snyder's bid to buy the Redskins was approved for him to do anything about Turner. At his first home game after he bought the team, Snyder said there were signs imploring him to fire Turner. "I was overwhelmed," he said in his office in Redskins Park. "I was a pure fan, and I was a little young."

Snyder couldn't wait to get the first notch on his belt. His trigger finger was antsy, but Turner ruined his plan. He won the NFC East in Snyder's first year with a 10–6 record, the first time the Redskins had been in the playoffs since 1992, Gibbs's final year. Then the Redskins beat the Lions in a wild-card game but lost in the next round in Tampa 14–13. The Redskins had a chance to win, but a botched snap on a field goal attempt from 51 yards with just over one minute remaining prevented the ball from getting into the air. Even so, the Redskins had something to build on.

Snyder then went out and tried to buy the Super Bowl. He signed Deion Sanders and Bruce Smith, two Hall of Famers whose best football had already been played. He signed safety Mark Carrier. Then he created a quarterback controversy by bringing in Jeff George to compete with Brad Johnson, who had just taken the 'Skins to the second round of the playoffs. Snyder wrote checks for over $40 million in signing bonuses. The Redskins also had the second and third overall picks in the 2000 draft. After the Browns selected Penn State defensive end Courtney Brown, the Redskins picked linebacker LaVar Arrington from Penn State and offensive tackle Chris Samuels from Alabama. Snyder and the Redskins had created a tremendous buzz around Washington and throughout the NFL.

That put the pressure on Turner to work all those new players into the team, not let a quarterback controversy split the locker room, and, of course, win games, get the Redskins into the playoffs again, and this time take them further than the second round. Snyder made it even more difficult for Turner by transforming training camp into an easy opportunity for opponents to scout the Redskins. The Redskins became the first team to charge admission to watch training camp practice. The price: $10 for anybody fourteen or older. The NFL has a rule that teams can't scout camp practices or scrimmages unless there is an admission fee. Then anybody can attend. There have been stories over the years about how teams spy on one another's training camp practices, but spying was not necessary with the Redskins in 2000. For $10, everybody was welcome, including opposing scouts, and teams did take advantage of the opportunity of seeing Washington up close.

Predictably, the Redskins were a disaster in 2000. Snyder couldn't wait until the season was over and allow Turner to leave in a dignified way. He fired him with three games remaining in an 8–8 season. Turner was 7–6 when he received his parting gifts. "I didn't hire him," Snyder said.

That led Snyder to hire Schottenheimer, an old-school coach with old-school values. Hard work. Discipline. Marty Ball. Snyder gave him total control, and Schottenheimer went 8–8. After the season, Snyder decided that giving all the power to one person was not in his best interests. Schottenheimer had the power and didn't want to give it up. There was only one thing for Snyder to do. He fired Schottenheimer.

"I like Marty and still do to this day. We are good friends," Snyder said nearly ten years later. "He'd still be here if he didn't want to do it all. He was insistent on doing it all. That was something that I don't think works. One guy can't do everything. He was a machine on that front. He wouldn't drop the personnel side and give us a chance at more of a team energy."

Snyder was going back on the deal. When he hired Schottenheimer, he gave him the control. Now he was taking it back. "I saw it for a year and said that is not going to work," he said.

Snyder had to pay for his decision. Schottenheimer was just one year into a four-year $10 million deal. Snyder was responsible for the $7.5 million left on the contract. It didn't take Schottenheimer long to bounce back from any scars he might have incurred from getting fired by a man a generation younger. He was hired immediately by the Chargers, and that reduced Snyder's financial obligations.

Snyder now had some work to do. That was two coaches fired—three if you want to count interim coach Terry Robiskie, who was not given the job permanently after Turner was dismissed. Who would be the next to make lots of money and be miserable?

Steve Spurrier, come on down. The University of Florida coach, a former NFL quarterback, was considered an offensive genius, so creative that not even the best defensive minds in the league would be able to stop him. Spurrier loved to be courted and had turned down the Tampa Bay Bucs' overtures in 1996 after Jimmy Johnson elected to go to the Dolphins and before the Bucs hired Tony Dungy. He had turned down Snyder the year before when Snyder hired Schottenheimer. Snyder was offering a five-year $25 million contract, and Spurrier signed on with full confidence that his Fun 'n' Gun offense could work in the NFL. "There is no doubt in my mind," he said.

Besides, he needed a job. He had unexpectedly resigned from Florida a couple of weeks earlier. Now he was Snyder's fourth coach in thirteen months. Spurrier ridiculed NFL coaches who felt they had to see the sun come up in the morning out their office window or they were not doing their job. "I like to believe I can spend two hours and get as much done maybe as some coaches do in four or five hours," he said.

He liked to needle opposing teams and coaches. Peyton Manning could never beat Florida, and when he elected to return to Tennessee for his final season, Spurrier couldn't help himself. "Peyton Manning came back to win the Citrus Bowl again," he said. "You can't spell Citrus without the UT."

The ol' ball coach, as he was known, lasted two seasons in Washington. He liked to play golf, and that was hard to do in November in Washington. He didn't care about defense, which is something that needs to be played in the NFL. He was outcoached. He wanted out so badly, he gave up the remaining three years on his contract. He left $15 million on the table and a 12–20 record as his legacy. He couldn't cut it against the big boys.

"I'll tell you this," Snyder said. "Spurrier is a heckuva guy. The NFL stumped him."

Snyder was reeling. He had a proven winner in Schottenheimer and forced him out in a power struggle. Spurrier was a coveted college coach, but that often doesn't translate into success in the pro game. "I took a chance, and I think everyone respected the chance I took," Snyder said. "I don't regret taking the chance trying to get Spurrier. He was a cool guy. I still get along with him."

Snyder then went for a can't-miss with Redskins fans. He brought back the legendary Joe Gibbs. He had retired after the 1992 season, and now it was 2004. Gibbs won three Super Bowls in Washington with three different quarterbacks and was still revered by the passionate Redskins fans. The issue was whether Gibbs had lost his fastball after all the years in the NASCAR pits. He stayed four years, made the playoffs twice, and was gone.

"We were very close in '05 to going all the way," Snyder said. "In '07, we went to the same place, Seattle, in the rain. Joe felt if we got through Seattle in '07 and '05, we might win the whole thing."

That was a bit of revisionist history. Or wishful thinking. The Redskins beat the Bucs in 2005 and lost in Seattle in the divisional round. If they had won that game, they would have played in Carolina in the NFC championship game. In 2007, the Redskins lost in the wild-card round to the Seahawks. If they had won that game, they would have played in Dallas and then played either the Packers or the Giants in the next round. In each case, they were a long way from the Super Bowl.

After the loss to the Seahawks after the 2007 season, Gibbs left the Redskins again. Snyder was devastated. He idolized Gibbs. "It was a spectacular experience," he said.

Snyder turned on all his charm in a futile attempt to talk Gibbs into coaching the fifth and final year of his contract. "I joked around with Joe at the end," Gibbs said. "You can't quit. He said, I'm not. I'm retiring. I pleaded with him not to retire. I love him. We are very close."

If Snyder had not been able to talk Gibbs out of retirement in 2004, he was close to hiring Jim Fassel, who had just been fired by the Giants. It almost happened again after Gibbs left, and this time the story got strange even by Snyder standards. After Gibbs had left, Snyder promoted Vinny Cerrato, his right-hand man, to be general manager and executive vice president of football operations. He had been with Snyder every year except the season Schottenheimer was in charge. When something went wrong, Snyder had an easy out. He blamed Cerrato. That would come in handy.

In the weeks after Gibbs retired, Snyder hired Jim Zorn, the quarterback coach for Mike Holmgren in Seattle, to be Washington's offensive coordinator. Snyder made that hire even though he didn't have a head coach. Fassel, who already had interviewed with Snyder and Cerrato, was so sure he was getting the head coaching job that he started to gather his belongings in Phoenix for the move to Washington. All that seemed to be in Fassel's way was Giants defensive coordinator Steve Spagnuolo, who just finished an incredible playoff run when New York's defense shut down Tony Romo and Brett Favre in the NFC playoffs and then held Tom Brady and the Patriots' record-breaking offense to 14 points in the Super Bowl. Snyder was not going to make any decisions until he had a chance to interview Spagnuolo.

Once the Giants returned from the Super Bowl, Snyder interviewed Spagnuolo for a total of twenty-eight hours. But Snyder already had hired Zorn as the offensive coordinator. Head coaches like to hire their own staff, but Snyder was caught off guard by Gibbs's retirement and felt he needed to start assembling a staff before all the quality assistants were off the market. Spagnuolo decided to return to the Giants. Snyder and Cerrato asked Fassel to speak to Zorn to see if he would be a good fit on his staff. While that was going on, there was a lot of negative feedback in Washington regarding what appeared to be the imminent coronation of Fassel, who had not been offered a head coaching job in the four hiring cycles after he was fired by the Giants following the 2003 season.

"We went through staffing. My fingerprints are all over that staff. We were framing a contract," Fassel said. "I didn't know it at the time, but Vinny knows and likes Zorn, and they had been close friends for a long time. Once Zorn got there and they had time on their hands, he is an engaging guy. Very glib, polished."

After Spagnuolo turned down the job, Snyder and Cerrato decided to interview Zorn to replace Gibbs. He was the tenth and final candidate to be interviewed. He was already in the building, so why not?

"We conducted a full search and ended up with the right guy," Snyder said after he hired Zorn.

After two disastrous seasons in which Zorn managed to win twelve of thirty-two games—the same record as Spurrier—

Snyder fired Zorn, and Cerrato resigned. Zorn was not ready to be a head coach. Snyder had to blame somebody. Instead of admitting he'd had the ultimate authority and made a mistake, he blamed Cerrato.

"The mistake he made is, this is where I learned a lot, the general manager needs to prevent the owner from hiring someone who's not qualified," Snyder said. "And that's why Vinny is no longer here, to be truthful with you. He's not here because his job was to prevent the owner from hiring a not-qualified coach. Having said that, we went in and had the worst two-year experience I ever dreamed. I apologized, according to my wife, ten thousand times. I apologize openly. I made a big mistake. It's a terrible experience when you know you got the wrong guy to lead the franchise."

Snyder then hired Bruce Allen, the former GM of the Bucs and the son of Redskins legendary coach George Allen, as general manager and Shanahan as coach. Snyder liked Shanahan from the first time he met him at the Pro Bowl after the 1999 season, the first year he owned the team. Snyder brought his parents, his wife, and his kids and was staying at the Four Seasons in Honolulu. One day walking around he bumped into Shanahan, then the Broncos' coach, who had struggled to a 6–10 record in the first season after Elway retired. Shanahan and Snyder had a few beers. They had dinner a couple of nights later. They were always friendly at the league meetings and sat near each other.

Snyder fired Zorn one year after Shanahan was fired in Denver. Shanahan sat out the 2009 season and was a natural fit for Snyder. He was also available. Shanahan spoke on the phone with Gibbs for ninety minutes before he took the job. "My job is to help the coach any way I can and support him," Snyder said.

Snyder has tremendous passion for the Redskins but hasn't figured out the right formula for success. Until the Redskins get to a Super Bowl, he will be viewed as a rich kid owner who has no idea how to win. He is the steward of one of the NFL's most treasured franchises, and he has a responsibility to reward the Redskins' loyal fans.

He has grown up in the years since he joined the NFL's exclusive ownership club in 1999. Both he and his wife, Tanya, are cancer survivors. He was diagnosed with thyroid cancer in 2001, and the *New York Times* reported that he underwent an eight-hour operation at the Mayo Clinic in Rochester, Minnesota, and now has a faint scar at the base of his neck. Tanya was diagnosed with breast cancer in 2008. She told the *Times* she underwent two operations for early-stage breast cancer one year apart. Tanya Snyder had been active in breast cancer awareness before she was diagnosed and later became the NFL spokeswoman for National Breast Cancer Awareness Month.

Snyder has faced difficult challenges that have helped put things in perspective.

"I'm a lot older now. I've had cancer, my wife had cancer. We have plenty of kids," Snyder said, sitting in his office. "It matures you. When you are young and full of energy and enthusiasm, you make mistakes."

If he keeps making them, he has a solution: You're fired.

THE JOY OF REX

Rex Ryan was leaning against a wall outside the fashionable Fairmont Hotel in New Orleans after his second season as coach of the New York Jets. Right off Canal Street and a few blocks from the famed French Quarter, the Fairmont is the hotel the NFL often uses for one of the teams when the Super Bowl is played at the Superdome. The lobby was crawling with NFL royalty as the billionaire owners and millionaire coaches were checking in at the front desk for the annual league meetings.

The NFL was in the middle of a 136-day lockout. The doom and gloomers were predicting that the 2011 season would be wiped out, but there was Rex just being Rex, which is what makes him so much fun and so different from all the other coaches in the league. The Jets had made it to the AFC championship game in each of his first two seasons, and now Ryan was predicting bigger things for the 2011 season, assuming there was a 2011 season. In the process of talking up his team, he somehow found a way to compare himself to Babe Ruth.

In one memorable sentence, Ryan referenced Teddy Roosevelt and the Babe.

"They talk about walk softly and carry a big stick. I love that. I agree with that 100 percent," Ryan said. "But I guess I feel more like Babe Ruth. I'm going to walk softly, I'm going to carry that big stick, and then I'm going to point, and then I'm going to hit it over the fence."

Walk softly? Maybe. Talk softly? That wouldn't be Ryan.

Baseball legend has it that Ruth pointed to center field during an at bat in the fifth inning of the third game of the 1932 World Series and on the next pitch blasted the ball over the center field fence at Wrigley Field in Chicago. Up to the plate steps the Rexino.

"It's like he had the courage to do that. I think I've got the courage," Ryan said. "Now granted, I can't hit anywhere close to Babe Ruth and I'm not as good a coach as Babe Ruth was a player."

His Jets didn't have the Babe's back in 2011. They were too busy stabbing one another in the back as the locker room became dysfunctional and the team limped to the finish line with three straight losses to complete a disappointing 8–8 nonplayoff season.

By then, Ryan's annual declaration of greatness had turned him into the boy who cried wolf. Going into the 2009 playoffs, he insisted that the Jets should be the favorites to win it all. They won two playoff games on the road against the Bengals and Chargers and then lost the AFC championship game in Indianapolis. Going into the 2010 and 2011 seasons, he proclaimed the Jets would win it all. They came close again in 2010, winning road playoff games against the Colts and Patriots, beating all-time greats Peyton Manning and Tom Brady back to back, but then lost the AFC title game in Pittsburgh. Their 2011 meltdown and inner turmoil left Ryan questioning the way he handled the team; he admitted he was oblivious to the tension in the locker room.

On the day he was introduced as the Jets coach, he promised a trip to the White House for his team, and he wasn't referring to one of those tours where people line up for hours and never come close to meeting the president. He was talking about being the invited guests as Super Bowl champion. Ryan wanted it all for the Jets: the Oval Office, the Rose Garden, a green and white jersey for the president, the "J-E-T-S Jets Jets Jets" chant reverberating through the halls of the West Wing. Basically, Mr. Ryan Goes to Washington.

A few months after he took the job, Ryan woke up the Patriots in New England when he told Mike Francesa in an interview on WFAN in New York: "I never came here to kiss Bill Belichick's rings." Ryan's players loved it. A few weeks later Ryan said, "I'm not intimidated by anybody. Does that mean I am disrespecting Belichick? No. I think he's a hell of a football coach."

Ryan had waited a long time for his chance to become an NFL head coach, and he wasn't going to hold back. This could be his one and only chance. In 2008, he had interviewed with the Ravens, Falcons, and Dolphins. Even though he was the defensive coordinator on Baltimore's staff and had been with the Ravens for ten seasons, owner Steve Bisciotti, after firing Brian Billick, chose to go outside the organization and hire John Harbaugh. It was a blow to Ryan's ego, but he accepted Harbaugh's invitation to remain on the staff as the assistant head coach/defensive coordinator. Ryan had a good relationship with Bill Parcells, who was then running the Dolphins, and the Tuna and Ryan's father, Buddy, really went at it when Parcells was coaching the Giants and Ryan was coaching the Eagles. But Parcells didn't hire Rex in Miami. He chose Tony Sparano, who had worked for him in Dallas. (When Ryan needed a new offensive coordinator in 2012, he chose Sparano, who had just been fired after four seasons in Miami.) Atlanta went with Jacksonville defensive coordinator Mike Smith. He and Ryan had worked together for four years in Baltimore.

When was Ryan going to get his opportunity? He was a hot candidate after the 2008 season in a year the Ravens made it to the AFC championship game, losing in Pittsburgh. On a Sunday during the postseason, when NFL rules permit assistants on teams still alive in the playoffs to interview for head coaching jobs, Ryan packed two interviews into one day in Baltimore the morning after the Ravens upset the Titans in the divisional round in Nashville. He first met with the Rams at the Ravens' facility in Owings Mills, Maryland. The Jets contingent of owner Woody Johnson, general manager Mike Tannenbaum, and front office executives Scott Cohen and Joey Clinkscales had flown down on Johnson's private jet and was waiting for Ryan in a conference room at Baltimore/Washington International Airport. His meeting with the Rams had run long. Ryan could not be rude and get up and leave. When the Rams finally ran out of questions, he called the Jets to say he was "flying" on the highway to get to BWI. The New York job was the one he wanted.

"I was getting concerned that him being forty-five minutes late would make Woody agitated," Tannenbaum said.

Ryan was aware that you get one chance to make a first impression and being late for a job interview is not recommended. He walked into the conference room knowing he was fighting from behind. "I think I had to make up some ground initially," he said. "I was just myself. I felt comfortable."

He compiled a sixty-two-page brochure with a color picture of himself on the cover with the title:

Rex Ryan
Head Coaching Candidate
January 2009

The brochure was filled with testimonials from Ravens All Pro linebacker Ray Lewis and other players Ryan had coached. One page caught the attention of the Jets. It was a large picture of the Super Bowl ring he had won as a defensive assistant with the Ravens in 2000. The Jets' only Super Bowl came on January 12, 1969, when Buddy Ryan was the defensive coordinator and little Rex used to run around the practice field and hang out in the locker room. His interview with the Jets brass lasted three hours. Ryan left, and the Jets knew they had their man.

"Woody, what do you think?" Tannenbaum said.

"He's exactly what you said he would be," Johnson said.

Tannenbaum considered that a positive review.

The next week, the Ravens had barely pulled off their uniforms after the loss in Pittsburgh when the Jets offered Ryan their head coaching job. Shortly after they introduced him as their coach, the Jets presented Ryan with the Jets green warm-up jacket his father wore as an assistant coach. He felt an obligation to live up to the standards his father helped create in the Super Bowl year. The Jets knew he would be the face of the franchise, but they couldn't have known all that would come out of his mouth.

Ryan surely is his father's son. Buddy stirred it up as the defensive coordinator of the 1985 champion Bears, often feuding with volatile head coach Mike Ditka, and is still the only assistant coach ever carried off the field after the Super Bowl. If he was brash with the Bears, he was off the charts when he became head coach of the Eagles. Buddy Ryan spoke in headlines. His press conferences as a whole were relatively mundane, but he would slip in a line or two that would get his players or the opponent or the media fired up. He was considered dangerous by the competition because he just didn't care who he offended, and that appears to be a dominant gene he passed down to Rex and Rex's twin brother, Rob, a longtime NFL assistant coach. Buddy often would get on his own players publicly. He once called Bears defensive tackle William "Refrigerator" Perry, taken in the first round, a wasted draft pick. Rex never does that. Publicly, he is always supportive of his players.

"Obviously, the biggest mentor of my life would be my father, from a football standpoint, from being a dad," Rex said. "It was the football thing that probably bonded us more than anything. He is a guy I truly respect and love. We were the only kids growing up who never had a curfew. But if he said to be home at eleven, we were going to be home."

Ryan learned a lot about defense from his father, and he also learned to be true to himself and speak his mind even if that got him into trouble. The NFL is a buttoned-down league. So many head coaches are afraid to say which ankle the backup guard injured on special teams for fear of giving the other team too much information. Ryan starts off every one of his in-season press conferences by running down the injury report and actually gives useful information. Belichick in New England would rather give up the code to his bank account than hint at what might be ailing Tom Brady.

Ryan changed the atmosphere around the Jets. He took over for Eric Mangini, a Belichick clone who set the record for number of times putting the media to sleep. He wasn't much more entertaining in team meetings. There was a faction in the locker room that was happy to see him go when Johnson fired him after the 2008 season. Mangini's problem was that he tried too hard to be Belichick. As a result, he came off as Belichick Lite. He was trying to be somebody he was not. Ryan has stayed true to himself, which means he is going to be occasionally outrageous. He tends to overrate his players, thinking he has the best at every position, but they love him for it.

When Ryan was hired, it was culture shock for the Jets. Mangini had sucked the life out of the building with his paranoia. He even made Johnson feel uncomfortable, and Johnson was the man signing the checks. The same players who were brainwashed by Mangini and were afraid to speak their mind suddenly took on the personality of their new coach.

"More than anything, I try to be myself about how I feel about the team, about the direction of the team, and know what I believe are my principles of what I think it takes to be successful to win," Ryan said. "It is never going to change. I know what I believe in. I guess it comes off as being outspoken. It's hard to describe. That's just who I am. Being true to myself. I believe we can be a transparent organization. You are going to know more about us in good times and bad times. That's okay. This isn't rocket science."

Ryan has sworn off predicting any more Super Bowls for the Jets, but not because he has stopped believing in his team. He reluctantly acknowledges that predicting greatness put too much pressure on his players when his ultimate goal was to put the pressure on himself and take the focus off the players.

He is still surprised that more coaches don't stand up and say how they really feel. "I think the money you make in this business from coaching is so much more than it ever was," he said. "Everybody is trying to hold on to their jobs. I wasn't born into money. I never got into coaching for money. I got in for the competitiveness. I love competing. The money has just come with it. I never took the job to have security. I came to be a champion. I have no problem saying that is what I plan on doing. I have the courage to say it. If others don't, it does surprise me. I understand maybe that they are trying to hold on. The old saying is you undersell and overproduce. I don't believe in the undersell. Why would you coach? You are going to coach my team and you don't expect to win? Are you kidding me? What kind of leader is that? It sounds like a guy that has got no courage, no guts."

Transparency is not how NFL teams usually operate, not when coaches truly believe that if one little piece of unwanted information is made public, it can be the difference between making the playoffs and getting fired. After acquiring Tim Tebow, the Jets did not run the Wildcat offense in the 2012 preseason games to prevent their opponents from getting a sneak preview.

Ryan was in character as the star of *Hard Knocks* on HBO in the summer of 2010, dropping f-bombs for sixty minutes once a week for a month on national television. That turned off more traditional coaches such as Tony Dungy, and HBO bleeped out the curse words when it replayed the show in the afternoon. But in the evening, it was Rex Unplugged. He was foulmouthed. "I do a thousand interviews a year, and not one time did I ever cuss," he said.

It's just different when he's around his team. "This is how I talk to the football team in certain situations," he said. "I certainly wasn't going to change because *Hard Knocks* was there."

Ryan's language may have caused an uproar, so it's a good thing the cameras were not in the Jets' team meeting room the morning after they beat the Bucs during the 2009 regular season. Shutouts are very hard to come by in the NFL, but the Jets' defense was dominating Tampa and rookie quarterback Josh Freeman. The Jets won the game 26–3 for their third straight victory, improving their record to 7–6 and putting them in position to make the playoffs. Ryan still found something to be unhappy about. Linebacker Bart Scott's third-down unnecessary roughness penalty prolonged a Tampa drive in the third quarter, leading to a Bucs' field goal, their only points of the game.

"I messed up the shutout," Scott said.

Scott, who had played for Ryan in Baltimore, was the Jets' first free agent signing after Ryan was hired. They were like father and son, so Ryan knew he could handle good-natured teasing. Ryan stood at the podium with a plastic bag on his hand. It was a tradition he had brought with him from Baltimore.

"Everybody was like, what's in there?" Darrelle Revis said.

He put the bag on the podium. Ryan then announced, "The dumb dick award goes to Bart Scott. Come down and get it."

Revis is laughing so hard telling the story that he can barely talk. Ryan then revealed what was in the bag. It was a facsimile of a penis. "It was huge. Everybody was laughing like, wow, I've never seen something like that before," Revis said. "Bart came down and got it. It was hilarious."

Scott once received the award in Baltimore, so he knew it was coming. "It's all good," he said.

He put it in his locker. "I think somebody stole it," he said.

Rex Ryan knew when he was hired by the Jets that he had two formidable obstacles to overcome: the Giants in his city and the

Patriots in his division. He was considered one of the best defensive coaches in the league, a players' coach, but that doesn't always translate into being a very good head coach. The league is littered with successful assistants who reached the level of their competence as a lieutenant, but when they went out on their own, when they became the decision maker rather than the sounding board, they couldn't handle the job.

Ryan ultimately will be judged by Super Bowls, and the Jets knew that he was going to work hard at it. But he had fallen into the trap of coaches who lose their perspective when he was an assistant coach working for his father in the two years Buddy was the head coach of the Cardinals in 1994 and 1995. Rex was the defensive line coach his first year and the linebacker coach the second year before they all got fired because Arizona had only twelve wins in the two years. Rex and Rob were on the staff, and it was the first NFL job for each of them. Rex didn't want anybody thinking he was cutting corners or getting special treatment because his father was the head coach. His wife, Michelle, was a schoolteacher working in Kentucky and was pregnant with their second child. Michelle worked all the way up to her due date. Rex was finishing a minicamp in his first year with the team at the Cardinals' training facility in Tempe, Arizona, and then planned to join his wife in Kentucky and be with her when she went into labor. He feared that if he left minicamp, it would be a bad reflection on his father. "I never wanted any of that to come down on my dad," he said. "Babygate."

He remained in Arizona, but he knew that it was a huge risk and that he really should be with Michelle. "Most people wouldn't have even thought about it," he said. "But I'm a coach. A real coach."

Michelle was already ten days late and could have the baby any day. Ryan had a flight booked for the day after the minicamp concluded. The phone rang the night before. "I never realized how stupid I was," Ryan said. "My wife called, and her water broke."

Rex panicked. Michelle was by herself. Her parents were on

their way but not there yet. Ryan called Kevin Carty, one of his best friends. They coached together at Morehead State. Carty now lives in New Jersey and comes to a lot of Jets practices and games. He was within driving distance of Michelle. "Kevin, go get her," Ryan said frantically. It was two o'clock in the morning. "He drove her to the hospital," Ryan said. "I missed it by a day."

The Ryans already had a young son, Payton, named for Walter Payton, the Hall of Fame running back who played for the Bears when Buddy Ryan was an assistant in Chicago. Now they had a second son, Seth. It still bothers Rex that he missed the birth. "Seth is over it," he said. Rex said Michelle understood because Arizona represented their shot "to get out of Division 1-AA."

When Ryan took the Jets job, his sons were already teenagers. Payton was in high school and preferred to remain in the Baltimore area, living with Ryan's brother-in-law. It was tough on the family, but Michelle regularly went back and forth to see him. Ryan saw him only every now and then. Seth moved with his parents, and Ryan was a constant presence at his baseball and Friday night football games at Summit High School in New Jersey. In his rookie year, Jets rookie quarterback Mark Sanchez would show up to watch Seth play in his football games. Sanchez was basically the Ryans' third son, but without a bedroom in the house.

Ryan developed a close relationship with Sanchez as a rookie. The Jets fell in love with Sanchez, who had started only sixteen games at Southern California, when they worked him out two months before the 2009 draft. Before they put Sanchez through passing drills, the Jets had Kansas State's Josh Freeman rated ahead of him. After working out both, Ryan thought Sanchez had a better arm and was more accurate. He was also impressed that twenty-four receivers showed up at Sanchez's private workout for the Jets at his high school in Mission Viejo, California. Freeman had two receivers when the Jets worked him out at Kansas State. The start of a field hockey game on the high school field overlapped with Sanchez's workout, and both teams agreed to delay the game until Sanchez was finished. That showed the Jets the respect Sanchez had earned. He sealed the deal over dinner. He picked a Mexican restaurant and ordered for the table. He was sure of himself, even with Johnson there with them. As the Jets contingent left and piled into a car, Sanchez jumped on a motorcycle.

"Okay, guys, see you later," he said.

Teams live in fear of their players riding motorcycles, especially franchise quarterbacks. Ben Roethlisberger almost killed himself in an accident in the streets of Pittsburgh in 2006. Sanchez was only kidding. After Ryan did a double take, Sanchez got in his car. Ryan loves that kind of personality. On draft day, the Jets traded up from the number seventeen spot to the number five spot in a deal with Cleveland, which now was run by Mangini, who was hired by the Browns less than one week after the Jets fired him. The Jets gave up their first-round and second-round picks and three backup players: defensive end Kenyon Coleman, safety Abram Elam, and quarterback Brett Ratliff.

Through three seasons, Sanchez had not developed as quickly as the Jets hoped, and they created a quarterback controversy when they traded for Denver's Tim Tebow. The Jets insisted that Sanchez was still their guy, but they were challenging him by bringing in the most popular player in the NFL to be his backup.

Ryan worked hard teaching Sanchez what it meant to be a professional, and that certainly didn't include doing anything to embarrass the opposition. But the rookie quarterback tested the patience of the rookie coach.

Ryan was seated comfortably on the Jets' charter flight home from Oakland after a satisfying 38–0 victory in his first season, the most one-sided regular season home loss in Raiders history. The turbulence on the flight home had nothing to do with any rough air current. It came after Ryan learned about Sanchez snacking on the sideline during the game.

Ryan had settled into his seat in the front of the plane when he was told of Sanchez's antics. He had removed him in the fourth quarter with the game out of reach. These are the best times on an NFL winning sideline. Players clown around. They root for teammates who otherwise rarely get on the field except for special teams. Sanchez was just a rookie and had the Jets perplexed with his lack of maturity. He was twenty-two going on fifteen. He had a lot of growing up to do in the biggest market in the country. There was no escaping the scrutiny. After Ryan removed him from the Oakland game with the outcome secure, Sanchez realized he was hungry and could not wait for the snack waiting in the locker room or dinner on the plane. The television cameras caught Sanchez sitting on the bench eating a hot dog as if he were competing in the annual Nathan's contest in Coney Island on the Fourth of July. He had his head down and he was trying to hide the hot dog. Sanchez was just a kid, and he was hungry. It remains a mystery how he acquired the hot dog. If he had gone into the stands in full uniform and bought it from a vendor, he probably would have been noticed as he walked up the aisle. He had a co-conspirator in the great hot dog caper and wasn't about to reveal that person's name. In the world of supersized egos that get insulted easily, this was worse than Kurt Warner once signing autographs for fans seated behind the Rams' bench with three minutes left in a one-sided victory over the Jets at Giants Stadium. The next day, he faxed a letter of apology to Jets coach Herm Edwards.

Ryan didn't know anything about Sanchez and the hot dog until he was on the airplane. "Oh, it pissed me off," he said. "I was pissed at him. It just brought attention to himself. You don't need that. Your team won 38–0; don't make the story be about you eating a hot dog. I was really disappointed in him."

Ryan lectured him at thirty thousand feet. "Dude, you showed up a team," he told him. "You were disrespectful to the game, and you were disrespectful to your opponent." Sanchez was ridiculed in the newspaper. He tried to restore his image a few days later by donating five hundred hot dogs and five hundred hamburgers, along with the rolls and buns, to the Community Soup Kitchen in Morristown, New Jersey. His goal was to buy a thousand of each, but there was not enough freezer space.

Ryan helped ease concerns that he was a pushover and too permissive with his players by the way he came down on Sanchez. He had to take a stand and not allow his quarterback to open a hot dog stand at the 50-yard line. Sanchez had burned a lot of calories during the game, but he chose the wrong time to try to replenish his system. Ryan didn't let it go after lecturing Sanchez. He told the team, "Make sure you guys eat your hot dogs before the game, not during the game, like Mark," Revis said.

It was interesting that Ryan was so critical of Sanchez's eating because it came at a time in his life when he was having big trouble controlling what he ate. After Ryan's first season, the Jets paid for him to go to the famous weight loss center at Duke University, where he took classes. But he decided to undergo lap-band surgery after consulting with former NFL offensive lineman Jamie Dukes. He checked into NYU under the alias Roy Rogers. He was forty-seven years old and weighed 348 pounds.

"I want to be around. I want to enjoy my kids. I want to see grandkids," Ryan said. "I don't need to get diabetes, high blood pressure, heart problems. I'm trying to avoid all of it."

In a little more than two years following the surgery, Ryan lost 106 pounds.

Ryan won over the Jets fans when he made the comment about Belichick's rings. They were tired of being bullied by Brady and Belichick and had had enough of the Jets taking a beating and not fighting back. Ryan had not even made it to training camp, and already he was imposing his will on his team, forcing it to take on his personality. The Jets might not win the fight, but at least they were going to fight.

Then, in the second game of Ryan's first season, the Jets beat the Patriots at Giants Stadium. They did it again in the second game of the 2010 season. Each year, however, the Jets lost the return match in New England. In the 2010 divisional round of the playoffs, the Jets beat the Patriots in Foxborough, completely confusing Brady. The picture on the cover of *Sports Illustrated* the next week showed linebacker Calvin Pace crushing Brady. "That was a great picture," Ryan said. "His eyes were this big. That one's up on the wall."

The playoff victory over the Patriots was the second most important in Jets history, right after Super Bowl III. It came one month after the Jets were embarrassed by the Patriots at Gillette Stadium 45–3 in a Monday night game. The Jets felt Brady was mocking them by being a little too enthusiastic after throwing a touchdown pass to make it 38–3 early in the fourth quarter and that Belichick was rubbing it in by having Brady play the entire game. Brady pointed to the Jets' sideline after the score, and Ryan later complained about Brady's "antics" and "Brady being Brady."

Football players want the coach to lead. They want him to set a schedule and tell them where they need to be and what time they need to be there. It's been that way since they started getting serious about football in high school. It's a sport that demands discipline. The players also want the coach to have their backs. Ryan was not afraid to criticize an opponent, and he encouraged his players to say what was on their minds. A few days before the playoff game against the Patriots, cornerback Antonio Cromartie made it clear that he didn't hold Brady in high regard. He told the *New York Daily News* that Brady was "an asshole. Fuck him."

Brady countered by saying he had been called worse. Playing for any other team, Cromartie would have earned a trip to the head coach's office. "I think that language was a little strong for me," said Ryan, looking for laughs.

That was the environment he created. It was the language he spoke on *Hard Knocks*.

"I'm surprised how vulgar Cromartie was. It didn't make a

lot of sense," said Damon Huard, a former Brady backup. "Tom looks at it like: What is this guy talking about? It's out of left field. In my mind it's classless. Maybe Rex Ryan doesn't care and lets guys get away with that. There is no place for that."

Ryan loves to get little digs in on Brady at every opportunity. He has said no one studies like Peyton Manning and implied that Brady's success is a result of having Belichick as his coach. When the Jets were playing the Colts on a Saturday night in the wild-card round before they eliminated New England the next week Brady was with his supermodel wife, Gisele Bundchen, attending *Lombardi* on Broadway. "Peyton Manning would have been watching our game," Ryan said. Brady later said he was monitoring the game on his cell phone and got home in time to watch the second half.

As much as the long-suffering Jets fans would love for Ryan to trash talk Belichick—they're still upset that he bailed on the team after one day as the head coach in 2000—Rex has never done it. Rex's brother Rob won two Super Bowl rings as an assistant working for Belichick. The Ryan family holds Belichick in high regard.

"There is no coach in the league I respect more than Bill Belichick," Ryan said. "That's the truth. But I got the same job he does. I'm going to try to kick his butt every time. He's going to try to kick mine. There is no question. I want to try to knock him off the top. There is no reason why my goal shouldn't be like that. Do the New England Patriots have an advantage over the New York Jets in the head coaching position? Absolutely. But I got news for you: They got it over every team in the league. The guy is a superstar in coaching."

The Jets have to deal with the Patriots twice a year. They have to deal with the Giants almost every single day. They meet only once every four years in the regular season, and they play a meaningless preseason game every summer. They elbow each other for attention in New York. The Giants let Ryan do all the talking, and they do all the winning. The Jets are starved for attention. After the Giants beat the Patriots again in the Super Bowl after the 2011 season, the Jets traded for Tebow and dominated the headlines for weeks. Eli Manning commented that the Giants just won the Super Bowl but he was just the third most talked about quarterback in "my own city."

The Jets' victory over the Colts in Super Bowl III was the greatest upset in pro football history. But in New York, the Giants were still the kings. Even though the Jets were the NFL champions, they didn't become the champions of New York until they easily defeated the Giants in their first-ever meeting that summer of 1969 in a preseason game at the Yale Bowl. For that short period, the Jets were the big brothers in their relationship with the Giants. As much as Ryan has made it his mission, the Jets have not been able to overcome the Giants' tight relationship with their loyal fan base. He attempted to make a case for it after the Jets advanced to the AFC championship game in his first two seasons while the Giants failed to make the playoffs. After his second season with the Jets, Ryan wrote a book, *Play Like You Mean It*. He antagonized the Giants when he said the Jets were the better team and the big brother and "we are going to remain the better team for the next ten years."

In the week leading up to the important Jets-Giants regular season game late in 2011, Ryan didn't tone down the rhetoric. The Giants were coming off a bad loss to the Redskins. The Jets had just lost to the Eagles. The winner would be in good shape to make the playoffs. The loser would be in big trouble. The game was at MetLife Stadium, the $1.7 billion stadium the teams financed as 50–50 partners. This was a Jets home game, which allowed them to dress up the stadium in green. The Giants and Jets had fought over who had the honor of hosting the first regular season game when the stadium opened in 2010. When there was no agreement, Roger Goodell flipped a coin, and it came up Giants. They opened against Carolina on a Sunday afternoon, and the Jets' consolation prize was opening against Baltimore on *Monday Night Football*. The Jets even came in second when they fought with the Giants over which team would get the home locker room closest to the players' parking lot. They lost that coin flip, too. The Jets considered themselves second-class citizens for the twenty-six years they played at Giants Stadium. As the Jets pulled into the parking lot, the big blue Giants Stadium sign was staring right at them. The Giants had their offices in the stadium and were there 365 days a year. The Jets were there for eight regular season games and two preseason games, and for all but the last two years their headquarters were in Hempstead, Long Island. The Sunday night traffic after games was brutal. It could take the players two hours to cross two bridges and get home.

When the teams agreed to work together on the new stadium, the Jets insisted that the Giants not have their offices and training facility in the stadium. They built a new training center in the outer reaches of the stadium parking lot. The Jets built a lavish facility in suburban Florham Park, New Jersey, about forty minutes from the Meadowlands. Still, when it came time for the grand opening of the new stadium, they felt like second-class citizens all over again. That was how they tried to make the Giants feel when they met in that 2011 regular season game. On the wall outside the Giants locker room are painted logos from their Super Bowl appearances along with paintings of their Vince Lombardi Trophies. The Jets players walk past that wall on the way to the locker room when they enter the stadium from the parking lot. That's why Jets management puts up a curtain in front of that wall for every home game. The curtain went unnoticed until the Giants played the Jets with the Jets as the home team. The Giants players were livid.

As far as the Giants were concerned, they had had enough of the Jets. They had had enough of Ryan talking big leading up to the game. They felt they were the big brother even if the Jets had had more success the previous two seasons. The Giants won the showdown game and credited Ryan for getting them fired up with his constant big brother–little brother talk. The Giants live by Tom Coughlin's motto of "Talk is cheap. Play the game." Coughlin reiterated that with all the stuff coming from the Jets leading up to the game. Ryan, who insisted that he respects Coughlin, lives by a different philosophy. "That's the old saying, Talk is cheap. Money buys whiskey. I understand all that. That's the truth, but I don't care about Tom Coughlin or anybody else," Ryan said. "I know how I believe, and I don't care if it's acceptable in everybody's opinion. I really don't care. I'm worried about my opinion. This is how I feel. Quite honestly, I couldn't care less what anybody thinks."

The Giants beat the Jets and did not lose again on the way to their fourth Super Bowl victory.

After the game, Ryan and Giants running back Brandon Jacobs came face to face on the field. Jacobs, at six feet four inches and 264 pounds is an imposing figure. Ryan is a large man who is not used to backing down.

He was not about to back down from Jacobs. Their mouths were inches apart, and their left shoulders were touching.

"It's time to shut up, fat boy," Jacobs said.

"Shut the fuck up," Ryan said.

Classy.

A little more than one month later, the Giants won another Super Bowl.

"Quite honestly, it's hard to argue. They did win the Super Bowl," Ryan said. "But the two previous years, we were better than they were. The game against them changed two organizations. Unfortunately, we couldn't respond, and they went on and won the Super Bowl. Even then, I'll still never consider myself a little brother. I'm going to be fighting you. I'm going to try to get to that big brother status. They are not going to shut me up."

Ryan does not have a filter. It's part genetic. He inherited that from Buddy. It's part environmental. Some of his formative years were spent without a lot of structure in the house.

After his parents were divorced, he lived in Toronto with his mother, Doris, his twin brother, Rob, and older brother, Jim. Rex and Rob were inseparable. "I was supposed to get deported. Absolutely. I wouldn't go to school. I think that was part of being dyslexic and struggling and all that stuff," he said. "I had a morning paper route, afternoon paper route, paid for everything, stole things. I wouldn't steal a kid's lunch money or anything like that. But we weren't anybody you wanted to mess with, my brother and I. We basically did what we wanted. My mom was teaching all the time or she was gone." By the time he reached high school, Rex was back living with his father.

Rex didn't want his sons to follow that same path of getting into trouble, but as hard as parents try, there are times kids just do dumb things. Both of Ryan's boys became a bit too mischievous one year before the Jets hired him. "I've had some issues with my kids. You can check the record," Ryan said. "It was harmless little pranks like Payton spray painting a sign. And they talked Seth into it, too. They had to do community service."

Ryan doesn't always set the best example for his children or as a role model. One week before the Saints were playing the Colts in Super Bowl XLIV in Miami, Ryan was in town for a mixed martial arts event in Sunrise, Florida. After an interview in which he promised the Jets would beat the Dolphins twice in 2010 was broadcast throughout the arena, he was verbally harassed by some fans. Ryan showed them his middle finger. A quick-triggered fan captured the moment on his cell phone camera, and it soon went viral. The Jets fined Ryan $50,000.

Did he learn his lesson? Not really. At halftime of a 21-point Jets loss at home to the Patriots in 2011—they were trailing only 13–9 in the first half, but the Pats scored a touchdown with only nine seconds left—Ryan was walking toward the tunnel behind the Jets' bench leading to the locker room when a fan shouted at him.

"Hey, Rex. Belichick is better than you," he said.

"Shut the fuck up," Ryan responded.

"Fuck you," the fan said.

That cost Ryan $75,000. This time the NFL fined him.

With all the theatrics that go on around Ryan's Jets and the way fans yell at Ryan, the Jets have a WWE feel to them.

"Fans cuss me constantly," Ryan said. "Usually, it's 'you fat ass.' You name it, I get it. I love that part of football. I don't want to be liked by the opposition. I want to be respected. The reason the opposing place can't stand me is because I can beat you. That's fine with me. They are great as long as they can kick your ass all the time. They know they can't do that with me. I'm not going to take my rightful place underneath their team. That's not flying with me. You can hate me; that's fine. But if I ever coached for that team, that team would love me because they know how passionate I am and how committed I am."

He found a way to control what goes in his mouth but not what comes out.

That makes him a unique and valued member of the fraternity.

ACKNOWLEDGMENTS

Sean Payton walked into the cafeteria of the Saints' headquarters in Metairie, Louisiana. It was December 2009, the first stop on my journey to go behind the scenes to illustrate the high-pressure world of NFL head coaches.

I first got to know Payton when he was on Jim Fassel's staff with the Giants and kept in touch with him when he spent three years working for Bill Parcells in Dallas. He had been disappointed at how things ended with the Giants after Fassel removed him as the play caller, but I remember telling him when he took the job with Dallas that working for Parcells and getting that on his résumé was the best thing he could do for his career.

I traveled from New York to New Orleans two months before Payton won the Super Bowl and a little more than two years before he was suspended for the 2012 season by Roger Goodell for his role in the bounty scandal. But on this day the Saints were undefeated, and Payton was making a name for himself as the best of the young coaches in the NFL. He had just finished taping his weekly television show when he sat down to talk with me.

"I've got about forty-five minutes," he said. "Then I have a team meeting."

After ninety minutes went by like it was fifteen, I was thinking that every question would be my last, but Payton was in a talkative mood, which was a good thing. I actually was hoping Payton didn't forget about his meeting. I could wait until it was over, I told him; I wasn't flying home until the morning. He gave me another twenty minutes.

I had intended to focus the Payton chapter on the role of the Saints in the rebirth of New Orleans and Payton being at the center of it. It's one of the most heartwarming stories the NFL has seen in the Super Bowl era. Then a couple of months after the 2011 season the NFL revealed that it was investigating the Saints for their pay-for-performance bounty program, which was against league rules. Sweetheart, get me rewrite, as they used to say in the newspaper business. I had to start over. A couple of days before Goodell announced Payton's suspension, I happened to be in the NFL office for a meeting with the commissioner. I was sitting in the reception area reading some e-mails on my phone when a man walking by called out to me. It was Payton, who was taking a brief break from his meeting with Goodell. Thirty minutes later, as Payton was getting set to leave the NFL office, Goodell told him I was in the reception area and offered to send him down a back elevator so that he could keep the visit private. "Too late," Payton told him.

I want to thank all the coaches and owners for their cooperation as I researched *Coaching Confidential*. They were giving of their time and their insights. It was fun to meet up with coaches whom I have known a long time and others I was getting to know better.

A few months after Dan Snyder hired Mike Shanahan in Washington, I traveled to Ashburn, Virginia, to discuss John Elway and Dan Reeves and Al Davis with Shanahan. He showed a side I had never seen before: great storyteller, great sense of humor. Then Snyder, whom I have been friendly with since the day he bought the Redskins in 1999, invited me up to his office, where we talked about the six coaches he had gone through in his first eleven years owning the Redskins before he hoped he found stability with Shanahan.

"You like peanuts?" Snyder asked.

"Sure," I said.

"What do you like to drink with them?"

"Diet Coke," I said.

He walked across his huge office at Redskins Park and came back with an oversized bag of peanuts in the shell and a couple of sodas for us. He put a towel on the floor and encouraged me to join him in tossing the shells on the towel. If I did that at home, who knows what the better half of my marriage would do to me. But here was one of the richest men in sports turning his office into a ballpark.

I drove down the New Jersey Turnpike and sat with Eagles coach Andy Reid as he opened up about the turmoil he went through when his sons were arrested in separate drug incidents in the Philadelphia area on the same day in 2007. He and his wife, Tammy, were on vacation in California at the time. He pointed out the spot where he often sleeps in his office, which Rex Ryan of the Jets also did when I visited him in his office.

Ryan and Tom Landry are two of my all-time favorite coaches to write about. They are a bit different, however. I covered the Cowboys as my first big job in the newspaper business, and the man you saw on the sideline in the fedora with the frown on his face was not the man I got to know and admire. Ryan is just fun to be around, doesn't take himself too seriously, and never flinches when I criticize him in the *New York Daily News*. Can't they all be like Rex?

The most scenic visit was at Dick Vermeil's house in East Fallowfield, Pennsylvania. He told great stories as we sat on his deck with a beautiful view of the Pennsylvania countryside. After I spent a few hours with Vermeil, he insisted that I take home a party favor. He went to his private stock and handed me two bottles of wine with the Vermeil label.

One white. One red.

The day after the Saints beat the Colts in the Super Bowl in Miami, I was in Bill Parcells's office at the Dolphins' facility in Davie. He was running the Dolphins but not coaching them. He had a small office with a big television so that he could watch tapes of college players. The Colts had used the Dolphins' facility during Super Bowl week, and Parcells made sure to visit the weight room so that he could spend time with Peyton Manning, one of his favorite players.

I have known Parcells since he joined the Giants as defensive coordinator in 1981. Parcells was always entertaining in his press conferences. There were days covering the Giants and later the Jets when Parcells filled up every page of my notebook. He's a charming guy when he feels like it, but he didn't like it when I disagreed with him, which was too frequent, as far as he was concerned.

When I wrote a column criticizing his decision to give up first- and third-round picks for Curtis Martin, I came home to find two messages from Parcells's secretary on my answering machine. Bill, she said, really wanted to talk to me. Of course I returned his call. We spent thirty minutes sparring. It turned out he was right about Martin, but it doesn't mean he was right about everything, and I was never afraid to write about it. I took it as a sign of respect that he would call to disagree. If he didn't respect me, he wouldn't care; at least that's how I looked at it.

I met with Tony Dungy in the coffee shop of the hotel he was staying in on Central Park South to talk about his coaching life. There isn't a classier man who has ever made his living on an NFL sideline than Dungy. Once Tebow Mania overwhelmed the NFL during the 2011 season, I decided to wait until the off-season to interview Broncos coach John Fox, who was on that same Giants staff with Payton. Tebow was his starter going into 2012 training camp, Fox said, but you never know what's going to happen in free agency, he cautioned. What happened was Peyton Manning. Fox agreed we needed to have a follow-up conversation to bring the story up to date.

My most poignant meeting was with Patriots owner Robert Kraft. I wanted to speak to him about Parcells, Pete Carroll, and Bill Belichick, the three coaches he's employed in New England. He invited me to meet him at his home in Chestnut Hill, Massachusetts. He buzzed me through so that I could drive past the front gate. I was caught by surprise when I rang the bell. There was a guard standing right inside the front door. Okay, Kraft is a wealthy, well-known figure; it made sense. On closer inspection, the guard was not real, just a statue. But a great deterrent nonetheless.

He invited me to dinner and asked if I would mind if his beloved wife, Myra, joined us. We had met many times over the years, and I always enjoyed her company. The three of us went to a local restaurant, and not only was Kraft forthcoming about his relationship with all three of his coaches, it was heartwarming to see how much he cared for Myra and attended to her every need. There was no indication that she was in a fight for her life, battling cancer. She died almost exactly one year later. I feel fortunate that I was able to spend those couple of hours with her.

Of course, I want to thank Sean Desmond, my editor at Crown, who as usual was so supportive. We worked together on my first book, *The Catch*, which detailed the 1981 NFC championship game between the Cowboys and the 49ers. It was a sad ending to a great game for Sean's Cowboys. I hope the Jimmy Johnson chapter chronicling the Herschel Walker trade makes up for it.

I've dedicated this book to my incredible family—my wife, Allison; daughters, Michelle and Emily; and son, Andrew. Michelle, the nutritionist in the family, provided encouragement and a guide to healthy book-writing snacks; Emily, a terrific writer, always had great ideas; and Andrew, with his vast knowledge of sports, assisted with the research. Allison, a big football fan long before we met, was consistent in her message: Keep writing.

And to Dad: You first got me hooked on the NFL when we went to the old Yankee Stadium and sat in end zone seats to watch the Giants beat the Eagles 7–6 in 1968, and you're a still a big Giants fan today. Finally, I want to remember my mother, who passed away in the summer of 2010 just as I started writing *Coaching Confidential*. Mom, I miss you every day.

INDEX